PARADOXES
OF
YOUTH
AND
SPORT

MAR 0 1 2003

SUNY series on Sport, Culture, and Social Relations
CL Cole and Michael A. Messner, editors

*A complete listing of books in the series
can be found at the end of the volume.*

PARADOXES
OF YOUTH
AND SPORT

EDITED BY
Margaret Gatz,
Michael A. Messner, and
Sandra J. Ball-Rokeach

STATE UNIVERSITY OF NEW YORK PRESS

Published by
State University of New York Press, Albany

© 2002 State University of New York

All rights reserved

Printed in the United States of America

No part of this book may be used or reproduced
in any manner whatsoever without written permission.
No part of this book may be stored in a retrieval system
or transmitted in any form or by any means including
electronic, electrostatic, magnetic tape, mechanical,
photocopying, recording, or otherwise without the prior
permission in writing of the publisher.

For information, address State University of New York Press,
90 State Street, Suite 700, Albany, NY 12207

Production by Cathleen Collins
Marketing by Michael Campochiaro

Library of Congress Cataloging-in-Publication Data

Paradoxes of youth and sport / edited by Margaret Gatz, Michael A. Messner,
    Sandra J. Ball-Rokeach.
        p. cm. — (SUNY series on sport, culture, and social relations)
    Includes bibliographical references and index.
    ISBN 0-7914-5323-5 (alk. paper) — ISBN 0-7914-5324-3 (pbk. : alk. paper)
        1. Sports—Social aspects—Congresses. 2. Youth—Social conditions—Congresses.
    I. Gatz, Margaret, 1944– II. Messner, Michael A. III. Ball-Rokeach, Sandra J.
    IV. Series.

GV706.5 .P365 2002
306.4'83—dc21
                                                                2001042646

10 9 8 7 6 5 4 3 2 1

Contents

Foreword

Paradoxes of Youth and Sport grew out of a 1997 conference at the University of Southern California titled "Youth, Sport, Violence and the Media." The conference brought together a wide range of scholars, youth sport administrators, community activists, coaches, and athletes. The organization for which I work, the Amateur Athletic Foundation of Los Angeles (AAF), was a cosponsor of the conference.

As a foundation that develops youth sport programs and makes grants to youth sport organizations throughout southern California, and particularly Los Angeles, the AAF welcomed the chance to be involved with the conference. The conference offered an introduction to the research and analyses of academicians who, operating from a variety of disciplines, had prepared papers on youth sport. Equally important to us was the opportunity to interact with the nonacademic participants, that is, the community representatives and sport administrators who brought with them a practical expertise born of firsthand experience providing sport programs, while assessing the impact of such programs.

This book offers the same sorts of opportunities to readers. Paradoxes of Youth and Sport, while somewhat more narrowly focused than the conference that inspired it, still addresses the same overriding issues, namely, What, if any, values does sport impart? Can sport be used to ameliorate social problems of poverty, poor schools, violence, drug use, and crime? Should we even attempt to use youth sport in this way? Underlying these overarching questions are the subtexts of race and gender, as well as the media's role in shaping our attitudes with regard to all of these issues.

For any person or organization involved in providing sports programs to young people, questions pertaining to the impact of sport on the lives of young athletes and the communities in which they live are fundamental. Throughout most of the twentieth century, in the United States, there had been a widespread, largely unexamined assumption that sport, crudely put, is a good thing for kids. Sport, so the argument goes, teaches valuable lessons that carry over into other walks of life, benefiting not only the individual athletes, but society as a whole. This attitude is pervasive, and two decades of critical examination by sport scholars, and to a lesser extent by sport journalists, have done little to erode the basic assumption.

At the "Youth, Sport, Violence and the Media" conference, the differences between the academic participants and people with experience in providing youth sports in urban settings was interesting to observe. It was evident even within the first couple hours of the conference.

Jay Coakley, a sociologist from the University of Colorado, Colorado Springs, presented an eloquent address urging the audience to think critically about the use of sport as a means of preventing youth violence and other forms of social deviance. He encouraged listeners to question why sport is viewed as a social control device, particularly one that can be used to "control" African American boys and young men. Coakley also questioned the sociopolitical agendas that underlie the desire of some people to use sport to address urban social ills.

A dramatically different perspective emerged in the following session when Ed Cabil, a high school teacher at John Muir Middle School in Los Angeles, discussed an afterschool program of sports and academic tutoring called "New ADAGE" that he has run since 1986. Cabil seemed unconcerned with the larger political and ideological implications of youth sport. His explanation of why he started New ADAGE was simple and direct: "I was tired of seeing my students die." Cabil noted that in contrast to the situation that existed prior to the establishment of New ADAGE, not a single student had been killed at his school since the program began. Furthermore, Cabil believed that New ADAGE had steered many students away from crime and drug use.

Social scientists might point out that it is hard to know whether Cabil's program really stopped the killing and reduced crime and drug use. After all, they would point out, it is difficult, if not impossible, to run a controlled experiment in the real world. Perhaps other factors unrelated to sport were the intervening variables. Many academics also might seek to analyze the social and political context in which a program such as New ADAGE exists.

The academic perspective notwithstanding, anyone who has had even limited contact with youth sport administrators, coaches, and parents involved with urban youth sport programs will know that most of them fervently believe in the value of sport. Most would accept Cabil's analysis at face value. In fact, many people at the grassroots level would argue that academic researchers with no "real" knowledge of low-income urban neighborhoods can not fully comprehend the role of sport in an urban setting.

My point here is not to credit or discredit either the arguments of academic critics or the beliefs of those who provide urban youth sport programs. In fact, the two camps share some common ground. Both agree that sport has significance. Both are motivated by a desire to effect social change. And, I suspect both groups would largely agree on what would constitute an ideal youth sports program. That said, the fact remains that academicians and practitioners have different professional agendas and different problem-solving methodologies. The value of a book like *Paradoxes of Youth and Sport* is that it gives voice and credence to both perspectives.

As these readings demonstrate through both empirical and anecdotal evidence, sport in urban settings clearly has an impact on peoples' lives. At the same time, readers will be struck by the difficulty of comprehending the nature of that impact and judging its worth. Sport is an immensely complex social institution. The fact that it intersects with so many other important institutions in modern society only makes the task of understanding it more difficult. *Paradoxes of Youth and Sport* performs the valuable function of affirming the relevance of youth sport while at the same time compelling us to reflect seriously on how we should attempt to structure sport and the broader social settings in which it exists.

Wayne Wilson, Ph.D.
Amateur Athletic Foundation of Los Angeles

Preface

This book addresses central cultural issues of our time—violence, structural inequities, and race—through the lens of sport. These issues permeate sport, and thus are promulgated in the public image of sport; at the same time, sport is offered as a tool for righting of social wrongs. The chapters of the book were originally developed as background papers for a National Conference on Youth, Sport, Violence, and the Media held in April 1997, at the University of Southern California (USC). That conference was sponsored by the Steering Committee for the Study of Sport in Society. The purpose of the steering committee is to bring together faculty and graduate students from various academic departments and professional schools with educators, executives, and community leaders from the public and private sectors for a researcher-practitioner exchange designed to understand and enhance the role of sport in society.

There would have been no conference, and no book, without generous support from several key sources. Sara Miller McCune and the McCune Foundation were the first to tell us that we had an idea worthy of support. Wayne Wilson has been a consistent source of sound advice and the Amateur Athletic Foundation of Los Angeles, where he serves as vice president for research, has been a crucial financial backer and host. The Bauer Foundation contributed much-needed financial support. The National Institutes of Health, through its Office of Behavioral and Social Sciences Research, awarded a small contract for book preparation. At USC, both the Annenberg School for Communication and the Social Science Research Institute, which housed the project, made critical and generous contributions. A small grant from the James H. Zumberge Faculty Research and Innovation Fund helped to fund consultants to the steering committee.

This undertaking would not have been possible without the help of a great number of people at every stage of development. Faculty who planned the conference included the editors of this book, Darnell Hunt and

Malcolm W. Klein. Graduate students and former graduate students Matt Hale, Faye Wachs, and Shari Dworkin played important roles in conference organization. Other key members of the steering committee include David Carter, John Callaghan, and Todd Boyd. Dean Geoffrey Cowan, and then deans Edward Blakely and Morton Schapiro were consistently supportive.

Highly competent assistance has been provided by Social Science Research Institute staff, especially Letty Baz, also Donna Polisar, Brianna Garcia, and Barbara Yuen in the Department of Psychology, and Shari Hoppin in the Annenberg School for Communication. Another round of appreciation goes to Ronald Helfrich, our editor at the State University of New York Press, and Cheryl L. Cole, coeditor of the SUNY series on Sport, Culture, and Social Relations.

Introduction

Framing Social Issues through Sport

We live in an era of increasing concern over dangers faced by children and youth: violence, school dropout, gangs, unwanted pregnancy, drug use, unequal access to quality education, and limited employment opportunities. This book explores emergent debates among academics, youth advocates, health educators, and sport practitioners concerning the extent to which sport can be a resource in the lives of disadvantaged children and adolescents, and the extent to which sport itself harbors and fosters social problems such as violence, racism, and sexism.

There appear to be two contradictory positions on sport. On the one hand, sports programs are touted as a violence prevention tool for urban youth; on the other hand, violence is an integral part of the sports world. Youth sport participation is promoted as an alternative to gang violence, but fights between professional athletes are jokingly celebrated on evening sports highlights shows viewed by these same youth. Sport venues are seen as places where adult mentors can have a positive influence on young people, yet some coaches, such as former Indiana University basketball coach Bobby Knight, verbally and physically abuse their players, and some parents get into fights at their children's soccer or little league games. Sport participation is viewed as a way to bridge difference, yet male and female athletes still have separate and unequal participation, access, and media coverage, and racism and homophobia are still rampant in many areas of the sports world.

This book plumbs these paradoxes of sport. We draw on the works of scholars from various academic disciplines, and the voices of people outside of the university—practitioners who are teaching sport to youth, athletes, and representatives of the media. Bringing these different and often

1

discordant voices together into an implicit conversation that unmasks major paradoxes in the study and application of sport is our central goal as editors of this book. The dialogue we hope to foster is grounded in conversations that we have had about our own ambivalent and contradictory engagements with sport and society. As an editorial trio, we represent diverse disciplines and different methodological perspectives—a community psychologist, a sociologist with a joint appointment in gender studies, and a sociologist housed in a school for communication. Margaret Gatz is a psychologist who has worked extensively in the area of mental health, including interventions with youth in schools. Though playing sports has always been part of her life, her interest in sport was not connected to her scholarly work until she became her university's faculty athletic representative to the National Collegiate Athletic Association (NCAA), from 1986 to 1993, and subsequently served on the association's research committee. This experience made clear to her both the clashes that can occur between athletics and academics and at the same time the inspiring role of sports participation and sports idols in the lives of many youth. Michael A. Messner is a sociologist whose research explores boys' and men's athletic experiences through a feminist lens. He is a noted critic of the racism, sexism, and violence in sports media. His critiques of sport, however, are grounded in his having both positive and negative experiences as the son of a coach, a high school and college athlete, a sports fan, and today, the father of two young boys who are exploring various aspects of sport participation. The sociologist Sandra J. Ball-Rokeach is a communication theorist and researcher with interests in the social roles of sport as presented in the media, both with regards to violence and community building. But to her, these are not simply abstract academic issues. Sport was an important part of her childhood, where she became a lifelong baseball fan, competed in tennis, and broke gender lines by playing on a boys' baseball team in the late 1940s. As a teacher, she is concerned about the dilemma that athletes face in their attempt to negotiate education and sport participation.

In our conversations, the three editors of this book became convinced that what we might previously have thought were simply our own individual ambivalences about sport actually reflected the paradoxical nature of sport in society. This paradox is apparent in the growing scholarship on sport. Not long ago, one of the editors attended a scholarly conference made up mostly of psychologists and sport practitioners. Many of the presentations were concerned with how to use social science to help coaches and athletes maximize their competitive performances. To the extent that social issues were discussed in this conference, sport was seen mostly as a useful tool in psychotherapy or for intervening in problems that existed outside of sport such as providing life skills learning for underprivileged urban youth. There was very little discussion of the possibility that sport might be contributing to social problems, nor was there much recognition or discussion of the burgeoning scholarship that is critical of sport. A few months later, the same editor attended a conference where scholars, this time mostly sociologists, presented their research on institutionalized sexism, racism, and homophobia in sport, on how sport promotes violence, and on how corporate media promotes images of sport that largely reproduce social inequalities. There was almost no discussion of the actual or potentially positive aspects of sport at this conference, nor was there much evidence that these scholars had read or thought about the works written by sport psychologists and practitioners.

Two things were particularly striking about the juxtaposition of these two academic conferences on sport. First, there was almost no referencing of work across the disciplines. Second, the public divergence between the "sport-is-good," "sport-is-bad" conference themes was not as absolute as it seemed. For instance, at the sociology conference, following a particularly critical session on the commercialization of sports, one scholar excused himself from an informal postsession discussion by somewhat sheepishly admitting that he had to get back to his hotel room to watch his university's football team on TV, while two others in the group remained behind to discuss their recent experiences as coaches in their children's soccer leagues. A parallel experience occurred when another editor attended an ancillary session at a sports psychology conference that was primarily focused on sport as a prosocial activity. Ambivalence was suddenly revealed as participants noted their concerns about the negative influences of poorly trained or carelessly selected coaches on young people's development.

In short, our public personae often force polarized stances on the virtuous or victimizing nature of sport that are betrayed by our private ambivalences. It is our view that the study and practical application of sport can be advanced by bringing ambivalence to the foreground in a more nuanced assessment of the paradoxes of sport. To this end, we have designed this volume as a venue for dialogue across three groups of people: "critical" sport scholars, scholars who see sport as a positive force for intervening in youth problems, and people who are out in the community working with youth and sport. The book continues a discussion held at the National Conference on Youth, Sport, Violence, and the Media that we organized at the University of Southern California.

The roots of our juxtaposition of perspectives on sport lie in public and academic conversations about sport and society over the past thirty years. Changes over time in the formal field of sports studies mirror our personal reflections about the paradoxes of sport.

The Ambivalence of Sport Studies

A quarter of a century ago, the value of sport was expressed in beliefs such as,
    "Sport builds character."
    "Sport participation is a stepping-stone to success for poor and minority youth."
    "Sport is a democratic equalizer, where everybody is judged by the same standards, and is held accountable to the same rules."

In the 1970s, athletes, coaches, sportswriters, and scholars began to provide critical views of sport: Former Major League baseball player Jim Bouton's celebrated 1970 book, *Ball Four,* pierced the image of the national pastime with its descriptions of baseball stars boozing and engaging in sexual activities and violence; National Football League player David Meggyesy's 1970 book *Out of Their League* criticized the dehumanization, racism, and sexism in professional football; and *The David Kopay Story* (1977) starkly reveals the sexism and homophobia that kept Kopay closeted as a gay professional football player. More recently, athletes have written about the use of performance-enhancing drugs, academic failures that were systematically covered up, and physical abuse of wives and girlfriends. In his 1996 book, *The Dark Side of the Game,* former professional athlete and current commentator, Tim Green, suggests that most football players can turn violence on and off, such that they are mean and vicious on the playing field, but not on the street. However, he goes on to write that "There are some, though, who cannot separate the violence of the game from real life. They mistake life for extension of the playing field where you hit hard and you hit first" (p. 65).

Reflecting this critique from inside of sport, social science research emerged in the 1970s and 1980s that challenged the all or none "sport is good" assumptions. The sport psychologists Bruce Ogilvie and Thomas A. Tutko (1971) mustered evidence to support their claim that "sport does not build character; it builds characters." The sociologist Harry Edwards (1970, 1984) claimed that a racist structure of opportunity disproportionately channels Black youth into sport. Most Black athletes, Edwards argued, do not experience sport as a way out of the ghetto. Rather, for most, sport is a "treadmill to oblivion." During the same period, feminist scholars disputed the democratic nature of sport by revealing how women had been systematically excluded from participation (Felshin, 1974; Oglesby, 1978), and how boys' and men's sports served to promote sexist ideas and male supremacist practices (Sabo & Runfola, 1980). Furthermore, media scholars argued that public awareness of the negative roles of sport in social relations was impeded by the commercial interests of the "sports-media complex" in fostering a positive image of sport as victimless entertainment (Jhally, 1984).

Sport studies scholars convincingly argued that the institution of sport was intricately intertwined with other social institutions such as families, schools, the economy, and mass media, and as such, it both reflected and reinforced inegalitarian beliefs, values, and power relations (Edwards, 1971; Eitzen & Yetman, 1977; Gruneau, 1983; Hoch, 1972; Scott, 1971; Tutko & Bruns, 1976; Theberge, 1981). Rather than promoting inclusive, democratic, egalitarian, cooperative, and peaceful values, they argued that sport offers youth a pedagogy of racial and sexual exclusion, gender hierarchy, violence, and destructively competitive values (e.g., that "winning is the only thing") in an increasingly commercialized context. Sport, in other words, was not immune from social problems; it was, rather, a major source of those problems. The logical practical outcome of this critical perspective was extreme: either radically change the institution of sport, or steer kids away from participating in it altogether.

Critical sport studies offered an important corrective to romanticized and uncritical acceptance of sport as an unambiguously positive institution. The emphasis on critique, however, drove out any discussion of the potentially positive aspects of sport. Most athletes, coaches, parents, youth sports organizers, and spectators (and, as we have just suggested, many "critical" sport scholars themselves) know from experience that sport participation has offered them numerous moments of pleasure, healthy exercise, friendships, mentoring relationships, and lessons about achievement, cooperation, and competition that spill over into nonsport contexts. The critical sport studies perspective thus rarely rings "true" as a complete story in the ears of sport participants.

By the 1990s, sport scholars had only begun to bridge the gap between critical analysis and concrete interventions that aim to reduce the negative and accentuate the positive potentialities in sport. Community organizers in inner cities, for example, offered sport participation (e.g., Midnight Basketball) as a way to deflect youth away from antisocial behavior and as a context for teaching life skills. Other community programs began to use professional and collegiate star athletes to encourage youth to imagine futures for themselves. Sport psychologists hypothesized that the same strategies found helpful in enhancing the performance of elite athletes could be applied in training programs serving ordinary people. A few social scientists began working as consultants to youth sports practitioners, conducting studies to ascertain the effects of youth sports programs.

Yet optimistic attempts to use sport to improve the lives of youth all too often ignore public argument and research evidence that suggests caution in the wholesale use of sport as an intervention tool. As an institution, sport has built-in positives and negatives. To paraphrase the sport sociologist D. Stanley Eitzen (1999), sport unites and it divides; sport is healthy and it is unhealthy; sport is fair and sport is foul. Moreover, as an institution, sport is not seamless. There are some aspects that may be far more positive and healthy for youth than others. For example, it appears that some boys' sports like high school cross-country are far less homophobic, and far less violent, than most high school football programs (Anderson, 2000). And though there is growing evidence that sport participation is generally a healthy and empowering experience for girls, it also appears that the highly professionalized, commercialized, and regimented worlds of big-time figure skating and gymnastics are correlated with dangerous levels of serious injuries, eating disorders, and emotional stress (Ryan, 1995). In fact, if we want to engage in work with youth, there is no intrinsic reason to choose to do so through sport, other than that sport is, simply, where we tend to find tens of millions of children and youth as active participants, spectators, and fans. The scholarship on sport suggests that when we choose to work with kids through sports, it must be done intelligently, that is, selectively. We need first to find the current aspects of (certain) sports that are good and useful, build our programs on them, and, then, undertake research to assess whether we achieved our goals. In parallel fashion, we need to critically analyze the negative aspects of current sports, and either act to change them, or steer kids entirely away from them (McKay, Messner, & Sabo, 2000).

The Present Volume

These are the issues that are addressed in greater depth in the various chapters of this book. The book has four sections. In part I, we ask the question, Under what conditions can sport for youth build character and prevent violence? Our focus is how to make sports participation an asset in the lives of marginalized urban youth. We touch on the broad array of social ills on which participation in sports programs may have an effect, although with special attention to violence. Contributors to this section furnish the rationale and provide examples, but also offer words of caution for using sport programs as a means of preventing violence and promoting positive values among young people. Part II is directly focused on media representations, particularly with regard to race, gender, and violence. Contributors discuss critical readings of sport media, and consider ways for scholars to be more involved in dialogue with sport media workers and consumers. Part III considers race: Under what conditions can sport promote interracial understanding and provide opportunities for social mobility, and under what conditions will this not occur? When should popular sports figures be seen as role models for disadvantaged youth and when should they not? In part IV, we focus directly on the problem of violence in sport, on and off the playing field. Contributors include violence researchers and violence prevention advocates who provide a context for considering sports violence and for considering the use of sport as a tool of violence prevention. Other chapters assess the extent to which sport might be a venue in which boys and men learn to normalize—even valorize—violence against other men, against women, and against their own bodies.

Within each section of the book, the chapters are sequenced to flow from a theory- and data-based description of social issues, to intervention strategies. Authors were selected deliberately to encompass disparate academic areas, from cultural studies to quantitative social science. Finally, each section ends with a conversation between one of the book's editors and a relevant sports practitioner. Thus, the organization of the book carries the burden of creating a dialogue between diverse academic scholars and community representatives, including directors of youth sports programs, policymakers, media, and the athletes themselves.

References

Anderson, E. (2000). *Trailblazing: The true story of America's first openly gay track coach.* Los Angeles & New York: Alyson Books.

Bouton, J. (1970). *Ball four.* New York: Dell Publishing.

Edwards, H. (1970). *The revolt of the black athlete.* New York: Free Press.

Edwards, H. (1971). The myth of the racially superior athlete. *Black Scholar, 3,* 56–68.

Edwards, H. (1984). The collegiate athletic arms race: Origins and implications of the rule 48 controversy. *Journal of Sport and Social Issues, 8,* 4–22.

Eitzen, D. S. (1999). *Fair and foul: Beyond the myths and paradoxes of sport.* Boulder, CO: Rowman & Littlefield.

Eitzen, D. S., & Yetman, N. B. (1977). Immune from racism? *Civil Rights Digest, 9,* 3–13.

Felshin, J. (1974). The triple option for women in sport. *Quest, 17,* 36–40.

Green, T. (1996). *The dark side of the game: My life in the NFL.* New York: Warner Books.

Gruneau, R. (1983). *Class, sports, and social development.* Amherst: University of Massachusetts Press.

Hoch, P. (1972). *Rip off the big game.* New York: Anchor Press.

Jhally, S. (1984). The spectacle of accumulation: Material and cultural factors in the evolution of the sports media complex. *Insurgent Sociologist, 12,* 41–57.

Kopay, D., & Young, P. D. (1977). *The Dave Kopay story.* New York: Arbor House.

McKay, J., Messner, M. A., & Sabo, D. (2000). Studying sport, men and masculinities from feminist standpoints. In J. McKay, M. A. Messner, & D. Sabo (Eds.), *Masculinities, gender relations, and sport* (pp. 1–12). Thousand Oaks, CA: Sage.

Meggyesy, D. (1970). *Out of their league.* Berkeley: Ramparts Press.

Ogilvie, B. C., & Tutko, T. A. (1971). Sport: If you want to build character, try something else. *Psychology Today, 5*(5), 61–63.

Oglesby, C. (Ed.) (1978). *Women and sport: From myth to reality.* Philadelphia: Lea & Febiger.

Ryan, J. (1995). *Little girls in pretty boxes.* New York: Warner Books.

Sabo, D. F., & Runfola, R. (Eds.) (1980). *Jock: Sports and male identity.* Englewood Cliffs, NJ: Prentice-Hall.

Scott, J. (1971). *The athletic revolution.* New York: Free Press.

Theberge, N. (1981). A critique of critiques: Radical and feminist writings on sport. *Social Forces, 60,* 341–353.

Tutko, T. A., & Bruns, W. (1976). *Winning is everything and other American myths.* New York: Macmillan.

PART I

Can Sport for Youth Build Character and Prevent Violence?

S port has been given a burden in American society of teaching more than simply physical fitness and athletic skills. The first section of the book takes on the question of whether and under what circumstances sport can serve as a tool for promoting youth development and for preventing delinquent or health-threatening behavior. The chapters were selected to advocate and to critique the notion that sports participation can teach social and emotional skills to youth. The section begins with a critical exploration of the conceptual bases of youth sport programs. Next, we move to an overview of the contributions of sport to youth development. Finally, we provide examples of programs designed to be sensitive to the pitfalls of assuming that the benefits of sports are automatic.

In chapter 1, Jay Coakley partitions the benefits claimed for sport into two distinctive dreams. In the one dream, sport provides diversion for "at-risk" youth who are otherwise likely to get into trouble. In this dream, sports participation is a social intervention to keep problem youth off of the streets and out of trouble. In the other dream, sport teaches values such as teamwork and positive approaches to competition, and thereby gives young people tools that will be of value when they begin their careers. In this dream, the targets are the future leaders of the community. Coakley goes to point out that both dreams are oriented toward individuals and neither dream addresses structural inequalities in society, such as racism and poverty, which may be important factors to include in a comprehensive violence prevention program. His unalloyed portrait of each model should help those who are developing sports programs more clearly to consider the messages embedded in the programs that they promote, both the explicit and the implicit goals.

Chapter 2 by Martha E. Ewing, Lori A. Gano-Overway, Crystal F. Branta, and Vern D. Seefeldt provides a literature review that details the claims made about the benefits to youth of participating in sports and the evidence in support of these claims. Areas in which it is claimed that sport may make a difference include physical fitness, work ethic, social skills, emotional regulation, moral values, self-confidence, self-esteem, and self-efficacy. In addition, participation in sport can have positive spillover to the classroom, both with respect to better grades and lessened school dropout. Similarly, a small amount of evidence indicates that the availability of sport may counteract juvenile crime.

Ironically, at the same time that sport is being proposed as a way to control deviant behavior, Ewing and her colleagues document the fact that participation opportunities are decreasing, most particularly in poor urban areas. Ewing and Steve J. Danish in chapter 3 each point to excessive concern about winning, because a focus on winning leads to limitation of participation opportunities only to the most talented.

Both Coakley and Ewing and her coauthors assert that accruing emotional and interpersonal benefits from sport participation does not happen automatically but requires that responsible adults use the sport experience deliberately to teach these life skills. Coakley catalogs conditions that must be met by a sports program in order for it to promote development; Ewing and her coauthors present ways in which coaches can make lessons in self-esteem and morality a part of the sports experience.

Danish argues that the focus must be the teaching of life skills—the behavioral and cognitive tools that individuals need in order to succeed, for instance, having positive expectations about one's future, managing anger, and making effective decisions. Life skills can be learned from sport and transferred to other life domains. He suggests that professional athletes will only be effective role models for youth if they publicly convey the qualities that lead to success in both sports and in other life venues. Danish describes two specific programs that teach life skills using sport: Going for the Goal (GOAL) and Sports United to Promote Education and Recreation (SUPER). In GOAL, life skills are taught through sports as a metaphor. In SUPER, there are both sports clinics and attention to life skills applicable to both sports participation and life.

Finally, in the interview with Marty Martinson, she describes a mentorship program that also uses sport as a vehicle, in this case, for bringing together adults and adolescent girls. She provides a firsthand description of the difficult work that is required for a program to function; the benefits are not at all automatic. Martinson attends especially to the assumptions that adults bring to their role as mentors. Her effort in training the mentors was to turn their concern with rescuing these girls into a search for the girls' strengths.

3 1833 04323 9265

In this section of the book, "youth" encompasses both boys and girls. However, there are important differences that warrant highlighting In discussions about potential benefits of sports, preventing violence, delinquent behavior, and gang membership is largely a male-oriented goal, in fact, an urban African American male goal. While less attention has been paid to girls, programs such as Martinson describes are beginning to appear. For inner-city girls, the interest is whether athletic participation can improve fitness, reduce teen pregnancy, and broaden social and academic opportunities. There is also an intriguing suggestion that girls may gain more advantages from sports programs than boys, because sports participation may challenge traditional gender role expectations (Hanson & Kraus, 1998; Miller, Sabo, Farrell, Barnes, & Melnick, 1998). For boys, in contrast, sport is consonant with dominant expectations about masculinity. Other differences between boys and girls with respect to sports are relevant to program planning. Girls are more likely than boys to participate in individual sports; boys are almost entirely engaged in team sports (Scully & Clarke, 1997). The idea of succeeding against oneself rather than by beating an opponent is embraced by girls more than by boys (van Wersch, 1997). Dropping out of sport in adolescence (age twelve and beyond) is a bigger problem for girls than for boys (Scully & Clarke, 1997). A final consideration is whether girls are better reached through single-sex or coeducational programs; currently practitioners are exploring both approaches.

Taken together, the chapters in this section provide a summary of available empirical evidence in support of the use of sport to enhance youth development, strong suggestions about the conditions that must be provided in order for programs to serve this purpose, and descriptions by Martinson and Danish of actual programs. These ideas should be provocative to researchers and of value to those who direct youth sports programs.

References

Hanson, S. L., & Kraus, R. S. (1998). Women, sports, and science: Do female athletes have an advantage? *Sociology of Education, 71,* 93–110.

Miller, K. E., Sabo, D. F., Farrell, M. P., Barnes, G. M., & Melnick, M. J. (1998). Athletic participation and sexual behavior in adolescents: The different worlds of boys and girls. *Journal of Health and Social Behavior, 39,* 108–123.

Scully, D., & Clarke, J. (1997). Gender issues in sports participation. In J. Kremer, K. Trew, & S. Ogle (Eds.), *Young people's involvement in sport* (pp. 25–56). London: Routledge.

Van Wersch, A. (1997). Individual differences and intrinsic motivations for sport participation. In J. Kremer, K. Trew, & S. Ogle (Eds.), *Young people's involvement in sport* (pp. 57–77). London: Routledge.

ONE

Using Sports to Control Deviance and Violence among Youths

Let's Be Critical and Cautious

JAY COAKLEY

The goal of this chapter is to encourage critical thinking about using sports as a means to control deviance and violence among young people. One way to accomplish this goal is to frame the topic in new and unexpected terms and to ask new questions about the topic. This helps us to break away from the dominant public discourse that usually occurs around the combined topic of youth, deviance, violence, and sports. I have found that many people in the United States have particular images in their minds when they think about using sports to control deviance and violence among youth. For the purpose of raising questions about those images, what would you think if I indicated that this chapter will focus on the following two questions:

1. Are corporate CEOs who participated in organized youth sports less likely than other CEOs to initiate and approve corporate policies that deviate from antitrust rules, do violence to the environment, or have violent consequences for residents in low-income inner-city neighborhoods?
2. Can we control corporate deviance and violence through youth sports programs offered to young people who are likely to acquire power as adults in this society?

Are these questions consistent with the images that most of us have in mind when we think about controlling deviance and violence through sports? How are they different? What are the origins of the dominant images that

13

many of us use when we think about this topic, and what are the consequences of those images for the way we think about policies, programs, and research agendas? My purpose in asking these two questions is not to distract us from important issues, but to force us to keep a wide range of important issues in mind as we discuss the possibility of using youth sports to control deviance and violence. As we think about this topic, it is important to ask at least eight additional questions:

1. How are deviance and violence defined in our research reviews and program discussions and what "counts" as deviance and violence, and what does not?
2. Who is identified as deviant or violent as we use our theories and frame our research?
3. What conceptual frameworks do we use to think about deviance and violence among young people, and on what assumptions are particular frameworks based?
4. Who and what escapes our critical attention as we use particular frameworks to discuss youth, deviance, violence, and sports?
5. How and why have youth sports have been identified as a potentially effective antidote to the wide range of problems facing some young people today—problems such as teen pregnancy, a lack of prenatal care, low-birth-weight babies, child malnutrition, lack of child care, underfunded schools, poor and unsafe housing, unemployed and underemployed parents, a lack of public transportation, high stress, high levels of environmental pollution, drug use, HIV and AIDS, assaults, murders, and gangs formed around desperate attempts to find hope or to express anger and despair?
6. What leads many people to think that youth sport programs might solve problems of deviance and violence when research clearly shows that these problems are related to a long history of economic decline, high rates of poverty, and feelings of despair in inner cities (Wilson, 1996)?
7. Why do many people see corporations as the new hope for solving the social problems affecting inner-city youth when these same corporations have moved jobs away from inner cities and demonstrated little interest in training and hiring workers from low-income areas in the United States?
8. Why do so many people today ask, "What if there were no sports?" instead of "What if there were no decent jobs enabling parents and their children to live with security and hope?"

These questions are important because we live in what might be called an "era of the corporation," and many of the images that influence public discourse about social problems are generated and distributed by those corporations. Those of us in the academic world realize this because we find that we must apply to corporations for grants when we seek support for research and programs related to social problems. We know that power and resources today rest primarily in the hands of the men who control large, transnational corporations. In the United States, over 98 percent of these powerful men are White. The policies set by these men and those who work for them serve to set parameters and to direct the focus for many of our grant proposals.

Although many of the White men who run these corporations and sit on corporate boards are good people who want to do the right thing, their jobs depend ultimately on maximizing dividends for shareholders. We should remember that the CEOs of major corporations do not receive incomes frequently in excess of $7 million per year (during the late 1990s) plus other perks because they have worked to solve social problems. Therefore, I frequently ask critical questions when the CEOs and public relations directors of large, transnational corporations generate and distribute the images used to frame many of our ideas about social interventions and social programs.

The images generated by corporations, including corporations selling athletic shoes and apparel, are so pervasive today that students in my classes now express their social concerns by asking the question, "What if there were no sports?" When I hear my students say this, I wonder if this question, first asked in Nike commercials in 1997, distracts my students from asking more critical and useful questions such as, "What if Nike hired low-wage workers in Indonesia and Vietnam, and there were no jobs in the inner city?" I think it does distract many of them. Therefore, we have class discussions through which my students quickly realize that having no job, coping with the legacy of racism, living in communities without strong and supportive social institutions, and facing the future without hope are indeed worse than having no sports to play.

With these issues in mind, I will critique some of the public discourse that increasingly frames our ideas about social intervention in the lives of young people today.

Dreams about Character, Behavior, and Sport Participation

I often am amazed by the pervasiveness of beliefs and assumptions about the character-producing and behavior-shaping potential of sport participation. Dreams of using sports to promote or redirect the development of young people, especially those who have been defined as problems and threats to society, has a long history in the United States. I will not discuss that history other than to say that these dreams have taken different forms depending on historical conditions, the prevailing political climate, and dominant beliefs about the populations of young people encompassed by the dreams.

Through U.S. history there have been two major recurring dreams about youth sports. The most prevalent one is the dream of using sports to control deviance and violence by constraining and constructively socializing young people who have been identified in dominant public discourse as lacking the character required to restrain themselves from disrupting the social order. This is what might be called "the social control and deficit-reduction dream."

This dream often corresponds with cultural climates in which certain young people have been identified as "problems" or "threats" to society. The dream focuses on changing the personal characteristics and behaviors of these young people so that they can escape their immediate environments and become productive citizens in the very same social and economic system that gave rise to the conditions that limited their lives in the first place. If this seems to be an ironic dream, it is.

This dream does not focus on the need for social justice, *or* on rebuilding strong community-based social institutions, *or* on reestablishing the resource base of the communities where these young people live, *or* on politicizing and then empowering these young people to be effective change agents working on behalf of their communities. Instead, it focuses on increasing self-esteem among young sport participants so that they can pull themselves up by their athletic shoelaces and escape the conditions that led others to label them as *at-risk,* mark them as problems, and see them in need of control and socialization. This dream consists of a modern version of the *pull-yourself-up-by-your-own-bootstraps* approach to solving social problems.

According to this dream, sport programs are forms of social intervention that can be used to "fix" the character and lifestyle defects of certain young people in inner-city areas, while controlling them at the same time. Success in this dream occurs if crime rates decline and if young people are less apt to disrupt the social order. The young people most in need of "fixing" in this dream usually come from low-income and ethnic minority backgrounds.

This *social control and deficit-reduction dream* is frequently described in dramatic terms by people in "the social problems industry"— a high-growth industry in our increasingly privatized political world. The people in this industry sell proposals that are based on the dream that sports can be used to eliminate character deficits in certain children and thereby minimize problems in the society as a whole. For example, when the Midnight Basketball League was founded in Glenarden, Maryland, in 1986, it was noted in *Sports Illustrated* that this program would take "Black inner-city males off the streets by keeping them in the gym during . . . the hours when they would be most likely to get into trouble" (Bessone, 1991). Subsequent discussions of "midnight basketball" have followed this dream theme. In fact, most of them have occurred in association with debates about crime bills at all levels of government. During these debates it has been clear that many people believe that these leagues can be used to control the behavior of young, Black, inner-city males—a segment of the population defined by many policy makers as an "urban other" in need of policing (Pitter & Andrews, 1997).

A second recurring dream about character, behavior, and sport participation involves using youth sports to expand developmental opportunities and to build leadership and other usable skills among young people defined as assets to the community. This is what might be called "the social opportunity and privilege-promotion dream." This dream also focuses on individuals, but the emphasis is on building their strengths rather than on reducing their deficits. The dream does not focus on young people learning to pull themselves up by their athletic shoelaces. Instead, it focuses on young people achieving success by learning how to take advantage of the privileged positions their parents have obtained in the society.

This dream, like the *social control and deficit-reduction dream*, has nothing to do with social justice, community development, or structural and cultural transformation. It assumes that the world is right as it is, and that the challenge for young people is simply learning to position themselves to benefit from how the world works.

Those who have this *social opportunity and privilege-promotion dream* see sports as microcosms of the larger world—a world in which competition prevails, where individual confidence makes a person a good competitor, and where teamwork is needed to put together the deals that lead to success in the marketplace. Those who have this dream assume that sport participation prepares young people for this world, that playing sports opens doors to opportunities and enables young people to live more successful lives than their parents.

My goal in this chapter is to first raise questions about the usefulness of these two dreams and then to argue that we need *alternative dreams* that fall outside the parameters set by either the *social control and deficit-reduction dream* or the *social opportunity and privilege-promotion dream*. Examples of *alternative dreams* would include dreams informed by a quest for community development rather than by a quest only for individual achievement, and dreams based on concerns for justice rather than on concerns only about individual freedom and choice. They would also include dreams that visualize young people growing into political and cultural change agents, not just young people who are aspiring stockbrokers and bank presidents. They would be dreams in which progress is defined in terms of maximizing the public good, not maximizing only individual and corporate bottom lines.

My point here is that we need dreams, including sport dreams, that go beyond images of smiling, airborne, athletic cultural icons that have magically escaped or transcended a world full of difficult social, economic, and political challenges to reach awesome heights of individual achievement. Of course, these "be like Mike" (i.e., Michael Jordan) images are comforting for privileged people who wish to think that difficult social, economic, and political problems can be solved if every individual would only try harder, run faster, and jump higher to achieve the American Dream. But they are *not* the images needed to inspire real social transformation.

Unfortunately, the *alternative dreams* that I have described do not inform dominant public discourse about social problems today. Where are the images that might be used to construct alternative dreams? Why are these images not seen in television commercials and halftime reports of sport events sponsored by corporations? Such images are difficult to find, and they are not included in commercials and halftime reports because they do not represent messages that are compatible with dominant corporate interests today.

Illustrations of Dominant Sport Dreams

Two events that occurred recently in the Denver metropolitan area serve to illustrate the *social control and deficit-reduction dream* and the *social opportunity and privilege-promotion dream.* The events, both involving youth sports and both covered by the *Denver Post,* also show how these dreams draw on and influence ideas about young people and about the social worlds in which they live.

During February 1997 there were two separate cases involving adults pleading for youth sport programs and facilities for young people in the Denver metro area. By chance, one case involved an ethnically mixed, working-class and low-income inner-city area encompassing a predominantly minority population in Denver. The other case involved a predominantly White, upper-middle-class suburb that is far from the inner city.

The texts of the media coverage of each of these cases were quite different, as were their implications and general tone. I realize that there are many ways to read news stories. But when these stories are viewed in the context of current historical conditions, prevailing political orientations, and dominant beliefs about young, poor, inner-city youths of color and beliefs about young, upper-middle-class, White suburban youths, we can identify at least some of the assumptions that inform them and influence how people read and interpret them.

I have selected quotes from the news coverage of each of these two cases to provide a sense of how the issues involved in each were conceptualized and portrayed in the stories told in the articles. My goal is to show how public discourse and community discussions about policy issues are related to, and informed by, each of the two major sport dreams I have described. My argument is that when these news stories are juxtaposed and viewed in connection with that discourse, they assume, use, and evoke powerful images and ideologies. The news coverage, as the quotes partially show, implies important unstated assumptions— assumptions about young people, sports, families, communities, ethnicity, adults in the lives of young people, and the organization of society in the United States. Please note that my argument is *not* solely based on these two cases and their associated media coverage. In fact, by themselves, these two cases are not very significant except that they are similar to many other cases that are and will continue to occur in the United States. Therefore, these two cases illustrate rather than provide the basis for my analysis.

The inner-city case. The first case involved a debate over which organizations in the city of Denver would have access to inner-city softball fields during the summer of 1997. The Police Athletic League (PAL) had been granted the bulk of field permits, and other organizations were questioning this decision because they had no fields on which to play games and run their leagues. The coverage of this story was informed by the *social control and deficit-reduction dream*.

As the debate about access to the softball fields occurred, the coverage in the *Denver Post* went like this:

> The controversy has been brewing. . . . Competition for the finite supply of fields and play times is always fierce. . . . [An aide to the mayor] said the summer [PAL] would "give kids an opportunity to do something besides hang out on the street and get into trouble."
>
> [The PAL director] said if the police league doesn't get the fields it was originally allotted, the summer baseball program may have to be scrapped altogether. "Summer baseball may not happen this summer. Where it's going to go from here, I don't know." (*Denver Post*, February 12, 1997, front page)

A day later, the follow-up story reported that

> Backers of the police league, meanwhile, claimed there
> would be "riots in the streets" if it isn't allowed to play summer
> ball. (*Denver Post,* February 13, 1997, p. B-1)

The underlying theme in the overall coverage of this issue was that the low-income, minority youths in this inner-city area need to be kept off the streets, and that if they did not have adult-supervised activities to keep them occupied, they might engage in disruptive behaviors. The arguments being used by the representatives of the Police Athletic League, and the newspaper coverage itself was grounded clearly in the *social control and deficit-reduction dream.*

When viewed in connection with dominant public discourse today, this coverage reaffirms certain assumptions about the characteristics of certain populations of young people and their families. I am *not* saying that these assumptions underlie everyone's interpretations of the coverage. But popular stereotypes and dominant cultural images strongly suggest assumptions that these inner-city youth are potentially dangerous and likely to get into trouble unless they are placed in structured settings where they are controlled by adults. Other assumptions that underlie a dominant reading of the coverage are that the parents of these young people are uninvolved and unable to control their children, that the young people are inclined toward deviance and should be protected from the environment and themselves, and that the streets and the community as a whole would be safer if these young people could be controlled and socialized through sports.

Before everyone who has ever used the "get-kids-off-the-street-and-keep-them-out-of-trouble" argument gets defensive, let me say that I realize the importance of any programs that provide young people with safe contexts in which they can develop competence and come to understand that they are valued members of the community. However, my point here is that when this argument is combined with dominant ideological orientations today, it ties directly into the *social control and deficit-reduction dream* that many people in positions of power use when they think about certain social problems and about how sports might be used to solve them.

When the political winds are blowing in a strong right-wing direction, many legislators do not think twice before taking that argument and using it to justify funding for new prisons instead of new athletic fields. They think that if getting people, especially people of color, off the street is the way to keep them out of trouble, nothing could be more effective than putting them behind bars. Funding priorities in most states suggest that this has already occurred.

Another danger with the "get-them-off-the-street-and-keep-them-out-of-trouble" approach is that it lets powerful people off the hook by reaffirming popular assumptions that identify young low-income and minority youth as "problems," as "at-risk," and in need of intervention in the form of externally imposed systems of socialization and social control. At the same time it allows them to ignore key questions that would force them to acknowledge important social issues. These issues include recent changes that have led to (1) a dislocation of economic activities in most inner-city areas populated by low-income minorities, (2) a resurgence of racial and socioeconomic residential segregation, (3) a gutting of city funds that could be used for social programs serving the needs of children in low-income communities, and (4) the reemergence of an ideology that blames children and their unemployed and underemployed parents for the problems they encounter as they live lives devoid of hopeful visions of the future (Pitter & Andrews, 1997).

The suburban case. At the very same time that the debate over access to inner-city softball fields was occurring there was coverage of two competing private, suburban soccer clubs that had joined forces to solicit corporate sponsorships. They also united to lobby the local suburban government to provide funds for a new thousand-seat soccer stadium and twenty-four state-of-the-art soccer fields for the young people in the two clubs. The coverage of this story was informed by the *social opportunity and privilege-promotion dream.* Consider the following segments from the newspaper coverage:

> Nike has already agreed to supply the combined club with equipment and pledged to open the doors to other companies interested in corporate sponsorship of the stadium.
> The combined club wants to build a complex in the southwestern part of the metro area. . . . But combining the clubs will do more than just build fields, club officials said. It will also allow them to bump up the caliber of soccer and increase the chances of their kids getting college scholarships.
> "It's [mainly about] getting our kids national exposure. They would have [the] college recognition they deserve," [the soccer club president] said.
> "The new club would be able to attract better-paid coaches for the competitive teams, and the club's staff could help train the recreational coaches, who are now often parents of the players." (*Denver Post,* February 13, 1997; front page)

The coverage of the suburban case emphasizes the hope that sport programs would provide young people in upper-middle-class communities with deserved exposure and recognition. It also was hoped that this exposure and recognition would maximize opportunities for these young people to attend college with athletic scholarships to pay their way. The assumptions associated with such coverage are that sport participation for these young people is secondary to developing competence and attending college, that these young people deserve opportunities to expand their contact with the world and prepare for the future, and that these young people are valued and have potential that should be developed. Also assumed is that their parents care enough to be coaches and to pay for trained and certified coaches for their children, and that communities are best served by giving these young people opportunities to develop their skills, gain recognition, further their education, and then achieve positions where they can make contributions to society.

Themes in the coverage and interpretation of both cases. If we view the media coverage of both of these cases as part of a public discourse in which youth sports are defined as vital sites for socialization experiences, there are at least six similar assumptions underlying the overall coverage of these and many other cases:

1. Change is grounded primarily in maximizing individual freedom and choice (as opposed to maximizing social justice).
2. Progress is best measured in terms of individual achievement (as opposed to community development).
3. Problems are best solved by fostering individual mobility (as opposed to transforming communities economically and politically).
4. Programs should focus primarily on increasing self-esteem (as opposed to creating change agents and community organizations to instigate structural and ideological transformation).
5. Controlling deviance and violence best occurs by making poor, young people responsible and accountable (as opposed to making transnational corporations and political leaders accountable).
6. Violence is associated with young people, especially those in gangs (as opposed to the corporate and government decisions and policies that have had devastating consequences for low-income, minority communities).

Learning from Experience

My purpose in the previous section was to use two everyday examples to illustrate that we must be cautious as we dream about using sports to control deviance and violence. If we are not cautious we may unwittingly reaffirm ideological positions that identify young people, especially young people of color as "problems," and then forget that the real problems are deindustrialization, unemployment, underemployment, poverty, racism, and at least twenty years of defunding of social programs that have traditionally been used to foster community development in ways that positively impact the lives of young people.

When we forget these latter issues, we let off the hook political and corporate leaders who have taken for granted that the bottom line must inform social action. Or worse, we end up letting those "bottom liners" frame our own social action in ways that focus almost exclusively on individual character development and behavior control and ignore issues of community development and social transformation. Of course, it is important to have strategies that increase individual achievement and boost standardized test scores. But strategies are also needed to address key structural problems such as underfunded schools, communities without services, poverty, racism, and the economic dislocation that has devastated inner-city areas and given rise to a generation of young people desperate for hope and support.

Regardless of how many sport programs are sponsored by public, nonprofit, and private organizations, there will always be an emphasis on using violence as a means of surviving and gaining status when young people live their lives in contexts where there are pervasive threats to physical well being, moral worth, the achievement of adult status, and in the case of young men, threats to masculinity. Abandoning projects that foster social justice and community development in favor of offering young people a choice between participating in sport programs so they can be saved through assimilation, or joining gangs and risking lives in prison, clearly misses the point (see Cole, 1996a, 1996b).

In addition to creative programs for young people, what we need today are programs and policies that make powerful people and the organizations they represent accountable for the forces that have gradually eroded and sometimes devastated working-class communities. The call for such programs and policies will not come until questions are asked about what counts as violence and who counts as deviant in our society. Assuming that chronic unemployment and the poverty and hopelessness it causes are best handled by using sport programs to socialize the children of parents who have no access to decent jobs is certainly questionable. If the provision of sport programs distracts attention from economic factors that have destroyed the foundations for community in inner cities, school-funding formulas that produce savage inequalities in the lives of children, and political decisions that have eroded inner-city infrastructures and social programs, the programs subvert the possibility of needed social changes.

Additional Reasons to Be Cautious about Our Sport Dreams

In addition to being cautious about sport dreams because of the ideological foundations on which they often rest, we also should be cautious because research on sport participation and behavior suggests that, *by itself,* playing sports is a poor antidote for deviance and violence. Those who play sports are less likely than comparable others to engage in deviant or violent behaviors *only when* participation is accompanied by an emphasis on a philosophy of nonviolence, respect for self and others, the importance of fitness and control over self, confidence in physical skills, and a sense of responsibility (Coakley, 2001; Trulson, 1986). Simply removing young people from "the streets" is just the beginning. Furthermore, if sport programs emphasize hostility toward opponents, aggression as a strategy, bodies as weapons, domination of others, and letting referees and coaches make calls that young athletes should learn to make for themselves, we can't expect rates of deviance or violence to decrease. Only when the meaning and experience of sport participation connects young people with others in supportive and positive ways can we hope for rates to decline.

Further caution is suggested by research showing that sport participation, under certain conditions, provides a context in which groups of young people develop a collective hubris that may be associated with extreme behaviors such as binge drinking and a range of assaultive behaviors (Donnelly, 1993; Snyder, 1994). When sport participation separates young people from the rest of the community and when young athletes see themselves as superior to others who are not part of their athletic fraternity, deviance and violence may be directed at those "outsiders" who are seen as undeserving of their respect (Coakley, 2001).

In general, we know that sport participation does not produce a catharsis in a psychoanalytic sense or a definitive set of moral lessons leading to special off-the-field sensibilities about good and evil. We also know that sports often *do* serve as contexts for important experiences in the lives of some young people, and that sport participation can produce positive developmental outcomes when it expands the number and types of connections with others and broadens young people's ideas about who they are, what the world is about, and how they are connected with that world. But when sport participation constricts relationships with others and encourages the formation of a unidimensional view of self, it often will be associated with negative developmental outcomes.

These are not earthshaking conclusions, but they do lead us to be cautious when we make generalizations about the consequences of sport participation in the lives of young people and when we frame sport programs as tools for constructively intervening in the lives of young people.

Making Dreams Happen

Although there are good reasons to be cautious about what we can expect in connection with sport dreams, I empathize with the dedicated youth sport coaches and program administrators who have used sports as a tool for connecting with and supporting young people. I especially empathize with those who have used sports as a life preserver for rescuing young people drowning in a dangerous mix of malnutrition, inadequate health care, poor housing, underfunded schools, homelessness, HIV and AIDS, dangerous and polluted environments, drug use, teen pregnancy, police brutality, gangs, assaults, murders, and parental unemployment.

Regardless of the social, economic, and political origins of that mix, young people must be rescued by any means available. However, if this rescue work is not accompanied by strategies that attack the origins of the problems, we will continue to run short of life preservers.

In the meantime, for those engaged in this rescue work there is encouraging empirical support for making the case that under certain conditions sports can serve as a life preserver for individuals. Support is found in research on sports, on psychosocial development, and on adolescence. The combined findings on these topics emphasizes the fact that young people, regardless of background, face an identifiable range of developmental challenges as they grow up, and that meeting those challenges is most likely when they have access to a variety of personal and social resources. Sport programs, under certain conditions, can put young people in touch with those resources. But this does not occur automatically, nor do young people automatically use accessible resources in positive ways. So making dreams happen through sports can be tricky, and it depends on our knowledge of the experiences of young people rather than on our knowledge of sports.

At the risk of oversimplifying an impressive array of research and theory on youth and youth development, I have concluded that positive transitions from childhood to adolescence to adulthood are most likely when young people live in a context in which they are physically safe, personally valued, socially connected, morally and economically supported, personally and politically empowered, and hopeful about the future. To the extent that sport programs serve these needs, we can expect them to contribute to the positive development of participants.

Being Physically Safe

Research indicates that threats to physical well-being produce withdrawal or defensive violence, neither of which is conducive to youth development. When sport programs provide young people with a safe environment they facilitate developmental possibilities. Actual positive development, however, depends on additional experiences. But the importance of providing safety cannot be underestimated, especially for young people who live in areas where violent and destructive forces are prevalent (Wacquant, 1992).

Research also suggests that feeling safe can be difficult when sport programs emphasize hostility as a motive for dominating opponents, aggression as a strategy, and bodies as weapons. Regardless of the sport, an explicit philosophy of nonviolence combined with respect for self and others is important if young people are to feel physically safe. Interestingly, research indicates that even in heavy contact sports such as boxing and the martial arts it is possible to teach participants a philosophy of nonviolence (Trulson, 1986; Wacquant, 1992, 1995).

Being Personally Valued

Research indicates that a positive sense of moral worth facilitates positive development. When sport programs teach skills, develop competence, and give young people opportunities to display that competence, self-esteem is promoted. If this occurs in settings where young people are treated and respected as whole persons, and learn how to clarify their experiences in the larger community in which they live, self-esteem may then grow into a general sense of moral worth. This is especially important in the case of young people who are members of groups that have been socially and culturally marginalized in society. However, when sport programs separate young people from the community, it is difficult for them to convert self-esteem in an athletic setting into a sense of moral worth in a larger social context. The ultimate goal is not to take young people off the streets, but to enable them to become agents of progressive change and social development in their communities.

Being Socially Connected

The experience of being connected with peers, of having close friends and belonging to a group in which experiences can be shared, is key to development. (This is why young people become members of cliques, crews, and gangs.) Sport programs contribute to development when they provide access to peers combined with learning experiences that enable young people to connect with those peers in deep and supportive ways. Such connections depend on being responsive to others, caring, being empathetic, being flexible, and having good communication and conflict resolution skills (Martinek & Hellison, 1997). These forms of social competence are especially important for young people who regularly face adversity and conflict in their everyday lives.

Being Morally and Economically Supported

Development during childhood and adolescence depends on receiving moral and economic support from adults, including parents, teachers, mentors, and advocates. Adults and adult institutions structure the life course of young people by providing opportunities to develop and use abilities in their communities. Adults also guide the moral and economic choices made by young people (Williams & Kornblum, 1985). When supportive adults and adult institutions are absent, development suffers and poor choices are common.

Marita Golden highlighted the importance of adult support in the lives of young African American males in her book, *Saving Our Sons* (1995). As she thought about what her own son would need to survive his life as an adolescent growing up in Washington, DC, she concluded that he would need "a 'congregation' of fathers, formal and informal, to surround him" (p. 62). And as she thought about the importance of those men in her son's life and in the lives of his peers, she noted that "all the 'male role models' in the world could not reach a boy unless he had been consistently, purposely loved and cared for, unless he already had been taught and was prepared to trust himself and others" (p. 64).

Golden's insights remind us that rhetoric about role models often distracts attention away from the fact that young people need advocates, as well as models, in their lives. Too often the call for role models is used by privileged White adults to justify why they should not be held responsible for providing moral and economic guidance for young people of color.

Being Personally and Politically Empowered

When sport programs are organized so that young people themselves have a voice in the program and are heard by those who run the programs, sport participation is likely to facilitate positive development in the form of autonomy (Martinek & Hellison, 1997). When young people have a voice they are much more likely to be seek information about the program in which they participate and the community context in which the program exists. Many young people desperately need experiences that show them they can exert control over their own lives and the contexts in which they live.

Using sport programs as sites for enabling young people to become critically informed about their connection with the world and the social, economic, and political forces that are at work in the world around them is rare. However, sport programs have been used to enable young people to gain more control over their personal lives and over the immediate sport settings in which they practice and play games (Martinek & Hellison,

1997). Of course, it is a big jump from exercising control over one's personal life in a gym and over the immediate context in which sport participation occurs to exercising control in the community at large. But the process is similar, and it would seem that there is the potential for learning to exercise such control in the community.

Being Hopeful about the Future

When sport programs expose young people to a wide range of possibilities and visions for their lives, they open the door for positive development. Hope is grounded in a sense of efficacy or the belief that goals can be achieved. After years of working with young people in inner-city areas, Martinek and Hellison (1997) note that hope exists in the lives of young people to the extent that they see significant others in their lives achieve goals and see some degree of predictability in their immediate social environment. Similarly, Golden (1995) notes that as young people grow up they "need to see their parents capable of providing for them [so they can] learn that the world is a fair and reasonable sphere for them to enter, one that they can trust" (p. 60). If they see parents unable to deal with their own problems and an environment in which events appear to be random and capricious, hopelessness is likely.

Sport participation may put young people in touch with significant others who can deal successfully with challenges in their own lives and who can serve as "hookups" to experiences and opportunities that provide young people with the exposure to possible futures and the hope of making positive things happen in their lives. But this clearly involves more than shooting baskets or running sprints. Many adults who work with young people in inner-city areas realize this and try to serve as "hookups" for as many youngsters as possible.

This list of needs can be daunting for anyone who considers how sport programs might positively impact the lives of young people, especially young people living in areas where economic dislocation and other social problems are pervasive. But unless these needs can be met, sport programs will never be a viable form of *social* intervention.

Summary

The purpose of this chapter is to help all of us keep sports in perspective in our discussions about youth, deviance, and violence. Strategically organized sport programs may serve to control rates of deviance and violence among those lucky enough to be included in them. But the long-term effectiveness of sport programs as forms of social intervention depends on how they are combined with critically informed strategies to alter the forces that have produced serious economic dislocation and other social problems in certain communities.

When sport dreams focus our attention strictly on issues of individual mobility and distract us from developing strategies for community development, they often do more to reproduce social and economic inequality than they do to produce meaningful social and economic transformation. In the absence of policies and programs designed to foster transformation, the provision of sport programs is likely to benefit corporate bottom lines more than it will ever benefit those who have been socially and economically marginalized to the point of desperation. And it is desperation that gives rise to deviance and violence.

References

Bessone, T. L. (1991). Welcome to night court. *Sports Illustrated, 12,* 20–21.

Coakley, J. (2001). *Sport in society: Issues and controversies.* New York: McGraw-Hill.

Cole, C. (1996a). American Jordan: P.L.A.Y., consensus, and punishment. *Sociology of Sport Journal, 13,* 366–397.

Cole, C. (1996b). P.L.A.Y., Nike, and Michael Jordan: National fantasy and racialization of crime and punishment. *Working paper in Sport & Leisure Commerce, 1* (1) (University of Memphis; http://www.hmse.memphis.edu).

Donnelly, P. (1993). Problems associated with youth involvement in high-performance sport. In B. R. Cahill & A. J. Pearl (Eds.), *Intensive participation in children's sports* (pp. 95–126). Champaign, IL: Human Kinetics Publishers.

Golden, M. (1995). *Saving our sons: Raising black children in a turbulent world.* New York: Doubleday.

Martinek, T. J., & Hellison, D. R. (1997). Fostering resiliency in under-served youth through physical activity. *Quest, 49* (1), 34–49.

Pitter, R., & Andrews, D. L. (1997). Serving America's underserved: Reflections on sport and recreation in an emerging social problems industry. *Quest, 49* (1), 85–99.

Snyder, E. E. (1994). Interpretations and explanations of deviance among college athletes: A case study. *Sociology of Sport Journal, 11,* 231–248.

Trulson, M. E. (1986). Martial arts training: a novel "cure" for juvenile delinquency. *Human Relations, 39,* 1131–1140.

Wacquant, L. J. D. (1992). The social logic of boxing in Black Chicago: Toward a sociology of pugilism. *Sociology of Sport Journal, 9,* 221–254.

Wacquant, L. J. D. (1995). The pugilistic point of view: How boxers think and feel about their trade. *Theory and Society, 24,* 489–535.

Williams, T., & Kornblum, W. (1985). *Growing up poor.* Lexington, MA: Lexington Books.

Wilson, W. J. (1996). *When work disappears.* New York: Knopf.

TWO

The Role of Sports
in Youth Development

MARTHA E. EWING, LORI A. GANO-OVERWAY,
CRYSTAL F. BRANTA, AND VERN D. SEEFELDT

Proponents of youth sports have enumerated many benefits associated with participation in organized youth sport programs. Specifically, Seefeldt (1987) proposed that through participation in sports children (a) develop physical skills that can contribute to a lifetime of physical involvement; (b) improve fitness; (c) learn social and emotional skills; (d) develop moral values; and (e) acquire a better sense of self through increased perceived competence, self-esteem, and self-confidence. However, the development of these competencies does not occur automatically. The action of coaches and parents determine whether or not youth acquire these positive aspects of sport. This chapter will provide an overview of six areas where participation in sport may contribute to youth development: (a) fitness, health, and well-being; (b) social competence; (c) physical competence and self-esteem; (d) moral development; (e) aggression and violence; and (f) education. In addition, we will address some of the barriers that have led to a decline in participation, particularly in urban environments.

Fitness, Health, and Well-Being

The relationship between fitness, health, and participation in sports is unresolved due to the continuing debate on the definition of fitness and the appropriate method for assessing fitness in youth. Corbin and Pangrazi (1992) reported that little evidence exists that children and youth are less fit today than in previous decades. This statement does not mean that all children have attained some acceptable level of fitness. Blair

(1992) argues that approximately 20 percent of children are probably at risk for problems associated with cardiovascular disease and that educators should make more vigorous efforts to help these children find more active lifestyles.

In 2000, Shalala and Riley's report on physical activity and health identified physical inactivity as a serious public health problem nationwide. The President's Council on Physical Fitness and Sport (1997) proposed several factors that might contribute to these national problems: (a) influence of television; (b) dwindling requirements for physical education in the schools; (c) the steep sport dropout rate among adolescents; (d) physiological issues such as high levels of cholesterol, high blood pressure, and diabetes; and (e) social pressures and personal misgivings of overweight individuals about physical activity. Additionally, in a study of preschool and elementary age youth (4–10 years of age) in a low-economic school district, Branta and Goodway (1996) found that children were unable to run the length of the gym without stopping. Some of the participants even became nauseated after only 2–3 minutes of continuous, vigorous movement. A few of the children were scared when they started sweating or when their hearts started pounding because they had never experienced sensations associated with vigorous physical activity. Therefore, children and adolescents are in need of opportunities to help them learn about fitness and health.

The problems of fitness and low-skill development are even more pronounced for girls living in poverty. In particular, girls living in poverty experience greater violence, family fragmentation, substance abuse, sexually transmitted diseases, and greater risk for unwanted sexual activity (President's Council on Physical Fitness and Sports, 1997). Added to this list could be the lack of athletic opportunity, low physical activity, and unsafe or unhealthy environments. Girls living in poverty are less likely to receive basic information about exercise, diet, and sport. Likewise, they are less apt to receive quality physical education and sports training at earlier ages, thereby restricting the development of motor skills (President's Council on Physical Fitness and Sport, 1997).

Youth who participate in sport programs should derive an appreciation of physical fitness. In fact, youth 10 to 18 years of age frequently identify some aspect of fitness (e.g., "to get exercise") among their top ten reasons for participating in sport (Ewing & Seefeldt, 1989). Youthful participants report experiencing some satisfaction from increased cardiorespiratory capacity, greater flexibility, stronger muscles, and less body fat. In addition, youth who participate in organized sport (including cheerleading and dance) had greater total daily energy expenditure and moderate-to-vigorous energy expenditure, and spent less time watching television than those who did not participate (Katzmarzyk & Malina, 1998). However, the fitness benefits derived from sports are variable. For example, soccer participants gain high benefits in the areas of aerobic capacity and muscular endurance but only moderate benefits in the areas of anaerobic capacity, muscular strength, total body coordination, and flexibility. Participants in baseball/softball gain low aerobic capacity and muscular endurance but high anaerobic capacity and muscular strength and moderate levels of total body coordination and flexibility (Seefeldt & Brown, 1995). Very few sports contribute to "high" total body coordination and flexibility; diving, gymnastics, and fencing are the exceptions.

Coaches must be aware of the youth on their teams who have low-skill levels and who are less fit. These youth will need extra encouragement and support while they develop sport skills and improve their fitness. In addition, the teammates of these low-skilled and low-fit youth must be sensitized to individual differences and discouraged from making derogatory remarks and/or "making fun" of youth who have perhaps the most to gain from being involved in sports.

The question receiving more attention today is how educators and promoters of youth sport programs can sustain the activity levels of early childhood across the late childhood and adolescent years. Freedson and Rowland (1992) indicated that children's habitual physical activity levels are low and that these levels decline rather dramatically from childhood through adolescence. These data parallel the research on attrition from youth sport programs, especially among males (Weiss, 1992). If we are to change the pattern of declining participation in sport and physical activity that occurs around 12 to 14 years of age (Seefeldt, Ewing, & Walk, 1991), Freedson and Rowland (1992) argue that "fun must be a primary component of any physical activity program for children to create the best possible scenario for them to maintain an active lifestyle throughout adolescence and the teenage years" (p. 135). Unfortunately, greater opportunities exist among children who grow up in middle and upper economic classes where resources enable adults to sponsor, organize, and administer youth sport programs (Ponessa, 1992).

Social Competence

While there are many benefits to being involved in sport, one of the most important contributions that sport makes to youth development is in the area of social and emotional development. Through interactions with adults and peers, children should learn appropriate behavior and learn how to manage their emotions. For example, the amount of physical play between parents and their preschool children has been associated with greater social competence of youth (MacDonald, 1987). Through the self-regulation process and the development of interpersonal and problem-solving skills, physical play is central to the development of social competence.

Participation in sport alone does not result in the development of positive social and emotional characteristics. For children who experience failure or disappointment, adult intervention is critical to help children understand "why" events happen in sport and to learn from the experience. For example, if a child goes to practice and attempts all the drills, and then arrives at the game and does not start or even get into the game until the outcome has been determined, she might conclude that the coach does not like her. An adult can help the child understand the concepts of sharing playing time and that not everyone can start. This lesson is hard for most children to understand and, without adult intervention, they may erroneously conclude that "no one likes them" or that they are "no good" at organized sport and withdraw from further involvement. If no one helps young participants to understand the "realities" of sport, these children may develop negative behaviors or attitudes about sport. Children may create problems to get the attention of their parents and the coaches when they feel that they are being treated unfairly. Sport provides many situations rich in lessons about how to interact appropriately in situations that seem unjust.

There is also a positive relationship between physical competence, interpersonal skills, and peer acceptance (Evans & Roberts, 1987; Weiss & Duncan, 1992). Weiss and Duncan (1992) found that boys and girls who believed that they were physically competent were actually competent as rated by their teachers. Those children who believed that they were physically competent were also those who perceived themselves to be accepted by their peers and were interpersonally competent as rated by their teachers. Involvement in sport influences the total child, including her physical, social, and emotional competence. Development of competencies also relates to self-esteem. When others acknowledge their successes in sport and physical activity, children gain a sense of worthiness and a growing sense of confidence in their ability to succeed in the execution of the skills.

Physical Competence and Self-Esteem

The relationship of self-esteem to continued involvement in sport is more complex. As children receive more instruction and practice, their physical skills should improve, which will result in more success and greater affect (i.e., pride and joy). Harter (1983) has proposed four dimensions underlying global self-esteem: (a) competence, or success in meeting achievement demands; (b) social acceptance, or attention, worthiness, and positive reinforcement received from significant others; (c) control, or feelings of internal responsibility for outcomes; and (d) virtue, or adherence to moral and ethical standards. Affect is central in formulations of self-esteem (Harter, 1981). The pride and joy or shame and disappointment that accompany perceptions of competence or incompetence are thought to influence motivated behavior. Thus, children need to be taught that a mistake is not synonymous with failure. Rather a mistake means that new strategies, more practice, or greater effort are needed to succeed at the task. What is often required when children perceive a mistake as a failure is for an adult to intervene and help children see other options rather than conclude that they lack ability at the task.

Self-esteem is tied closely to children's perceptions of competence. During the preschool years, children determine their perceptions of competence at a task by doing the task. As one child stated, "I know that I am good at jumping because I tried and tried to jump high and then I did." High for this child was several inches! By age 6 children begin to use social comparison as a way of determining their ability at a task. In sport, children ages 8 and 9 rely upon game outcome and parental feedback as primary informational sources of competence. Older children (ages 10 to 14) depend more heavily on social comparison to peers as well as evaluation by peers as sources of information about competence (Horn & Hasbrook, 1986, 1987; Horn & Weiss, 1991).

The highly visible arena of youth sports provides children with many opportunities to determine their ability when compared with others on their team or on the opponent's team. Unfortunately, given the influence of other factors such as maturation, previous knowledge of the sport, or ability to perform a sport skill, children often reach incorrect conclusions about their abilities. The findings of Horn and her colleagues (1986, 1987, 1991) suggest that early involvement of parents and coaches is critical in the development of more accurate assessments of competence in sport for youth who are learning sport skills. Without adults helping youth to differentiate the issues of effort and ability, children may decide too quickly that they are not good or competent at a sport and, thus, lose interest in continuing to work at developing their skills.

The impact of coaches' feedback on the development of self-esteem of youth was described in a classic study by Smith, Smoll, and Curtis (1979). Youth baseball players whose coaches had been educated to use a "positive approach" to coaching, that is, more frequent encouragement, positive reinforcement, and corrective feedback, had significantly higher self-esteem ratings over the course of a season than children whose coaches used these techniques less frequently. The most compelling evidence was found for children who started the season with the lowest ratings of self-esteem. In addition to evaluating themselves more positively, they evaluated their coaches more positively. In a follow-up study, Barnett, Smoll, and Smith (1992) reported identical findings. In addition, they found that one year later, 95 percent of the youth who played for coaches who had been educated to use the positive approach signed up to play baseball compared with 75 percent of the youth who played baseball with untrained volunteer adult coaches.

The role of coaches' feedback in developing perceptions of competence is not as straightforward as providing only positive comments to an athlete. Horn (1985) examined the influence of coaching behaviors on the self-esteem and perceived competence of female softball players ranging in age from 13 to 15 years. Coaches' patterns of verbal and nonverbal reinforcement were observed in both practice and competitive settings across the entire season. Although Horn reported that skill development was the primary contributor to positive changes in self-perceptions of ability, certain coaching behaviors also significantly influenced perceptions of self-esteem during practice situations only. Players who received more constructive criticism in response to performance errors had higher perceptions of competence than players who received more frequent positive reinforcement or no reinforcement related to performance. Horn attributed these findings to their contingency and appropriateness to player behavior. Too many times coaches give positive reinforcement, such as "Good job, Mary," when the effort did not achieve the desired outcome. The coaches' use of criticism, however, was often associated with a direct response to a skill error and usually contained skill-relevant information on how to improve (e.g., "That's not the way I taught you to hit a ball! Put both hands together and keep your elbows away from your body."). Thus, the quality of coaches' feedback, specifically the contingency to athletes' behavior and the appropriateness of the information given, rather than the quantity of the feedback and the use of only positive statements, is crucial to children's cognitions about the meaning of these messages.

Moral Development

Sport provides a dynamic domain for the development and expression of moral values and behavior. Sport activities provide participants with the opportunity to demonstrate (a) values such as working hard, striving to achieve, and playing fair; and (b) appropriate moral behavior toward others or good sportsmanship (Shields & Bredemeier, 1995). However, participation in sport alone does not lead to moral attitudes, judgments, or behaviors. Participation in physical play and sport can both facilitate and/or undermine the moral development of youth.

Children learn moral behavior from engaging with others, watching the behaviors of others, and/or being taught ethical behavior. Youth in a Tae Kwon Do class that emphasized physical skills related to fighting plus the philosophy underlying Tae Kwon Do (i.e., reflection and meditation) reported lower levels of anxiety and aggression, increased self-esteem, and improved social skills in comparison to those students who received training in self-defense skills only (Trulson, 1986). Thus, participation in sport does not necessarily lead to sportsmanlike behavior (e.g., lower aggression and improved social skills) unless sportsmanship is emphasized within the program.

The goals emphasized by a coach, parent, or program may affect the moral development of the participants. Athletes who focus on personal improvement reported that the purpose of sport was to teach values such as working hard, cooperating with others, and becoming good citizens (Duda, 1989). In addition, these athletes did not endorse cheating, but expressed approval for sportsmanlike behaviors in contrast to individuals who placed an emphasis on beating others. Individuals who focused on demonstrating greater ability than others more often viewed intentional, injurious acts as legitimate and were more tempted to violate sportsmanship attitudes and behaviors (Duda, Olson, & Templin, 1991).

Coaches are most effective in developing moral values when they teach youth appropriate behaviors as situations arise in games and practices. The effectiveness of teaching for moral development was demonstrated in a study involving two moral intervention programs that were introduced at a youth sport camp. The first program involved teaching one moral concept a week (e.g., fairness, sharing, and aggression) over five weeks. The instructors (coaches) also exposed moral issues as they arose in play and coached children through to an appropriate resolution of the issues. Children (ages 5 to 7) in this six-week intervention program had higher scores on measures of moral understanding than children who did not receive such training. The second intervention involved the instructor displaying moral behavior when appropriate. The children in this group also did better than children who participated only in the sport program where the coach did not always demonstrate appropriate moral behavior. However, the demonstration of appropriate moral behavior was slightly less effective than teaching about a moral value each week (Bredemeier, Weiss, Shields, & Shewchuk, 1986). Children learn moral behavior directly from instruction and active engagement and indirectly by observing the responses of instructors.

Both direct teaching of moral behavior and modeling appropriate behavior have been combined into intervention strategies in an attempt to alter aspects of moral development among high school basketball players, delinquent-prone fourth graders, and physical education students (DeBusk & Hellison, 1989; Gibbons & Ebbeck, 1997; Wandzilak, Carroll, & Ansorge, 1988). All of the programs were successful in positively influencing indicators of moral growth.

Comparative research has revealed that being involved in sport alone is not sufficient to ensure that participants will learn sportsmanlike attitudes and behaviors. In fact, sport may be a domain that suspends moral obligation or encourages unethical behavior for strategic gain in competition particularly when winning is overemphasized. Therefore, Shields and Bredemeier (1995) suggested that it is not the physical skills that are sportsmanlike or unsportsmanlike but the "social interactions that are fostered by the sport experience" (p. 178) that determine the character-building qualities.

Sport can be an effective arena for developing moral understanding only when the goals of the program are in line with moral attitudes and behavior and when specific teaching strategies are carried out to promote a positive change in moral growth. Therefore, sport participants must be led by individuals who believe in the principles of fair play and sportsmanship and who are willing to discuss the situations experienced in games and practices. Through this process of teaching moral reasoning and modeling moral behaviors, the moral development of sport participants can be influenced. To be most effective there must be a strong match between the philosophy of the program and an emphasis on appropriate behavior by coaches and parents so that children do not receive "mixed" messages regarding appropriate and inappropriate behavior.

Aggression and Violence

Just as sport is a tool for teaching appropriate moral values and behaviors, youth sports may be considered a venue for reflecting or shaping society's acceptance or disapproval for violence and aggression. Youth who watch sports on television or on the local playing fields can learn deviant and violent behavior through observation of the actions of athletes, coaches, and even sport commentators. Modeling of deviant behavior that is seen displayed by professional athletes, coaches at all levels, and peers can strongly influence the behavior of youth. Even though professional athletes and coaches are *punished* for their deviant acts, youth seldom *see* the consequences.

Children can learn both appropriate and inappropriate behavior through participation in sport. The impact on youth development of adult-supervised activity (including sport), safe havens from negative influences, academic enrichment programs, and community service activities is dramatic. Fox and Newman (1997) suggested that when youth are sent to the streets after school with no responsible adult supervision or constructive activities, such situations are associated with massive increases in juvenile crime. They found that juvenile arrests declined by 75% when an after-school recreation program was instituted in a housing project, while arrests increased by 67% in a comparison project without an afterschool project. Likewise, boys and girls clubs operating in housing projects reduced juvenile arrests by 13% and drug activities by 22% compared to projects without a club. Additionally, Jones and Offord (1989) conducted a nonschool intervention in two housing projects in Ottawa, Canada. The program included sports and skill development in other activities. Participants at the experimental complex had a decrease in juvenile charges for crime, a reduction in quantity of security reports, fewer fire calls, and fewer serious offenses when compared with the participants in the control complex. Since prosocial change rarely lasted more than a year after the out-of-school intervention was withdrawn, Jones and Offord argued that poor children need to be assimilated into leagues and other ongoing programs to accrue the most lasting effects. While participation in sport will not curb all violence and deviant behavior, it is a highly effective tool for teaching youth skills and values, helping children develop a positive sense of self, and providing a health-promoting alternative for youth who have nothing else to do.

Education

In addition to the need for sport in the afterschool hours to help keep youth from engaging in deviant activities, evidence is mounting that supports a positive relationship between involvement in sport, as well as in other cocurricular activities, and success in the classroom. Jeziorski (1994) reported that participants in cocurricular activities (e.g., sport teams, debate teams, music groups, and student governance) generally earned higher grades, behaved better in the classroom, and dropped out of school less than students who did not participate in cocurricular activities. Based on interviews with teachers and school administrators, Jeziorski (1994) suggested that these positive outcomes were attributable to the discipline and work ethic associated with cocurricular activities, which carry over into the classroom. The United States Department of Education's National Center for Educational Statistics (1988) reported that participants in high school cocurricular activities put more time into completing homework, had higher scores on the standardized tests, and were much less likely to have a 2.0 or lower grade point average than nonparticipants.

Marsh (1992) concluded from his rigorous analysis of data obtained from the High School and Beyond Study that participation in sport has little effect on academic achievement after controlling for preexisting conditions. However, sport did have a positive effect on educational aspirations and subsequent attainment. In addition, Marsh reported that sport participation had positive effects on social and academic self-concept, educational aspirations, enrollment in math and science courses, time spent on homework, and school attendance. The data did not support an effect of participation on grade point averages and academic test scores. Fejgin (1994), using data from the National Educational Longitudinal Study collected between 1988 and 1992, reported that participation in school sports ranging from intramural to varsity had a positive effect on grades, self-concept, educational aspirations, and locus of control. Additionally, participation in sport resulted in fewer discipline problems for high school athletes.

The opportunity to interact with coaches who model responsible behavior provides athletes with an additional avenue to learn responsible behavior in the classroom as a way to maintain eligibility. Benson, Galbraith, and Espeland (1998) have identified many "assets" that teenagers need for success in school and life. The more "assets" adolescents have, the more likely they are to engage in positive behaviors. Participation in sport, or in other youth programs, provides an environment for youth to learn better than half of the assets needed to be successful in school. Unfortunately, high school students acknowledge that they would rather succeed at sport than academics and that failure in sport was perceived to be far worse than failure in academics, particularly for adolescent males (Duda, 1985). The key is to link participation in sport, which is highly valued by adolescent youths, to academic performance.

The relationship between academic achievement and involvement in high school sports, while positive for most participants, has not been uniformly advantageous for all competitors. For Hispanic and White females and White males, athletic participation was positively related to higher grades (Women's Sports Foundation, 1989). For Hispanic males and Black females and males, the correlation between athletic participation and grades was smaller. Sports participation from all six ethnic and gender subgroups produced higher scores on the standardized achievement tests in vocabulary, reading, and mathematics when compared to nonparticipants. Melnick, Vanfossen, and Sabo (1988) reported that for high school girls sport participation was strongly related to extracurricular involvement and modestly related to perceived popularity, and only slightly related to delinquency and educational aspiration. Athletic participation was not related to psychological well-being. With respect to African American and Hispanic boys and girls, athletic participation was found to enhance popularity and contributed to greater extracurricular involvement. However, involvement was unrelated to grades and standardized test scores.

Although not directly related to educational outcomes, females participating in sport reported lower rates of sexual activity than female nonathletes. They also have lower incidences of pregnancy, which could impact their educational achievements when compared to nonparticipants. No differences in sexual activity were found among male athletes and nonathletes (Miller, Sabo, Farrell, Barnes, & Melnick, 1998). Therefore, the issue of whether sport participation contributes to educational benefits for youth of color and girls is less clear.

Barriers to Participation in Youth Sport Programs

In recent years the availability of non-school-sponsored programs has increased in the suburbs but decreased quite dramatically in the urban environments. Participation rates in Detroit, for example, have dropped to approximately 10 percent of the children compared to 75–80 percent in the suburbs (Seefeldt, Smith, Clark, VanderSmissen, & Bristor, 1995)! There are several potential causes of this dramatic drop within urban environments. White (1992) placed the barriers that restrict sports participation into six categories: (a) failure of the American public to understand the role of exercise and sports, (b) lack of motivation to do what is good and right for ourselves, (c) intellectual snobbery about exercise and sports, (d) racism, (e) sexism, and (f) the low national priority for participation in exercise and sports. Ewing, Seefeldt, and Brown (1993) added three additional barriers: (g) low socioeconomic status, (h) fear for personal safety, and (i) overzealous promoters.

Reduction in sports participation results when youth are less fit and are more sedentary, which is true for today's youth compared with youth ten years ago. Concurrently, the reduction in elementary physical education programs, which may be connected to intellectual snobbery of school administrators and teachers, has resulted in fewer youth learning the fundamental motor skills that are essential for learning sport skills. In addition, the lack of qualified coaches to teach sport skills and appropriate dietary and weight reduction practices have parents concerned about their child's safety in some sports.

Racism and sexism continue to discourage subsets of individuals from participating through lack of opportunity or through the belief that certain individuals should not participate in certain sports or will not be interested in participating in sports. Numbers of participants increase for both race and sex of participant in high schools where opportunity is more open to all students. Given the priority to participation of elementary youth in sport by the community recreation programs, many adolescents are forced to withdraw from participation in sports unless they can earn a spot on an interscholastic team. Within the urban environment many youth are unable to participate in sport because of the lack of monetary resources, lack of access to safe playgrounds, and the view that winning is the only goal of sports participation because it will lead youth out of the low economic conditions in which they may live.

Urban youth, especially minority youth (Rauch, 1989), are often growing up in poverty (Center for the Study of Social Poverty, 1992). Branta and Goodway (1996) reported that urban youth in their study had no safe outdoor play sites. Fourth graders in their investigation did not know how to self-organize and play relatively simple games such as kickball. Because of the decline in, or elimination of, quality physical education programs in urban schools and the paucity of community activity programs (Branta & Goodway, 1996; Seefeldt, Smith, Clark, VanderSmissen, & Bristor, 1995; Taylor, 1996), urban youth have few opportunities to receive instruction from qualified adults in developing their skills. Additionally, Goodway (1994) found that children from very low economic areas of a city were less skilled in sports and physical activities initially than were their peers from a higher economic status, but responded equally to a skill instruction intervention.

To overcome the barriers previously mentioned, sports organizers must reexamine their programs to see if (a) programming opportunities exist to meet the diverse interests of people in the communities, (b) children can reach the park or community recreation center safely, (c) coaches/volunteers are qualified to teach children and youth the skills and values of sports, (d) programs are meeting the needs of the participants rather than the needs of coaches, and (e) the values of physical exercise as well as competition are promoted. Certainly a major issue in many urban communities is the cost associated with offering sport programs. Communities must become more creative in order to offer programs that will reach the masses of youth with limited resources. The decisions that are made regarding the use of existing resources are often shortsighted. For example, it is hardly a responsible decision to eliminate opportunities for youth in the afterschool hours as it has been shown that between the hours of 2:00 P.M. and 7:00 P.M., nearly half of all violent juvenile crime takes place (Fox & Newman, 1997).

The supposition that sport can be used as a venue to alleviate the problems of adolescent violence and stress, social alienation and disaffection, and unhealthy behavior seems inappropriate to some who maintain that more direct interventions are required to alter this behavior. However, there is ample evidence that the involvement of youth in sports has led to the inculcation of responsible social behaviors and greater academic success (Jeziorski, 1994).

Sports have often been cited as the medium that provided contact between wayward youth and influential individuals. Sport has been credited with providing a sense of affiliation, a feeling of confidence in one's physical abilities, an appreciation of one's personal health and fitness, and the development of social bonds with individuals and institutions. The key is to get children involved early and to provide a variety of opportunities in sport. Not all youth want to compete; some do not have the skills necessary to compete. Many youth have indicated that they would participate in sport if the program were more focused on recreation than on competition and elitism (Cumming, 1998).

Summary

Clearly, sport has the potential to contribute to the development of children and adolescents in many ways. Critics of youth sport will argue that children, particularly those living in poverty, should be discouraged from participating in sport as it is a deterrent to acquiring the necessary education that will help impoverished youth get jobs. However, sport should not be viewed as the way to change one's economic status; rather, sport contributes to learning the skills and values necessary to succeed in education, in the workforce, and throughout life. Several questions arise, though, related to these developmental benefits. One, how many youth sports programs are designed to teach the physical, social, moral, and educational benefits so often attributed to sport participation? Two, are adults who conduct programs consistent in their philosophies and behaviors so that youth benefit fully from sport? And, third, are communities and business leaders ready to understand the long-term advantages of funding youth sports programs of quality for their youth? The answers to these questions help to determine if youth benefit from sport participation. Therefore, the key to youth development through sports is the quality of the youth sports program and adult leadership.

References

Barnett, N. P., Smoll, F. L., & Smith, R. E. (1992). Effects of enhancing coach-athlete relationships on youth sport attrition. *Sport Psychologist, 6,* 111–127.

Benson, P. L., Galbraith, J., & Espeland, P. (1998). *What teens need to succeed.* Minneapolis, MN: Free Spirit Publishing.

Blair, S. N. (1992). Are American children and youth fit? The need for better data. *Research Quarterly for Exercise and Sport, 63,* 120–123.

Branta, C. F., & Goodway, J. D. (1996). Facilitating social skills in urban school children through physical education. *Peace and Conflict: Journal of Peace Psychology, 2* (4), 305–319.

Bredemeier, B. J., Weiss, M. R., Shields, D. L., & Shewchuk, R. M. (1986). Promoting moral growth in a summer sport camp: The implementation of theoretically grounded instructional strategies. *Journal of Moral Education, 15,* 212–220.

Center for the Study of Social Policy. (1992). *1992 KIDS COUNT Data Book: State Profiles of Child Well-Being.* Washington, DC: Center for the Study of Social Policy.

Corbin, C. B., & Pangrazi, R. P. (1992). Are American children and youth fit? *Research Quarterly for Exercise and Sport, 63,* 96–106.

Cumming, S. (1998). The influence of children's achievement orientations and perceived competence on their desire to participate in sports organized in various ways: Preliminary report. Institute for the Study of Youth Sports, Michigan State University, E. Lansing.

DeBusk, M., & Hellison, D. (1989). Implementing a physical education self-responsibility model for delinquency-prone youth. *Journal of Teaching in Physical Education, 8,* 104–112.

Duda, J. L. (1985). Goals and achievement orientations of Anglo and Mexican-American adolescents in sport and the classroom. *International Journal of Intercultural Relations, 9,* 131–150.

Duda, J. L. (1989). The relationship between task and ego orientations and the perceived purpose of sport among male and female high school athletes. *Journal of Sport and Exercise Psychology, 4,* 24–31.

Duda, J. L., Olson, L. K., & Templin, T. J. (1991). The relationship of task and ego orientations to sportsmanship attitudes and the perceived legitimacy of injurious acts. *Research Quarterly for Exercise and Sport, 62,* 79–87.

Evans, J. R., & Roberts, G. C. (1987). Physical competence and the development of children's peer relations. *Quest, 39,* 23–35.

Ewing, M. E., & Seefeldt, V. D. (1989). *Participation and attrition patterns in American agency-sponsored and interscholastic sports: An executive summary.* Final report to the Athletic Footwear Coucil of the Sporting Goods Manufacturers Association.

Ewing, M. E., Seefeldt, V. D., & Brown, T. P. (1993). *Role of organized sport in the education and health of American children and youth.* Paper commissioned by The Carnegie Corporation of New York.

Fejgin, N. (1994). Participation in high school competitive sports: A subversion of school mission or contribution to academic goals? *Sociology of Sport Journal, 11,* 211–230.

Fox, J. A., & Newman, S. A. (1997). After-school crime or after-school programs: Tuning in to the prime time for violent juvenile crime and implications for national policy. Executive Summary of a report to the United States Attorney General, Washington, DC.

Freedson, P. S., & Rowland, T. W. (1992).Youth activity versus youth fitness: Let's redirect our efforts. *Research Quarterly for Exercise and Sport, 63,* 133–136.

Gibbons, S. L., & Ebbeck, V. (1997). The effect of different teaching strategies on the moral development of physical education students. *Journal of Teaching in Physical Education, 17,* 85–98.

Goodway, J. D. (1994). The effect of a motor skill intervention on the acquisition of fundamental motor skills of preschoolers who are at-risk. Unpublished doctoral dissertation, Michigan State University, East Lansing.

Harter, S. (1981). The development of competence motivation in the mastery of cognitive and physical skills: Is there a place for joy? In C. H. Nadeau (Ed.), *Psychology of motor behavior and sport—1980* (pp. 3–29). Champaign, IL: Human Kinetics.

Harter, S. (1983). The development of the self-system. In M. Hetherington (Ed.), *Handbook of child psychology: Social and personality development* (Vol. 4). New York: Wiley.

Horn, T. S. (1985). Coaches' feedback and changes in children's perceptions of their physical competence. *Journal of Educational Psychology, 77,* 174–186.

Horn, T. S., & Hasbrook, C. A. (1986). Information components influencing children's perceptions of their physical competence. In M. R. Weiss & D. Gould (Eds.), *Sport for children and youths* (pp. 81–88). Champaign, IL: Human Kinetics.

Horn, T. S., & Hasbrook, C. A. (1987). Psychological characteristics and the criteria children use for self-evaluation. *Journal of Sport Psychology, 9,* 208–221.

Horn, T. S., & Weiss, M. R. (1991). A developmental analysis of children's self-ability judgments in the physical domain. *Pediatric Exercise Science, 3,* 310–326.

Jeziorski, R. M. (1994). *The importance of school sports in American education and socialization.* Lanham, MD: University Press of America.

Jones, M. B., & Offord, D. R. (1989). Reduction of antisocial behavior in poor children by nonschool skill-development. *Journal of Child Psychology and Psychiatry, 30,* 737–750.

Katzmarzyk, P. T., & Malina, R. M. (1998). Contribution of organized sports participation to estimated daily energy expenditure in youth. *Pediatric Exercise Science, 10,* 376–386.

MacDonald, K. B. (1987). Parent-child physical play with rejected, neglected, and popular boys. *Developmental Psychology, 23,* 705–711.

Marsh, H. W. (1992). Extracurricular activities: Beneficial extension of the educational curriculum or subversion of academic goals? *Journal of Educational Psychology, 84,* 553–562.

Melnick, M. J., Vanfossen, B. E., & Sabo, D. F. (1988). Developmental effects of athletic participation among high school girls. *Sociology of Sport Journal, 5,* 22–36.

Miller, K. E., Sabo, D. F., Farrell, M. P., Barnes, G. M., & Melnick, M. J. (1998). Athletic participation and sexual behavior in adolescents: The different worlds of boys and girls. *Journal of Health and Social Behavior, 39,* 108–123.

National Center for Education Statistics. (1988). *National educational longitudinal study of 1988: First follow-up: Student component data file user's manual* (Vol. 1). Washington, DC: US Department of Education, Office of Educational Research and Improvement.

Ponessa, J. (1992). Student access to extracurricular activities. *Public Affairs Focus, 23,* 1–8. Princeton, NJ: Public Affairs Research Institute.

President's Council on Physical Fitness and Sport (1997). *Physical activity & sport in the lives of girls: Physical & mental health dimensions from an interdisciplinary approach.* University of Minnesota: Center for Research on Girls & Women in Sport.

Rauch, J. (1989, August). Kids as capital. *Atlantic Monthly,* pp. 56–61.

Seefeldt, V. D. (1987). *Handbook for youth sports coaches.* Reston, VA: National Association for Sport and Physical Education.

Seefeldt, V. D., & Brown, E. W. (1995). *Program for coaches' education.* Carmel, IN: Cooper Publishing Group.

Seefeldt, V. D., Ewing, M. E., & Walk, S. R. (1991). *Overview of youth sports in the United States.* Paper commissioned by the Carnegie Council on Adolescent Development.

Seefeldt, V. D., Smith, Y. R., Clark, M., VanderSmissen, B., & Bristor, J. (1995). *Recreating recreation: An assessment of needs.* Report to the Skillman Foundation, Detroit.

Shalala, D., & Riley, R. (2000). *Physical activity and health: Adolescent and young adults.* U.S. Department of Health and Human Services. Washington, DC.

Shields, D. L. L., & Bredemeier, B. J. L. (1995). *Character Development and physical activity.* Champaign, IL: Human Kinetics.

Smith, R. E., Smoll, F. L., & Curtis, B. (1979). Coach effectiveness training: A cognitive-behavioral approach to enhancing relationship skills in youth sport coaches. *Journal of Sport Psychology, 1,* 59–75.

Taylor, C. S. (1996). Sports and recreation: Community anchor and counterweight to conflict. *Peace and Conflict: Journal of Peace Psychology, 2* (4), 339–350.

Trulson, M. E. (1986). Martial arts training: A novel "cure" for juvenile delinquency. *Human Relations, 39,* 1131–1140.

Wandzilak, T., Carroll, T., & Ansorge, C. J. (1988). Values development through physical activity: Promoting sportsmanlike behaviors, perceptions, and moral reasoning. *Journal of Teaching in Physical Education, 8,* 13–23.

Weiss, M. R. (1992). Motivational orientations in sport. In T. Horn (Ed.), *Advances in sport psychology* (pp. 61–100). Champaign, IL: Human Kinetics.

Weiss, M. R., & Duncan, S. C. (1992). The relation between physical competence and peer acceptance in the context of children's sport participation. *Journal of Sport and Exercise Psychology, 14,* 177–191.

White, S. (1992). Sports: Barriers to participation. *National Forum, 112,* 2, 50.

Women's Sports Foundation. (1989). *The Women's Sports Foundation Report: Minorities in sports.* New York: Women's Sports Foundation.

THREE

Teaching Life Skills through Sport

STEVEN J. DANISH

S port is a major influence in the lives of America's youth. Estimates by the Athletic Footwear Association (1990) suggest that there are 20 to 35 million 5- to 18-year-olds participating in nonschool sports and another 10 million 14- to 18-year-olds participating in school sports in the United States. Only family, school, and television involve children's time more than sport (Institute for Social Research, 1985). Whether what is learned in sport, both through participation and by observing others play, contributes positively or negatively to one's identity and competence is a topic of debate by both professionals and nonprofessionals alike. On the one hand, almost every coach, athlete, and sport administrator believes that participation can have a beneficial effect on psychosocial development (Sabock, 1985). Furthermore, they generally believe that what is learned transfers directly to the classroom and to the boardroom. On the other hand, Ogilvie and Tutko (1971) believe that sport is as likely to produce "characters" as it is to build character.

The influence of sport is not confined to those who participate. Millions of children and adolescents watch sport on television, there are at least two magazines directed at youth that are devoted to sports, and marketing research (Zallo, 1995) indicates that sports stars are the overwhelming choice among teens in advertising (first among boys and second among girls). Therefore, to understand the impact of sport on youth, we must also examine how the media portrays sport.

The purpose of this chapter is twofold: (1) to consider how sport, be it participatory or as a spectator, influences the psychosocial development of youth and to present a series of propositions about this relationship; and (2) to describe specific interventions that use sport as a vehicle to reduce violence and enhance development.

49

Sport and the Psychosocial Development of Youth

Proposition 1:
Sport has always been more than a game in our society.

The belief that sport provides a training ground for life has its roots in the turn of the century. It was assumed that through sports, children and adolescents would learn good sportsmanship and other values and skills that would serve them well as they prepared for the rest of their life. Through sport, it was believed that youth could be taught to accept the prevailing norms and use their free time constructively. By the 1970s, the philosophy concerning the value of sport had changed. Critics of sport were concerned about its increasing focus on competition and winning as opposed to play and developing mastery (Martens, 1978; Orlick & Botterill, 1975). This change in the role of sport is accelerating. Sport has become less an activity for all, as it is in many other countries, and more a business and a means of entertainment. In the schools in our country, resource diversions from intramurals—which emphasize participation for all—into interscholastic athletics—which emphasize participation only for the talented—is increasing exponentially. In contrast, Australia, and especially New Zealand, have a much higher percentage of individuals participating in sports than does the United States. In our country, sport, both professional and collegiate, has become *big* business.

Much of this change has been fueled by the media. We sometimes disparagingly refer to certain sports events as made-for-media events (e.g., track meets among various football, basketball, and baseball players). However, many mainstream sporting contests are designed for or by the media. For example, the World Series has been moved to the evening to take advantage of prime-time viewing; college basketball games are arranged for television and sometimes start at 10:00 P.M. EST. As a result of increased media exposure, professional athletes are among the most recognized individuals in our country (Lupica, 1996; Zallo, 1995). What are some of the implications for youth?

Proposition 2:
Elite athletes represent dreams or fantasies
rather than role models for youth.

We know little about who our elite athletes are. With very few exceptions, adolescents don't have *real people* to look up to; they have one-dimensional caricatures. Too often these adolescents end up chasing dreams like "being like Mike," but the Mike they chase exists only in commercials, movies, and on brief clips of his best basketball moves. What is missing is information about what it took for these elite athletes and sports stars to get where they are.

In 1987, I was involved in developing a program for the United States Olympic Committee to assist active and recently retired Olympic and Pan American Games athletes in planning for, and coping with, their transition out of elite competition (Petitpas, Danish, McKelvain, & Murphy, 1992). The program, entitled the "Career Assistance Program for Athletes" (CAPA), provided participants with a forum to share concerns about disengagement from sport and to learn the basics of the career development process—self-exploration, career exploration, and career implementation. One of the key activities involved helping these athletes identify what they had learned through their participation in sport that was transferable to their next career. Most did not feel they were prepared to enter a "next career" because they had "not yet had a career." They felt that they had been out of the "real world" by being involved in their sport career, and had nothing to show for it. They did not understand that to be successful in sport required using both their mind *and* body and that some of what they had learned in sport had value beyond sport to other aspects of their lives. If the athletes do not make this connection, they will not be conveying it to youth who admire them.

Don't misunderstand me. I am all for adolescents having dreams, even if they are unattainable. However, there must be some connection between the dream and what it takes to achieve the dream. Without such a connection, the dream is unlikely to become a reality.

Proposition 3:
The media contributes both to the dehumanization of athletes and to the increase in violence in sports.

It is easy to assume that the media causes the problem and that the individual viewer is just a passive observer. This assumption is consistent with what is referred to as "cultivation theory" (Gerbner, Gross, Morgan, & Signorelli, 1986)—the more media watched, the greater the likelihood that the viewer's behaviors, values, and attitudes will be affected. However, research does not support such a view. Moreover, it runs counter to our understanding of human development.

Most developmental theorists believe that individuals are self-directing, proactive agents who are capable of shaping rather than just solely responding to their environment. Therefore, we must recognize that viewers are not just passive recipients of what they watch. They make decisions about what they want to watch and experience the programs differently depending on their needs and motives for watching.

Television is one of the greatest teachers we have. Anything that occupies 16,000 hours of an adolescent's life by age 14 (4,000 more hours than the adolescent spends in school) has to be an important influence. Clearly, television does play a strong role in building the fantasies about who athletes are and what they do. In fact, it could be said that athletes are the creation of the media. Television perpetuates myths and drama about sports and the players of sport. One of these dramas is that every sporting event is a battle between opponents who do not like each other. The event becomes the equivalent of war. While such a perspective helps ratings and sells advertising, for some young viewers it increases the likelihood that sport becomes an arena for violence (Anderson & Meyer, 1988).

On the other hand, many poor youngsters of all ethnic groups see sports as *the* way to get out of poverty. It has been reported that as many as two thirds of youth between the ages of 13 and 18 believe they can be professional athletes despite the fact that the chances are about 1 in 10,000. For them, watching sports on television serves a number of purposes. First, it provides a form of self-evaluation by comparing their self-worth and value with the athletes they see playing. Second, it provides an opportunity for self-enhancement in that the viewer may seek to maintain a biased but positive view of herself as a means of protecting her self-esteem (Martin & Kennedy, 1994).

Individuals who have low self-esteem may be predisposed to have more frequent comparisons with elite athletes to shore up their esteem. However, they also may feel inadequate in comparison and use dysfunctional strategies, including fighting, to rectify this perceived inadequacy. Perhaps this need to maintain self-esteem is a partial explanation why many youth are so eager to copy any elite athlete's behavior they can—and it is much easier to copy wearing certain shoes and apparel, "trash talking," and fighting than to copy their athletic skills. Third, and clearly not the least important, if they are using sports to lift themselves out of their circumstances, they may see their opponent as the enemy and the game as a war.

In sum, the media are the dream merchants who sell the myths about elite athletes and the sports they play. With very few exceptions, they do not present the human side of sport or the athletes. However, they are too easy a scapegoat. As will be discussed in the next section, sport, and especially youth sport, is a significant contributor to the increase in violence and to the lack of life skills present among adolescent athletes.

Proposition 4:
Sport contributes to the successful development of youth
only if the focus of the activity is to teach life skills.

There is nothing magical about a ball, or for that matter, about any sport object or sport venue. It is not sport per se that teaches life skills. The lasting value of the sport experience lies in the application of the principles learned through sport participation to other areas of life. Of the millions of children who play sports, only a tiny fraction will parlay those activities directly into a career in sport despite their dreams. For the rest, growing up means further defining their identity, discovering other skills and interests, and applying some of the valuable principles learned during sport participation to other pursuits. These transferable behaviors are called "life skills" (Danish, 1995).

Life skills are often discussed but rarely defined. For some, such skills refer to being able to balance a checkbook; for others, it means to be assertive in refusing to engage in behaviors that compromise health. Hamburg (1990) is one of the few authors who has tried to define this elusive concept. With the founding of the Life Skills Center, in 1992, we set about trying to define what exactly we meant by life skills.

Life skills are those skills that enable us to succeed in the environments in which we live (Danish, 1995; Danish & Donohue, 1995). They can be behavioral (communicating effectively with peers and adults) or cognitive (making effective decisions); interpersonal or intrapersonal. Some of the environments in which we live are families, schools, workplaces, neighborhoods, and communities. As one becomes older, the number of environments in which one must be successful increases. Environments will vary from individual to individual, and individuals in the same environment will be dissimilar from each other as a result of the life skills they have already mastered, their other resources, and their opportunities, real or perceived. For this reason, programs to teach life skills must be sensitive to developmental, environmental, and individual differences and to the possibility that the needed life skills may not be the same for individuals of different ages, ethnic, and/or racial groups, or economic status.

Life skills and sport skills have several similarities. First, both are learned in the same way—through demonstration, modeling, and practice (Danish & Hale, 1981). Second, the skills learned in one domain are transferable to other areas (Danish, 1995; Danish & Nellen, 1997; Danish, Petitpas, & Hale, 1993). Some of these skills are the ability to perform under pressure, solve problems, meet deadlines and challenges, set goals, communicate, handle both success and failure, work with a group and within a system, and receive feedback and benefit from it. Sport can provide a valuable vehicle for teaching life skills *when these lessons are learned and transferred.*

However, the process of transferability is not a natural one. As De Coubertin (1918), the founder of the Olympic movement, noted, "How many daredevil cyclists there are who once they leave their machines are hesitant at every crossroads of existence, how many swimmers who are brave in the water but frightened by the waves of human existence, how many fencers who cannot apply to life's battles the quick eye and nice timing which they show on the boards!"

For this reason I believe that teaching adolescents athletic skills without life skills sends the wrong message, especially when it is done by an organization that has a child's welfare as a major concern. I am afraid that it will reinforce the belief that their world can change if they become better athletes. For the overwhelming majority that is not true. On the other hand, when both sets of skills are taught together, and avenues to transfer skills from one domain to another are known, the effect can be very powerful. It is the opportunity that sport provides to know ourselves rather than to prove ourselves that enables us fully to develop our potential in sport and in life.

Proposition 5:
Being successful in sport is not the same thing as winning.

How does sport help youth learn life skills? When one can experience success and know what it has taken to be successful, confidence is increased and a feeling of competence is developed. However, knowing when one has been successful is not so easy to identify. A common way is to compare one's performance with that of another. Success becomes synonymous with winning. However, focusing on winning through beating the other person or team may take the spotlight off an individual's performance and put it on the performance of the opponent. If athletes lack a realistic yardstick with which to measure their success, it is hard to develop any confidence in their abilities. If winning is the criterion, the competition is not about the game but about personal respect, and anything or anyone that is in your way becomes an enemy. If this drive for self-respect is transferred into other areas, life becomes a competition against others, and the nature of interactions with others, both friend and foe, almost parallels the sport environment—someone has to win and someone has to lose.

An alternative is to develop a "win-win" environment. However, to learn how to win while others win, adolescents first must be taught to change the nature of how they compete. *They must learn to compete against themselves (their last and best performances) and against their own potential rather than against other people.* Although no one actually beats their potential, such a perspective teaches youth to focus on their performance rather than on others. The result is that they see changes in their competence, experience some "life wins," and feel less need for others to fail in order for them to feel successful (Danish, 1996). By adopting this perspective, score becomes less important and the quality of play and execution level becomes the focus. Instead of celebrating others' failures, the focus changes to experiencing successes.

From Ideas to Actions

We at the Life Skills Center have been developing programs to teach life skills. Our mission is to develop, implement, and evaluate life skill programs for children, adolescents, and adults. The two programs to be described use sports to teach life skills. In the first program, sport is used as a metaphor for teaching life skills; in the second program, sport is used as a context for teaching life skills. Both enable participants to experience "life wins" by providing opportunities to succeed and to develop a future-orientation.

The Going for the Goal (GOAL) Program

GOAL is our largest and best-known program (Danish, Meyer, Mash, Howard, Curl, Brunelle, & Owens, 1998a, 1998b). It is the 1996 winner of the Lela Rowland Prevention Award given by the National Mental Health Association, been honored by the United States Department of Health and Human Services as part of its Freedom from Fear Campaign, and received an honorable mention by the Points of Light Foundation.

GOAL is designed to teach adolescents a sense of personal control and confidence about their future so that they can make better decisions and ultimately become better citizens. To be successful in life it is not enough to know what to avoid; one must also know how to succeed. For this reason our focus is on teaching "what to say yes to" as opposed to "just say no."

The GOAL Program is a ten-hour, ten-session program taught to middle school or junior high school students. The program is generally taught in school (e.g., as part of the health curriculum) but has also been taught after school or at special venues such as clinics sponsored by U.S. Diving.

In the first workshop, *Dare to Dream,* participants discuss the importance of dreams and practice dreaming about their future. In the second workshop, *Setting Goals,* they learn that a goal is a dream they work hard to reach. They also learn the value of goal setting and practice recognizing reachable goals. The four characteristics of a reachable goal are that it is stated positively, is stated specifically, is important to the goal setter, and is under the goal setter's control. In the third workshop, *Making Your Goal Reachable,* the students apply what they learned in the second workshop. They write a reachable goal to be attained within the next two months that meets the four characteristics learned in the third workshop. We have found that developing such goals is difficult for adolescents and adults alike and learning and applying this process is a key aspect of the program. In the fourth workshop, *Making a Goal Ladder,* they learn how to make a plan to reach their goal by identifying all of the steps needed to reach their goal and then placing them in order on rungs of the ladder. In the fifth workshop, *Roadblocks to Reaching Goals,* the students learn how various roadblocks such as drug abuse, teen pregnancy, violence, dropping out of school, and/or lack of self-confidence can prevent them from reaching their goals in life. In the sixth workshop, *Overcoming Roadblocks,* they learn and practice a problem-solving strategy called "STAR" (stop and take a deep breath, think of all your choices, anticipate the consequences of each choice, and respond with the best choice). In the seventh workshop, *Seeking Help from Others,* the students learn the importance of seeking social support in order to achieve goals. In the eighth workshop, *Rebounds and Rewards,* they learn how to rebound when a goal or a step on the goal ladder becomes too difficult to reach. They also develop a plan to reward themselves for their accomplishments. In the ninth workshop, *Identifying and Building on Your Strengths,* the students identify their personal strengths and how to further develop these strengths. They are also asked to identify an area in which they want to improve and a plan for how they can work toward improvement. In the tenth and final workshop, *Going for Your Goal,* the students play a game, "Know-It-All-Baseball," which provides an opportunity for them to integrate the information covered (Danish, 1997).

There are several unique aspects in the design of GOAL. First, we chose skills as our focus because they are concrete, easily taught and learned, and when directed toward areas of our everyday lives, empower us. Teaching facts such as the danger of using drugs has not proven to be effective. Teaching skills requires learning how to do something. Second, the teachers of GOAL are high school student leaders chosen by their schools for their academic performance, leadership qualities, and extracurricular involvement. They receive special training on how to teach the program. Following the training, the student-leaders teach the skills to the middle/junior high school students. The ratio is approximately 2 to 3 high school student-leaders to between 15 and 18 middle/junior high school students. Successful high school students serve as concrete images of what early adolescents can become. Because these high school students have grown up in the same neighborhoods, attended the same schools, and confronted similar roadblocks, they serve as important role models and thus are in an ideal position to be effective teachers. Third, there is a printed Leader Manual given to each high school student and a Student Activity Guide given to each junior high/middle school participant.

The GOAL Program started in Richmond, Virginia, in 1987 and has been taught to almost 25,000 students. As a result of support from the Athletic Footwear Association and the Sporting Goods Manufacturing Association, GOAL has expanded to twenty-eight sites in the United States and internationally. It has been evaluated from several different perspectives and in several different contexts and found to be effective both in reducing the incidence of various problem behaviors, including violence, in teaching goal setting, and in improving means-ends problem solving (Danish, 1996; O'Hearn, 1998; O'Hearn & Gatz, 1996, 1999).

The SUPER (Sports United to Promote Education and Recreation) Program

The goals of the SUPER program are for each participant to leave the program with the understanding that (1) there are effective and accessible student-athlete role models, (2) physical *and* mental skills are important for both sport and life, (3) it is important to set and attain goals in sport and life, (4) roadblocks to goals can be overcome, and (5) effective participation in sport requires being healthy and physically fit.

SUPER is a 25–hour, 10–session program. Sessions are taught like sports clinics with participants involved in three sets of activities: learning the physical skills related to a specific sport, learning life skills related to sports in general, and playing the sport. Sometimes the students learn several sports within a SUPER program; other times the focus is on one sport. As with GOAL, we have developed manuals to facilitate dissemination (Danish, 1999a, 1999b).

Some of the life skills for which we have or are developing sessions include (a) learning how to learn; (b) communicating with others; (c) managing anger; (d) using positive self-talk (being your own coach); (e) giving and receiving feedback; (f) working with a team and within a system; (g) increasing focus and concentration; (h) learning how to win, lose, and respect your opponent; (i) performing under pressure; (j) solving problems; (k) meeting deadlines and challenges; and, most of all, (l) setting goals and attaining them.

For the most part, SUPER is taught by college students who are either athletes or physical education majors and therefore have some coaching and athletic skills teaching experience. Occasionally, skilled high school students serve as coleaders. The student-athlete leaders learn many of the skills the GOAL leaders are taught about leading and managing groups. They also review how skills are learned, how to teach sport skills to individuals who are less able and experienced, and how to use sport observation strategies. In teaching sport observation strategies, leaders are told that when they instruct, demonstrate, and conduct practices, they need to focus on *how* the students are participating as opposed to just *how well* they are performing and participating. Understanding *how* provides information on the life skills that the participants have, for example, (a) Are the students attentive when given instructions or observing demonstration? (b) Do they become frustrated with themselves when they cannot perform the activity to their expectations and does this frustration impede or enhance later efforts? (c) Are they first to initiate questions when they do not understand something being taught or do they wait quietly for someone else to talk first? (d) Are they first to initiate conversation with group members or do they wait for someone else to talk to them first? (e) How do they react when they have a good performance or a bad performance? (f) How do they react when others have a good performance or a bad performance? (g) How do they react when someone gives them praise or criticism? (h) Do they give up when they can't do as well as they would like, or as well as others, or do they continue to practice in a determined manner to learn the skill? (i) Do they compete or cooperate with the other youth? We expect that the leaders will spend at least several minutes with each individual to discuss the "hows" of their performance (separate from the "how wells") during each session of the sport clinics (Danish & Nellen, 1997).

We have completed a pilot of the SUPER Program. The Virginia Commonwealth University women's basketball team-taught the program to seventy-three middle school girls during the fall of 1998. It is our plan to have the program ready for use by others by the year 2000.

Summary

It is commonplace in today's society to look for villains and victims and certainly big-time sports and the media qualify as villains and youth have become victims. However, blaming parts of our society for what happens to youth, although easy to do, will not improve this situation. Action is necessary. Programs such as GOAL and SUPER are not a panacea for reducing violence; neither are teaching or learning life skills. However, such programs are part of a solution. And right now, we desperately need to make some progress.

References

Anderson, J. A., & Meyer, T. P. (1988). *Mediated communication: A social action perspective*. Newbury Park, CA: Sage.
Athletic Footwear Association (1990). *American youth and sports participation*. North Palm Beach, FL.

Danish, S. (1999a). *The SUPER Program: Leader Manual.* Department of Psychology, Virginia Commonwealth University.

Danish, S. (1999b). *The SUPER Program: Student Activity Book.* Department of Psychology, Virginia Commonwealth University.

Danish, S. (1997). Going for the goal: A life skills program for adolescents. In T. Gullotta & G. Albee (Eds.), *Primary prevention works* (pp. 291–312). Newbury Park, CA: Sage.

Danish, S. (1996). Interventions for enhancing adolescents' life skills. *Humanistic Psychologist, 24,* 365–381.

Danish, S. (1995). Reflections on the status and future of community psychology. *Community Psychologist, 28* (3),16–18.

Danish, S., & Donohue T. (1995). Understanding media's influence on the development of antisocial and prosocial behavior. In R. Hampton, P. Jenkins, & T. Gullotta (Eds.), *When anger governs: Preventing violence in American society* (pp. 133–155). Newbury Park, CA: Sage.

Danish, S. J., & Hale, B. D. (1981). Toward an understanding of the practice of sport psychology. *Journal of Sport Psychology, 3,* 90–99.

Danish, S., Meyer, A., Mash, J., Howard, C., & Curl, S., Brunelle, J., & Owens, S. (1998a). *Going for the goal: Leader manual* (2d ed.). Department of Psychology, Virginia Commonwealth University.

Danish, S., Meyer, A., Mash, J., Howard, C., & Curl, S., Brunelle, J., & Owens, S. (1998b). *Going for the Goal: Student Activity Book* (2d ed.). Department of Psychology, Virginia Commonwealth University.

Danish, S. J., & Nellen, V. C. (1997). New roles for sport psychologists: Teaching life skills through sport to at-risk youth. *Quest, 49* (1), 100–113.

Danish, S. J., Petitpas, A.J., & Hale, B. D. (1993). Life development intervention for athletes: Life skills through sports. *Counseling Psychologist* (Major contribution), *21,* 352–385.

De Coubertin, P. (1918).*What we can now ask of sport.* Address given to the Greek Liberal Club of Lauranne, France, February, 24, 1918. Translated by J. Dixon. *The Olympic idea: Discoveries and essays* (1966). Kolm, Germany: Carl Diem Institut.

Gerbner, G., Gross, L., Morgan, M., & Signorelli, N. (1986). Living with television: The dynamics of the cultivation process. In J. Bryant & D. Zillman (Eds.), *Perspectives on media effects* (pp. 181–226). New York: Guilford Press.

Hamburg, B. (1990). *Life skills training: Preventive interventions for young adolescents.* Report of the Life Skills Training Working Group, Carnegie Council on Adolescent Development, NY.

Institute for Social Research. (1985). *Time, goods & well-being.* Ann Arbor: University of Michigan.

Lupica, M. (1996). *Mad as hell: How sports got away from fans and how we get it back.* New York: Putnam.

Martens, R. (1978). *Joy and sadness in sport.* Champagne, IL: Human Kinetics.

Martin, M., & Kennedy, P. (1994). Social comparison and the beauty of advertising models: The role of motives for comparison. *Advances in Consumer Research, 21,* 365–371.

O'Hearn, T. (1998). The effect of training in goal setting and goal attainment on urban adolescents: A replication and extension. Unpublished doctoral dissertation, University of Southern California. Los Angeles.

O'Hearn, T., & Gatz, M. (1996). The educational pyramid: A model for community intervention. *Applied and Preventive Psychology, 5,* 127–134.

O'Hearn, T., & Gatz, M. (1999). Evaluating a psychosocial competence program for urban adolescents. *Journal of Primary Prevention, 20,* 119–144.

Ogilvie, B. C., & Tutko, T. A. (1971). Sport: If you want to build character, try something else. *Psychology Today, 5*(5), 61–63.

Orlick, T. D., & Botterill, C. (1975). *Every kid can win.* Chicago: Nelson-Hall.

Petitpas, A., Danish, S., McKelvain, R., & Murphy, S. (1992). A career assistance program for elite athletes. *Journal of Counseling and Development, 70,* 383–386.

Sabock, R. (1985). *The coach.* Philadelphia: W. B. Saunders.

Zallo, P. (1995). *Wise up to teens.* Ithaca, NY: New Strategist.

"Kids of Value"

A Conversation with Marty Martinson

M arty Martinson was codirector of the mentor program at Sports-Bridge, in San Francisco, during the second year of that program. She is a former college student-athlete who has taught physical education and coached intercollegiate volleyball at Mills College, Oakland, California. Martinson has also coached high school volleyball in San Francisco. She currently works as the Fitness Center Director and a personal trainer at the Albany YMCA in Albany, California.

Ed.: How would you describe the purpose of the mentor program?

MM: In the mentor program, we were trying to create and nurture an environment to connect adults with young girls, using sport as a common interest and a common space. Hopefully, we were fostering an interest on the part of young girls in sports, introducing them to a wide range of sports and to the enjoyment that can be gained through sports, such as the sense of team, responsibility, and personal achievement. We were conscious too that not only were the girls learning and gaining from the experience, but so were the adults. The mentor program was not set up as one person serving the other, but rather bringing together people to get to know one another, learn from one another, and develop community.

As indicated by the organization's name, SportsBridge, we deliberately used sports as the glue. Middle school is a time during which many girls lose interest in sports or end their participation. There are any number of reasons why this occurs, from lack of resources in schools for sports programs, to peer pressure to be traditionally feminine, and to girls beginning to see sports as contradictory to femininity. We were trying to put sports forward as a place for expression, leadership, development, and fun.

Ed.: The program had two groups of participants—the middle school girls and the mentors. How did you find and choose the mentors?

MM: SportsBridge is a volunteer organization. In fact, it was difficult finding qualified people willing to put in the time and effort necessary for this comprehensive mentor program. Once we identified volunteers, we conducted interviews to assess why the person wanted to become a mentor and to assure that the volunteer appreciated the time and responsibility that would be required. We wanted mentors who had a true interest in sports, a willingness to share with the young person, and perhaps most importantly, an understanding of who they would be mentoring. At Sports-Bridge, we worked with a culturally diverse middle school population, mostly from low-income families. The volunteers were mostly White middle-class women. Therefore, we selected volunteers who had some experience working with youth of color or an understanding of social justice issues relative to class, race, and ethnicity.

Ed.: What characterized the more successful mentors?

MM: The more successful mentors were those who were willing to both learn from and share with the young person. The mentor was willing to listen, to ask questions and to reveal aspects of herself in order to establish a meaningful relationship with the girl whom she mentored. A successful mentor was sensitive and self aware—getting to really know the young girl rather than making assumptions about her. Mentors who approached their role as a one-way relationship, thinking "I'll teach this girl how to do things right" or assuming "I'm going to save this child" were doomed to failure. The girls in the program could pick up that condescending attitude right away.

Ed.: On what basis did you pick the girls?

MM: The first year of the program we worked with one middle school; the second year with two middle schools. We chose twenty girls from each school. We worked with physical education teachers and principals to identify and interview girls who they thought would be interested in SportsBridge as a sports-oriented program and who could get something out of having an adult mentor. Some of the girls had an extensive sports background. Other girls were chosen knowing that they didn't have much of a sports background. These girls had shied away from organized participation for various reasons: fear of failure, negative body image, or discomfort with competition.

Basically, these were young people who we thought could benefit from having some extra support in their lives. As a result, we did at times find ourselves with students who had needs that went beyond what our volunteer mentors were capable of handling or qualified to address.

Ed.: You prefer to avoid referring to these youth as "at-risk"?

MM: Yes, I think the categorization of *at-risk* youth, well intentioned as it may have initially been to identify young people who could use some extra support, has become a very dangerous term. If one identifies a young person as "at-risk," one cannot help but ask, How would that person feel knowing that she is labeled as *at-risk?* How does the label impact her sense of herself and her ideas about what is expected or not expected of her? The label *at-risk* positions the problem at the level of the individual, asserting that the child is at-risk as opposed to there being bigger systemic problems that need to be addressed, and leads to the creation of programs to fix or save these children. We need to create a nurturing environment for young people, as opposed to a judgmental accusing one.

One of the most important points that we tried to get across to the mentors before they met the girls was that you are here to build a relationship with this person and to get to know this person and to support the girl in her interests, curiosities, strengths, yearnings, and joys; not to impose your idea of what she should be learning or what success means or what she should be dreaming about. That is a tricky thing—when you are set up as a role model, sometimes it is hard to sit back and listen. Mentors sometimes are tempted to have preset agendas, for instance, responsibility looks like this, proper English sounds like this, and all these things you must learn so you can get a job in a corporate world and be successful. The problem with such an agenda is that it is not necessarily related to the girls' interests; it's about the mentors' interests and cultural biases.

In chapter 1, Coakley writes about the need for sports programs to be thoughtful interventions. He makes the point that developing a sports program does not automatically support character-building in young people. My point is that we have to be similarly cognizant in the way that we develop mentor programs. Having a mentor will not automatically be a wonderful experience for a child. We have to be very thoughtful about how mentor-mentee relationships are constructed.

Ed.: Do the girls also come with preconceptions and assumptions?

MM: One of the first preconceptions we noticed was that the mentors would be younger. At one of the first meetings, one of the girls said, "my mentor is so old; my mentor is so old." She was twenty-five. This girl had one of the youngest mentors in the group. We as adults view these mentor programs in the social service tradition, but why the girls oftentimes want a mentor is because they want a friend. Then they discover it is a very different thing to have a friend who is ten years older than you or more. And so the age dynamic, the relationship between the adult and young person, was one of many interesting differences to bridge. There were also preconceptions and assumptions about race, class, religion, and sexual orientation.

Ed.: How is the mentor program structured?

MM: It is expected that the mentor and student get together once a week for a year. During this time, they might take a walk and talk, play sports, do homework, go out to eat. They spent time together doing anything that might be fun and connecting. SportsBridge organizes monthly events during which all the students and mentors come together for a sports-related activity. For example, we went camping, sailing, ice skating, and hiking. We had a day where a local women's martial arts group came and provided instruction. We also took the students to women's intercollegiate athletic games. At the end of the year there is a graduation. Some of the matches continued their relationship beyond the one-year SportsBridge program; others did not.

Ed.: You've referred to barriers to sports participation—shying away from competitiveness, not having the right body, lack of opportunity, peer pressure, schools not having resources. Are there other barriers specific to these girls?

MM: Within the population of Latina, African American and Asian American middle school girls with whom we worked, there existed a wide range of culturally-defined gender rules. Strict gender codes and homophobia definitely affect girls' participation in sports programs. In my experiences coaching high school and collegiate volleyball and working with the girls in the mentor program, I have seen many female athletes struggle with feeling a need to assert what they've learned to be appropriately feminine behaviors especially in light of being accomplished athletes. So much of what we see in terms of homophobia in women's sports is connected to this issue of socially approved gendered behaviors. In other words, you can be a successful athlete, but you better also be feminine and you must definitely NOT be a lesbian. That would be the ultimate betrayal of your female role. This social code then promotes a distancing from all lesbians and all perceived lesbians . . . sometimes leading to a distancing from sports. The middle school girls involved in SportsBridge talk about sex all the time. There was an interesting dynamic of distancing that developed among the girls when one of them discovered that her mentor was a lesbian and another girl asserted, loudly enough for other girls to hear, "At least my mentor isn't a lesbian." There was a tone of defensiveness and even self-reference in her assertion as if you say, "At least I am not a lesbian." Sociocultural factors involving expectations of what a girl is supposed to be—feminine and heterosexual, for example—definitely affect girls' participation in sports.

Another big barrier is schools' lack of funding for sports programs. Consequently, schools sometimes hire coaches who do not know the sport, or officials don't show up for matches. This lack of attention to quality programs leaves the girls with the sense that these activities are not viewed as very important. So, resource deficiencies send a message that athletic participation is not valued for girls.

Ed.: Did you build program evaluation into the mentor program?

MM: We hired a program evaluator. We had forty matches, forty mentors; that is a lot of relationships to keep track of! Having an evaluation was critical in terms of helping to guide the continued organization of the program.

There are mentors from two years ago who still have contact with their students, for instance, get together and have dinner. The majority of the relationships just last for that year. That is not to say that they were not valuable. One thing that a lot of the volunteers and students found out was that this program took a lot more time and energy than they thought. It was a commitment to a relationship not just meeting once a month for a fun event; some people found they were involved in a little more than they had bargained for.

Ed.: What did you learn from the experience?

MM: SportsBridge is one of a few youth sports programs specifically for girls, and the mentor program gave it a meaningful twist. The notion of women athletes serving as role models for younger girls was very compelling to teachers, volunteers, students, and funders. It sounds like such a great idea. You bring adult women together with young girls and you do sports together and what a great experience. But, as it turned out, it was much more complex than that. These cross-generational and often cross-cultural relationships took a lot of work. We often had to remind the adults to just step back and listen to what the young people were saying and to catch themselves in their own assumptions about who these young people are. The matches that did work—those who were able to have their relationship really last through the year and beyond, beyond the SportsBridge supported year, were able to say they learned and grew a lot.

One thing really strikes me about working with young people, particularly when we are talking about "inner-city youth"—which usually means youth of color, particularly African American and Latino youth. As we are developing programs in which young people can participate, it is so important to remember that these are kids of value, as opposed to kids who are troublemakers, or broken, or somehow less than whole. This is not to deny that some of these girls live in some very difficult circumstances, but the assumptions that we make about what those difficult circumstances then mean to that child can sometimes be really dangerous. We must approach these young people as valuable and educable rather than trying to manage or control or "deal with" them. Rather than stifling their growth and movement, we should be asking what can we bring out in this young person? What within her can we help nurture? How can we help her realize her dreams?

PART II

Reading Social Issues

Sports Media, Literature, and Pedagogy

Millions of people participate in sports each year, as active participants and as spectators. In recent years, some scholars have begun to point to the profound impact that the mediated spectacle of sport may have on spectators' values concerning race, gender, violence, and the commodification of everyday life. Children's relationships to sport media, in particular, are being scrutinized. A 1999 survey by the Amateur Athletic Foundation of Los Angeles (AAFLA) found that 82% of boys, and 58% of girls, interact with sport media—most often television—at least once a week. What do they see when they watch sports on television? Mostly men's sports, it turns out. A 2000 study done by the AAFLA found that only 8.7% of airtime on televised sports news, and only 2.2% of airtime on ESPN's popular sports highlights show, *SportsCenter,* were devoted to coverage of women's sports. A 1999 study commissioned by the advocacy group Children Now found that the televised sports (and their accompanying commercials) that boys watch most present consistent messages that violence is to be expected, and that men are rewarded with money and sexy women when they are aggressive, take bodily risks, and win.

Sport as popular culture—especially as encoded and sold through the mass media—is a multibillion dollar industry that is both a source of conservative values, and a site where these values may be questioned or perhaps openly contested. The chapters in this section look at sport as popular cultural "texts," and raise questions about how people might variously (and more consciously) "read" these texts.

In chapter 4 Mary Jo Kane and Kimberly D. Pearce conduct a textual analysis of gender and race in 1990s novels about adolescent female athletes. Nearly all of the novels portray girl athletes being subjected to some

sort of sexist treatment, and nearly all of them contain a "resistance narrative," with girls fighting for their right to play sports. Kane and Pearce also
examine the various ways in which the texts treat racial diversity among
girls, sometimes erasing race through a liberal "people are people" narrative, while at other times treating racial difference as an "exotic/flamboyant
spectacle." They observed that what they call "diversity dominant" novels
tended to be more realistic about the problems (e.g., eating disorders) that
some girls athletes face than were the majority of "White/dominant novels"
that tended to present girls' sports as devoid of any social problems.

In chapter 5, Sarah Banet-Weiser sheds light on current race/gender
dynamics in sport from a different angle. In her comparison of recent
media coverage of the (men's) National Basketball Association (NBA) and
the Women's National Basketball Association (WNBA), Banet-Weiser
explores an emergent tendency for media to mark Black male players' bodies as sexually aggressive and uncontrollably greedy. By contrast, women
basketball players seem to be presented as "pure," and the WNBA as a
refreshing "return to the game."

While Kane and Pearce show how young adult sports novels simultaneously reaffirm, modify, and challenge cultural assumptions about race
and gender, Banet-Weiser illuminates shifts in popular representations of
race and gender. Will people passively accept the dominant ideologies
encoded in these books and media texts, or will (some) publics engage in
critical analyses of popular representations of sport? Chapter 6 by Jim
McKay takes us affirmatively in this direction. McKay draws from theories
of radical pedagogy, peace studies, and feminism to discuss ways in which
students can be actively involved in their own critical analysis of sport
media, particularly in terms of the ways in which masculinity and violence
are portrayed in sport. In chapter 7 Lawrence A. Wenner moves us from
pedagogy to creative resistance. Wenner challenges sport scholars and
organizations to take an active role in criticizing the sports media's cele-
bration of violence. Wenner suggests that an annual "sports violence profile"—an analysis of media's treatment of violence in sport—be compiled
and distributed, accompanied by an annual "Bad Sport Award" and a
"Good Sport Award" given out to deserving individuals and organizations.

This section of the book is rounded off with an interview with David
Davis, a Los Angeles area sports journalist who is well-known for his commitment to illuminating social issues through the prism of sport. Davis sheds
light on issues raised by scholars in this section, particularly on how and why
mainstream sports media tend to focus on certain things—for instance, men's
sports—instead of others. He responds to scholars' criticism that sports media
tend to celebrate, rather than criticize, violence in sports. And he reflects on
the difference it might make as to *who* is looking at and describing sport.

FOUR

Representations of Female Athletes in Young Adult Sports Fiction

Issues and Intersections of Race and Gender

MARY JO KANE AND KIMBERLY D. PEARCE

Cultural representations found in sport media outlets both produce and reveal who and what matter in this culture. As Mary G. McDonald (1996) puts it, representations of Michael Jordan, be it in Wheaties or Nike commercials, or in off the court portrayals as an "engaging, thoughtful, private family man" (p. 345), go far beyond telling a story about a single sports superstar: Such representations allow for a complex analysis of some of the most powerful influences in American life such as race, class, and gender. Until recently, who mattered most in sports were almost entirely male, and a twenty-five-year history of sport media scholarship more than bore that out. Research that examined written, visual, and oral texts in print and broadcast journalism found that male athletes were significantly overrepresented (Duncan & Messner, 1998; Tuggle, 1997), and that even when athletic females were given coverage, the focus was on their physical attractiveness and heterosexual status rather than on their accomplishments as highly gifted athletes (Birrell & Theberge, 1994b; Kane, 1996). The weight of this research makes it clear that sport media promote widely held assumptions and practices that equate "sport" and "athlete" with males and masculinity.

Another area where cultural representations reveal who and what matter is the world of sports fiction. In 1982, Alan Tomlinson argued that sports fiction can be fertile ground for developing a "critical social consciousness" (p. 255) not just about sport, but about the larger social,

69

political, and economic issues embodied in sport. This is because the task of the cultural analyst is not to rate sports fiction as better or worse than other forms of literature, but to examine if and how this particular literary genre perpetuates and critiques traditional relations of power within a sport context. At the end of his article, Tomlinson calls for an analysis of sports fiction that is clustered around particular social types and age groups because this type of exploration unmasks the dominant characteristics and contradictions of our cultural life.

Unfortunately, few scholars have heeded Tomlinson's words; until the mid-1990s, there was only one published article that examined sports fiction. In 1985, Pat Griffin did precisely what Tomlinson suggested when she isolated a particular set of novels around a specific age level and social group. Griffin analyzed representations of adolescent female athletes in young adult sports fiction (YASF) and found that representations of athletic females both challenged and reinforced stereotypical assumptions about sport and gender. Two studies recently expanded the scope of Griffin's investigation. In 1997, LeeAnn Kriegh and Mary Jo Kane examined representations of female-athlete-as-lesbian in YASF written since the 1970s. They discovered that girls who wanted to play sports such as football frequently had their status as "true" females called into question. In a follow-up investigation, Kane (1998) also analyzed YASF written since the 1970s. She found that girls who tried out for boys' teams were characterized as being at greater risk for injury due to their so-called limited physical capacity, and that relationships among teammates on girls' teams emphasized heterosexual desire rather than solidarity and camaraderie.

The purpose of the current investigation is to further expand scholarly analyses of YASF. In this study, we shifted our focus away from novels that featured high school adolescents (ages 14–18) and concentrated instead on a middle school population (ages 11–13).[1] We also wanted to limit our analysis to those novels written in the 1990s to get a more contemporary feel of what is being said about athletic females during a time period of unprecedented interest in women's sports.[2] A third area of expansion involved an examination of race. None of the previous studies had analyzed beliefs about race or racism that are deeply embedded in sport. The failure to analyze racial narratives (or the lack thereof) is most egregious when it comes to women of color. As Susan Birrell (1989) has pointed out, "[scholars'] focus on race has been, in reality, a focus on Black male athletes" (p. 213). Such an analysis obscures the fact that women of color are silenced by the dual oppressions of racism and sexism, or what Mathewson (1996) calls the "function at the junction."

Young Adult Sports Fiction

Sports fiction written for a teenage audience is commonly referred to as "young adult sports fiction" and is considered a subgenre within young adult literature (YAL). Specifically targeted for young people who wish to see their peers at the center of a novel (Donelson & Nilsen, 1989), YAL has become increasingly sophisticated in character development and in the nature of topics (e.g., teen suicide) it will address (Kriegh, 1996). These developments are also reflected in YASF: Sports stories written in the early years were highly predictable, with formulaic plots that featured male protagonists who overcame insurmountable odds to lead the team to victory. These narratives have been replaced with stories that more accurately reflect the realities of today's adolescents.

Determining the scope and influence of YASF is difficult,[3] but it seems safe to assert that reading fictional accounts of other adolescents' lives enables young people to think critically about themselves, as well as the effect they have on others (Copeland & Lomax, 1992). Despite the increasing level of sophistication, books with female sport protagonists remain small in number: Sports fiction with male protagonists is still six times more common (Rueth-Brandner, 1991). This finding is especially troubling because, as Forrest (1993) points out, sports fiction with female protagonists can help girls counteract the limitations of gender stereotyping. With this in mind, we wondered what present-day messages were being given to girls who read YASF, particularly as those messages relate to race and gender.

Intersections of Race and Gender in Sport

Birrell (1989) was one of the first scholars to call for a theoretical blending of cultural studies and feminist analysis as a way to deepen our understanding of the complexities of sport forms, ideologies, and practices structured along racial and gender lines. A more profound approach, according to Birrell, is to view race and gender as culturally constructed markers that reproduce relations of privilege and oppression, to see identities constructed around racial and gender characteristics as contested, and to ask how relationships of power based on race and gender are reproduced through sport. Mathewson (1996) and Smith (1992) also argue that any comprehensive analysis of race and gender should avoid viewing African American women as the additive sum of separate, independent components ("add race and sex and stir").

It is clear from these theoretical frameworks and empirical investigations that sport is an important cultural site for the interplay of power, dominance, and subordination structured around race and gender. It is equally clear that representations of such interplay can be found in popular cultural outlets such as YASF.

Method

Sample and Data Collection Procedures

To be included in the sample, a novel had to meet several a priori conditions: Target a young adult audience, feature an athletic female of middle school age as the protagonist, have sport as a major venue, and be published during the 1990s. To obtain the sample, a "cast a wide net" methodological procedure was undertaken given the underrepresentation of females in YASF. First, computer searches of national databases were conducted using key phrases such as "girls in sport" and "young adult sports fiction" to identify novels and locate bibliographies. We also conducted a search of two Internet booksellers—Amazon.com, Inc. and Barnes & Noble, Inc. Finally, the Women's Sport Foundation's "Reading List for Girls" was obtained.

The final sample consisted of 12 novels representing a full range of sport participation. Six of the novels featured individual sports, 2 focused on team sports, while the remaining 4 featured girls who played on or against boys' teams. Nine of the 12 books portrayed persons of color, and of those 9, 7 featured a female athlete of color. This latter figure is somewhat misleading in that 4 of the 7 books were part of a gymnastics series in which one of the main characters is African American. Of the 3 remaining books portraying female athletes of color, 2 featured African American girls, while 1 featured a girl of Hispanic descent. It is important to note that in spite of such diversity, there was only one instance where a young girl of color served as the protagonist.

Textual Analysis

Our critique of YASF was informed by feminist and cultural studies methods of textual analysis. Such an approach allows for a systematic means by which visual, written, and oral texts can be understood beyond their face value. Sociology of sport scholars have increasingly used textual analysis to conduct in-depth readings that expose gaps, inconsistencies, and contradictions in the text (Davis, 1993; Duncan, 1990; Kane & Disch, 1993). Following on that tradition, we "read between the lines" and focused "on the cultural assumptions built into the text rather than the text itself" (Dworkin & Wachs, 1998, p. 5). This permits an "oppositional reading" whereby one not only identifies the dominant or "preferred reading" (messages an author means to convey), but also examines what series of propo-sitions (cultural assumptions) are behind those messages (Hall, 1980a).[4] Oppositional readers engage in the "politics of signification" (Hall, 1980b), so that, for instance, differences in hair texture among young girls of color in the novels we examined can be read as signifying racial "differ-ence." Such racial scripts reaffirm the so-called natural racial hierarchy that places "White" people at the apex, and works to maintain Whiteness as the dominant center of American culture.

It is especially useful to engage in textual analysis from an opposi-tional perspective when conducting research on traditionally marginalized groups. Newfield (1992) developed a list of questions by which to critically examine texts for their racial and racist overtones. These questions, modi-fied to include feminist theoretical activity, guided our readings of YASF: Who is the narrator or protagonist of the story? Whose values are taken as automatic givens? What are the gendered and racial assumptions of the text? What are the absences or silences of the text? In the resolution of the plot, what ideological position is revealed? Informed by these questions, we independently analyzed each of the twelve texts under consideration and categorized various themes related to race and gender.

Results and Discussion

The first category we discovered relates to the number of people of color who occupied each of the texts. There was a clear demarcation between those books in which the vast majority of characters were White and mid-dle-class and those in which a significant number were females and males of color. In the former category, a typical story line involved a young girl of color who serves as best friend and sidekick to the White female pro-tagonist. The American Gold Gymnasts Series and *Swimmers in Deep Water* (Wyeth, 1996), exemplify this type of narrative. In contrast to these texts were two books that featured people of color: *Run for Your Life* (Levy, 1996)—the only book where the female protagonist is a girl of color—and *Never Say Quit* (Wallace, 1993). What is remarkable about this demarcation is how consistent the themes *within* each of these types of novels are, especially as the themes deal with race and racism. For ease and brevity of explanation, we have categorized the first set of novels as "White/dominant" and the second set as "diversity/dominant."

White/Dominant Novels

White/dominant novels obscured race by emphasizing a "people are peo-ple" narrative whereby individuals of color are present, but "there is no attempt to reflect a culture distinct from the shared dominant one" (Bishop, 1992, p. 24). Even though specific characters may be Black, Asian, and Latina or Latino, their experiences are portrayed as universal, meaning that White and middle-class is the dominant (or the only) reference point. The findings from this investigation more than reflect such character portrayals. None of the girls of color is ever subjected to racist comments or innuendo, nor do they ever, in any explicit way, emphasize their racial backgrounds or heritage. The reader is thus left with the impression that regardless of their race, girls of color are just the same as their White counterparts. The one exception to this finding comes from the American Gold Gymnasts Series in the person of Monica Hales, a twelve-year-old African American who is best friends with Kelly Reynolds, the White protagonist. Monica and Kelly are members of the Sugar Loaf Gymnastics Academy in Atlanta. In *Split Decision* (Charbonnet, 1996), Monica, concerned that she is becoming too tall to remain a gymnast, looks for other outlets such as her love of animals. She volunteers at a local veterinary clinic and meets Dr. Thayer, an African American veterinarian and a former collegiate tennis player. Much of the novel involves Monica's being torn between her two competing desires: Staying with the gymnastics team and being loyal to her best friend Kelly, or quitting the team to spend more time with her role model, Dr. Thayer. This struggle is revealed in the following exchange:

> Kelly: "[I]t's really great that you like going [to Dr. Thayer's office] so much but I'm worried that it might get in the way of what's really important—gymnastics."
> Monica: "Is gymnastics what's really important, Kel? . . . I mean I can't even do a simple squat vault [because I have gotten so tall]. . . . But at Dr. Thayer's I do everything right. . . . I don't pull muscles or land badly or work so hard that my arms shake. And I really admire Dr. Thayer. It makes me think I can do anything and be good at it." (pp. 66–67)

Kelly persists in her efforts to keep Monica on the team, but the pressure of getting to practice, going to school, and working at the vet clinic takes its toll on Monica. Feeling forced to choose, she quits the team though she knows it will break Kelly's heart. Toward the end of the novel however, Monica rejoins the team after a conversation with Dr. Thayer in which she convinces Monica that she (Monica) could go onto college (and eventually vet school) by getting a gymnastics scholarship. In one of the only exchanges throughout the series that even hints at a person of color's racial heritage, Dr. Thayer tells Monica that she used tennis as a way to pursue her dreams of becoming a vet: "I was never going to be the next Althea Gibson" (p. 125) . . . "[but] I used my talent to *pursue my dream*" (p. 126). Monica's initial response to this story is quite startling, and reveals the extent to which girls of color in White/dominant novels are seen (and see themselves) as insulated from the "problems" of being Black in America:

> Monica didn't know what to think. Most gymnasts at [her training facility] were aiming for the Olympics, or at least for the world championships. Monica hadn't heard anyone talk about his or her *sport as the means to achieve other goals.* (p. 126, emphasis added)

In spite of her initial reaction, Monica soon realizes that Dr. Thayer has given her a way out of her dilemma: She can cut back on her hours at the clinic, and even though she may not be good enough to compete for the Olympics, she can still go to college on an athletic scholarship. With this solution in hand, she returns to the gymnastics team and is reunited with Kelly. At novel's end, Monica's position in the (White) world is firmly reestablished: "Monica caught Kelly's eye, and they burst out laughing. It felt good to be home" (p. 135).

Our analysis is not meant to suggest that Monica's desire to connect with an African American role model serves no important function. On the contrary, Monica tells her teammates how wonderful Dr. Thayer is, and how much she identifies with her, including their common racial heritage: "She's a woman, and she's Black. And guess what? She's from New Orleans, like me. She's really tall too" (pp. 26–27). But such a connection occurs in only one of the four novels in the series. Monica's admiration for Dr. Thayer is also never contextualized in any depth, the Althea Gibson reference notwithstanding. Why, for example, might it be especially important for African American girls to have role models given the history of racism and sexism in this country? An exploration of this particular (and ongoing) history could have been, in fact, a useful venue by which to explore the complex intersections of race and gender.

The finding that representations of Monica focus primarily on her "Whiteness"—and that these representations secure her position as a sympathetic, even exemplary, character—is consistent with arguments advanced by a number of scholars who suggest that White Americans not only accept, but are quite gracious toward, "exceptional Blacks" as long as they do not insist upon asserting their so-called Blackness (Andrews, 1996; Davis & Harris, 1998). Monica's work-hard ethic, as well as her struggles around loyalty and commitment to her teammates, also offer proof that African Americans can "make it" if they possess the right (meaning White) values (Wenner, 1995).

Another White/dominant novel that features a "people are people" narrative is *Swimmers in Deep Water* (Wyeth, 1996). This novel also portrays a young girl of color who is best friends with the White female protagonist. Rosa Gonzalez and Kristy Adams are members of the local swim club. Like Monica, Rosa never experiences any difficulties because of her race. But unlike the previous novel, the reader is given so few clues about who Rosa is, and where she comes from, that we can only guess as to the specifics of her racial background beyond a more global category of Hispanic. Perhaps the most telling example of how race is made invisible in this novel involves the identification of the two main characters' surname. Halfway down page 1 we are introduced to "Kristy Adams"; at the bottom of the same page we meet "Rosa." Even though we are given some stereotypical hints along the way that Rosa might be a girl of color—she is described as having "curly black hair" on page 5—it is not until page 21 that we learn her last name is Gonzalez.

Our reading of these young girls of color is not meant to suggest there were no racial scripts across White/dominant novels. But when these scripts did appear, they were consistently used to describe racial "difference" between the characters based on physical characteristics and personal attributes. In addition, these types of descriptions, used as an overt mechanism to differentiate girls of color from their White female counterparts, marked the only time throughout the novels where notions of difference were emphasized. This is important because no such differentiation—at least to the same degree—occurred for White characters, even though there are many physical differences among Whites (e.g., hair and skin color) that could have easily been highlighted. Emphasizing physical difference for people of color tells readers that "Whiteness" is the taken-for-granted norm, and that people of color need to be referenced in relationship to that norm. In the following section we document numerous examples where girls of color were marked as different from their White counterparts. Not surprisingly, these examples reaffirm widely held beliefs about race and racial relations.

Race as exotic/flamboyant spectacle. Laurel R. Davis (1997) examined representations of "bathing beauty" models who have appeared in *Sports Illustrated's* (SI) annual (and infamous) swimsuit issue. She discovered that *SI* executives use notions of exoticism to select the (often foreign) country that will be featured. Davis also found that these same executives reflected the belief that people of color are "vastly different from the culturally known Western self" (p. 103). Representations of girls of color in White/dominant novels also reflected the notion of race as exotic. To return to Rosa Gonzalez, we are told almost immediately that she likes "big hoop earrings" that are "definitely you" (p. 3). Of all the characters in the novel, it is Rosa who is most concerned with fashion and style, especially that which is considered exaggerated (i.e., flamboyant) by Western standards. In one revealing exchange, Rosa offers Kristy her "Purple Passion" lipstick so that a boy named Jason will be interested in her (Kristy). Kristy declines the offer, so Rosa decides to wear it instead:

> Kristy: "Be my guest. But don't put on too much. You might end up looking like the bride of Dracula."
> Rosa: "[Sighing as she] applied the lipstick heavily. 'Kristy, you should read more magazines. Dark lips are the fashion.'"
> (p. 84)

The notion of race as exotic and flamboyant also appeared in the characterization of Monica Hales throughout the American Gold Gymnasts Series. Even though this series contains numerous female characters, it is Monica who cares most about fashion. In *Competition Fever* (Charbonnet, 1996), Monica tells her teammates Kelly and Maya that if it weren't for her, the gymnastics team "would have no style at all" (p. 35) because she alone wears leotards that are "swirls of neon red, neon blue, and sunburst pink" (p. 36). In *The Bully Coach* (Charbonnet, 1996) we are also informed about Monica's interest in fashion. Here Monica uses her "flashy" style as a way to impress a new head coach:

> [It] was Monica who was really going to make a splash. . . . The tallest girl on their team and the only African American, she already stood out. But today she was wearing a vivid black-and-white zebra-print leotard. . . . [S]he was fussing with a red, green, and black scarf printed with a traditional African pattern. She had looped it around her puffy dark brown curls and was wrapping it across her forehead almost in a turban effect. (p. 23)

By highlighting this passage we do not mean to imply that Monica should not be proud of her African heritage, but it is rather curious how that heritage was equated with an exotic sensibility.

There is another important way in which representations of Monica's sense of fashion can be read as racial (and racist) scripts. In this passage, Monica is wearing a "black-and-white *zebra*-print leotard" (p. 23, emphasis added). In *Competition Fever,* she is described as wearing a "purple *leopard* print" leotard (p. 2, emphasis added). In both instances, Monica's outfit is linked to an exotic animal found in Africa. Though there are numerous descriptions of other girls' outfits throughout the series, none is ever identified with an animal-print leotard. These representations call to

mind racist stereotypes of "savage" Africans, as well as the "animaliza-
tion" of African Americans that resulted from the legacy of a White
supremacy that first biologized Africans as "creatures" rather than as fully
developed humans (Goldberg, 1990). Portraying African Americans as
primitive and closer to nature (Collins, 1990) has often occurred in the
world of sport. Coakley (1998) points out that sportswriters of the 1930s
and 1940s frequently described Joe Louis—the legendary heavyweight
boxing champion—as a savage beast from the African jungle. Though we
are not suggesting that Monica Hales was portrayed like Joe Louis, it is
more than curious that the only gymnast ever linked to "exotic wildness"
just happened to be African American.

Race equals physical superiority. Monica Hales and Rosa Gonzalez had
many things in common when it comes to racial stereotypes. They also had
another thing in common, only this time it went against a traditional race
narrative: Neither of them was ever portrayed as a superior athlete. Perhaps
this is because the sports they participated in—gymnastics and swimming—
are considered "White" sports. But in one of only two books that featured
both a Black female athlete and a "Black" sport, descriptions of superior
athletic ability abound. *Who Let Girls in the Boys' Locker Room?* (Moore,
1994), tells the story of three eleven-year-old girls who love to play basketball. When budget cuts eliminate the girls' team, they try out for and make
the boys' team. We are first introduced to the African American character
by the narrator of the story, Michelle Dupree: "The Awesome Keisha, an
African American girl . . . [looked] very cool in a white oversized T-shirt,
black jeans and matching sneakers" (p. 23). It is important (not to mention
disturbing) to point out that we learn Michelle's full name on page 1, but
are not given Keisha's last name until page 62 of a 144-page novel.

   Keisha's surname is made invisible because it is irrelevant to the way
in which her identity is constructed. In fact, everything the reader is told
about Keisha relates to her athletic prowess. Representations of Black athletes as inherently superior to White athletes have been well documented in
sport media scholarship. For example, Derrick Jackson (1989) points out
that sports commentators typically credit White basketball players' success
to intelligence and hard work, yet equate the success of Black athletes with
innate physicality. Though readers are told that Keisha works hard and is
a dedicated athlete, we are given far more information about the mental
strategies used, and the exhausting practices endured by, Michelle Dupree.

   By failing to develop Keisha's character beyond the most superficial
and stereotypical level, the author misses an opportunity to explore issues
of race and racism with her readers. The failure to explore how Keisha may
have experienced racism also obscured the intersections of race and gender.

This was especially frustrating because this novel contains the only narrative in the sample where a girl of color is subjected to overt sexism. Recall that the plot involved girls trying out for a boys' basketball team. When they do so, they meet with fierce resistance as when Michelle is told by her brother that she and the other girls should "Stick to the girls' league where you belong" (p. 34) because "everybody knows you can't win with a bunch of giggling girls on the team" (p. 35). As the plot develops, the boys' resistance increases, but it is always confined to sexist put-downs. By ignoring the possibility that another form of resistance—racial slurs and innuendos—could have easily been directed toward the best (and therefore the most threatening) female player, the reader is not forced to grapple with the thorny and interactive effects of racism and sexism.

Diversity/Dominant Novels

There were two books in which the majority (or at least a critical mass) of characters were people of color. As with White/dominant novels, themes within this category were remarkably similar. Both books, for example, contained narratives that can best be described as a "ghetto to glory" motif—the widely held assumption that a primary path to success for people of color, and especially African Americans, is through sport (Davis & Harris, 1998; Messner, 1992). In sharp contrast to the economically secure, White middle-class existence of the previous novels, diversity/dominant books focus on crime, poverty, and abuse. In *Run for Your Life* (Levy, 1996) Kisha Clark is the thirteen-year-old protagonist living in a housing project in Oakland, California. What sets this book apart from White/dominant novels is that it contains immediate and explicit references to race. Within the first few pages, Kisha recalls seeing pictures of her aunts "wearing African dashikis. They have huge Afros sticking out about five inches from their heads" (p. 4). She also tells us about drug pushers and "popping sounds" that refer to gunfire and pervasive poverty. Such danger and turmoil reflect the circumstances of Kisha's own family where domestic violence dominates her home life:

> I heard the front door slam. BANG. My dad came stomping into the apartment in a fury, like a bat out of hell. He was yelling and cussing, . . . "Money, money, money. Is that all you ever think about?" he yelled. . . . "Because we don't have any," my mother shouted [back]. . . . I hear a CRACK. Then my mom cries out. (pp. 74–75)

Kisha seeks refuge from "life in the projects" through her involvement with the girls' track club at the local community center. As the novel develops, Kisha's father becomes increasingly abusive and eventually shoots Kisha's mother in the leg. Kisha's response is to sink into a deep depression, but, in the end, her love of track, and being a member of the team, pulls her out of it: "Once I got out on the track, I felt more alive. The wind lifted me up and took me to some other place where there were no demons and bogeymen" (p. 193). In spite of her improvement, Kisha is filled with doubt about the role of track in her life. She resists the efforts of her close friends and family to go to an important track meet in Philadelphia, a meet that affords her the opportunity to begin her journey out of the projects. But Kisha is worried she will fail and tells everyone, "I'm not going. I can't" (p. 206). Toward the end of the novel this dilemma is resolved in a scene that reads like a Hollywood script, the classic "ghetto to glory" narrative. Kisha's mother tells her daughter,

> "I know what it's like to be shackled to a prison you can't get out of. I don't know if I'll make it. But *you* can. Go to the meet. That's your way out of here. Your ticket to a scholarship—a good education. Go. Run. *Run for your life!*" (p. 207)

Rising above life's circumstances was also a major theme that appeared throughout the other diversity/dominant novel, *Never Say Quit* (Wallace, 1993). This book features a multicultural cast of characters including Asians, Mexicans, African Americans, and Whites. In this novel, a group of self-described misfits—kids from the "other side of the tracks"—are told they are not good enough to make their middle school soccer team. They believe this decision has little to do with their abilities as athletes, and everything to do with discrimination based on race and class. Justine Smith, the White, working-class protagonist, is the leader of this multicultural group, who, with the help of an alcoholic, broken-down coach, form their own team and dedicate themselves to beating the White, middle-class team that rejected them.

As with the characters in *Run for Your Life* (Levy, 1996), Justine and her teammates are faced with seemingly insurmountable odds such as economic pressures, family members in jail, domestic violence, and the abuse of alcohol and drugs. But over the course of the novel, characters learn that sport is a vehicle for proving they belong in a White, middle-class world. In one revealing scene, Justine and her teammates try to convince the down-and-out (but former soccer great) Mr. Reiner to become their coach. He doesn't understand why it matters so much that they start a team. Justine provides the answer:

> "Because we want to beat those guys." I swallowed the lump in my throat. "We want a team so we can play them and beat them! . . . They make us feel like we don't belong. They make

us feel like we're not even good enough to go to the same school. But we are, Mr. Reiner. We *do* belong. We're just as good as them. . . ." (pp. 54–55)

White/dominant novels paint an entirely different picture of growing up in the 1990s: People are accepting of each other's backgrounds; families are loving, supportive, and intact; and the realities of such unpleasantries as violence, drugs, and sexual assault never surface. White/dominant novels even ignore widely reported social concerns in women's athletics such as the prevalence of eating disorders in women's gymnastics (Ryan, 1995). In over five hundred pages throughout the American Gold Gymnasts Series there is never a hint that any of the characters may be struggling with this life-threatening disorder. In fact, readers are given just the opposite impression. For example, the gymnasts often met at a local hangout and routinely ordered ice cream cones and banana splits. As the following quote indicates, gaining weight was hardly a concern: "[Eating ice cream] hits *all* the spots, Monica [said], licking her usual rocky road double cone" (Charbonnet, *Competition Fever*, 1996, pp. 40–41).

Although diversity/dominant novels provided a much-needed contrast to such simplified versions of modern America, we nevertheless had concerns with the "ghetto to glory" texts. These were the only two novels that contained more than a token presence of people of color. Yet in both instances their narratives were confined to a "better yourself" story line in which those who make a commitment to sports always rise above their circumstances. Though we do not disagree that individuals can reap tremendous rewards for participating in sports, and that sports have served a useful function for a number of minority groups (including Whites), neither book ever mentions the downsides of "making it" such as the exploitation of intercollegiate athletes and the far too frequent occurrence of debilitating physical injuries (Early, 1998; Messner, 1992). By focusing exclusively on an upward mobility narrative, these novels reaffirmed commonsense beliefs that Black people achieve only (or primarily) through sports. This racial script—combined with White/dominant novels where race is sanitized through a "White" lens— obscures the fact that racially defined groups are not passive recipients of the dominant culture, but "active creators of their own social worlds" (Birrell, 1989, p. 215). Though you would never know it from reading diversity/dominant novels, large parts of those worlds have little to do with sports in general, and ghetto to glory narratives in particular.

Gender Narratives

We have made the argument that White/dominant and diversity/dominant novels are different in many respects, but there are some themes that appeared across both types of novels. One area that stood out involved representations of gender. Across all twelve novels, athletic females, particularly those who want to play with and against males, are routinely subjected to sexist behaviors and remarks. The one exception to this finding occurred in the American Gold Gymnasts Series where young girls' sports participation was never problematized. Perhaps this is because gymnastics, with its emphasis on prepubescent bodies, and routines that emphasize grace and aesthetic beauty, offers little threat to traditional expectations of femininity. But when girls wanted to compete against boys in combative sports such as football and basketball they met with a great deal of resistance.

Several books in the study—including those that portrayed girls of color—contained a resistance narrative. Based on traditional assumptions about what girls can and should do, these narratives centered around three interrelated themes. First was that girls who wanted to try out for boys' teams were accused of "stepping out of line." This charge was linked to a second theme that emerged: Girls were told to "get back where they belong" because they didn't possess the physical capacities necessary to compete against boys. The third theme followed logically from the first two—girls who persisted in their efforts to play against boys were considered to be at greater risk for physical injury, or had their status as "true" females called into question. These findings are consistent with the work of a number of scholars who argue that sport has been constructed as a "male preserve" and that any efforts by females to encroach upon this space will be fiercely resisted (Birrell & Theberge, 1994a). They also mirror strategies that have been used to keep women out of sports altogether, or confined them to certain sports if they did participate. Such strategies range from freezing women out (e.g., by refusing to pass them the ball), to verbal intimidation and physical assaults.

Female athletes in our sample were subjected to all of these strategies and then some. In *Molly Maguire* (Sullivan, 1992), the female protagonist possesses the "fastest legs in the whole fifth grade" (p. 1). At recess one day, Molly tells her best friend she wants to play football because "it's the most fun thing to do in the whole world" (p. 3). Even though Molly knows she is a great athlete, she also realizes she must disguise herself as a boy if she wants to play football. Much of the plot involves Molly's exchanges with her nemesis, Jason Jenson, the class bully who taunts her with sexist remarks. After she makes the football team disguised as "Lee," Jason becomes her unwitting teammate. Not realizing he is really talking to Molly, Jason tells his new teammate why girls like Molly shouldn't be allowed to play football:

My dad says girls like that should be put in their place. She's the kind of girl who thinks she should be able to drive a truck or be an astronaut. . . . My dad says girls should stay home and learn to cook. That's their place. (pp. 48–49)

Over the course of several practices "Lee" wins the respect and admiration of her new teammates and during a big game she leads the team to victory while ignoring a mean and dirty opponent who tries to intimidate her. In one dramatic scene Molly makes a diving catch and scores the winning touchdown just at the moment he crashes into her and breaks her leg. While Molly is lying on the ground, Jason removes her helmet; her identity is revealed when "her long red hair cascaded out over the grass" (p. 98). Even though Jason thinks she pulled a "pretty dirty trick" (p. 103), Molly has won him over by proving she can rise above her biology and "be one of the guys" (p. 104). It should be pointed out that in spite of Molly's obvious athletic abilities, she was the only player who ever suffered an injury, let alone one that was season-ending. The reader is thus left with the impression that girls who want to compete with and against males are indeed at greater risk for injury.

Because it is assumed that girls don't belong in boys' sports, and because that assumption rests on the belief that females and males are fundamentally different due to their biology, girls who want to play on boys' teams are seen as foolish at best, and abnormal at worst. In the former category is Bobby Lorimar, the fifth-grade female protagonist in *Blowing Bubbles with the Enemy* (Jackson, 1993). Even though Bobby is as "tough, talented and athletic" (p. 4) as the sixth-, seventh-, and eighth-grade boys when it comes to playing basketball, she is told by her older brother Tim that she has "totally lost your marbles this time" and that she should "try out for the girls' team instead of making a fool of yourself in front of the whole school" (p. 22). But Bobby hasn't lost her mind. Her desire to play on the boys' team has a straightforward and logical explanation: "I had nothing against playing basketball with other girls. But it was simply that I knew that I was better than the girls on Mrs. D's team. I wanted to play basketball where I really belonged" (pp. 19–20).[5] Apparently Bobby doesn't realize that, for girls, "belonging" in men's sports goes far beyond one's athletic abilities and desires.

Whereas Bobby is told she is being foolish, other girls are accused of being abnormal. In *Who Let Girls in the Boys' Locker Room?* (Moore, 1994), Michelle and Keisha are told by a "real" female—cheerleader Stephanie—that they are "probably going to be the only girls in the district playing [basketball] with guys. You're not cool. You're freaks" (p. 79). Stephanie is not alone in her feelings. As a way to intimidate Michelle and

Keisha, the boys decide to publicly humiliate them by challenging their status as "normal" girls. Shortly after Michelle and Keisha make the team, a poster with the team schedule and picture is posted in the local grocery store. While Michelle is standing in the checkout line, she becomes aware of what her male teammates have done:

> Then she saw it. Someone had taken a Magic Marker and painted black mustaches on all the girls' faces. Michelle shook her head, totally shocked. Who would do such a mean thing? And why? It had to be someone who hated girls being on the Eagles team. (pp. 103–104)

Kane (1995) has argued that when athletic females so deviate from traditional expectations of femininity, their "biological standing as a 'real' female is called into question" (p. 210). The way in which female characters were treated in this novel more than confirms Kane's position.

Counternarratives. In spite of the unrelenting resistance that has just been described, young girls repeatedly fought back and established their right to play sports, even with and against boys. In this sense, many of the novels contained counternarratives, meaning that authors offered alternative and liberating possibilities for what it means to be female and athletic in the 1990s. For example, Michelle Dupree challenges her male teammates to stop treating the girls like they're too fragile, and points out that the only way they will beat their archrivals, the Barracudas, is if they play together as a team:

> [T]he not-so-fragile girls banged shoulders against the boys. . . . Then the girls knocked the boys with their not-so-fragile hips. . . . "We [girls] don't think about chests or behinds when we play, . . . We think about putting the ball in the hoop." . . . "If you guys can do the same, we have a good chance of finally beating the Barracudas." (p. 129)

Another example of a counternarrative involved Kristy Adams, the protagonist in *Swimmers in Deep Water* (Wyeth, 1996). Kristy is a star athlete on the local swim club who has a mad crush on Jason, a boy who swims for a rival team. After a visit to Kristy's house, where Jason has an argument with Kristy's brother about who has the better swim team, Jason stops calling Kristy. Convinced that Jason doesn't like her anymore because he thinks she's too competitive—"I'd give [my trophies] all away . . . if Jason would only like me again" (p. 111)—Kristy decides to skip an important swim meet so that she won't have to compete against Jason's team. To the rescue comes Rosa, Kristy's best friend and teammate, who chides

Kristy for her decision: "I never thought I'd see the day when Kristy Adams would wiggle out of a swim meet just because she wanted to please a boy" (p. 117). After this conversation, Kristy realizes she can't let her team down. She calls Jason and tells him,

> "I guess I'll get to the point. I'm going to be swimming at the invitational. My brother was definitely being a jerk that day. . . . But I will be competing against you at the meet. If you have a problem with it, I'm sorry." Kristy's heart lifted a little when she put down the phone. She didn't know whether she felt happy or sad. But she did feel like herself. (pp. 120–121)

At novel's end, Kristy's team wins the big match. But in a modern-day twist on the relationship between sport and gender, Kristy is able to be a great athlete *and* get the guy. The last paragraph of the novel describes her feelings about her two loves:

> Her gym bag was packed with a fresh drag suit, a cap, and goggles. She touched her cheek where Jason had kissed her, and closed her eyes. She had all night to dream. But the next day, she'd be back in the water. (p. 130)

Sexual identity as heterosexual desire. One area that provided little possibility of a counternarrative was sexual identity. The most universal theme that emerged across all twelve novels was that athletic females—as well as every other character—were unequivocally heterosexual. This was true regardless of a young girl's race, or whether she played on a boys' versus a girls' team. Bobby Lorimer may have been a better basketball player than most of the boys in her school, but she was also in love with "Leslie Crane, the tall, skinny basketball-playing boy of my dreams" (Jackson, *Blowing Bubbles with the Enemy,* 1993, p. 4). Monica Hales may have spent time in the gym perfecting her death-defying maneuvers on the balance beam, but she also "[scanned] the gym for the light of her life, Beau Jarrett . . . she'd had a killer crush on him for at least six months" (Charbonnet, *The Bully Coach,* 1996, p. 8).

Even if there wasn't a direct reference to a girl's sexual interest in boys, readers are told early and often that female protagonists are interested in activities traditionally associated with femininity and thus heterosexuality. We suggest that such an exclusive emphasis on "heterofeminine" interests and desires confirms for the reader that athletic females are, by definition, heterosexual. Given the historical association between women's sport and lesbian identity (Kane & Lenskyj, 1998), it is especially curious that there was never an instance where it was even suggested or implied that some female characters might be gay. The absence of a lesbian narrative also meant that exploring the complexities of another intersection in young girls' lives would not be possible. We are not, for example, given the opportunity to learn how it might feel for lesbian athletes to confront the combined effects of sexism and homophobia. Lesbian narratives could also further our understanding of an even more complicated intersection—being a lesbian athlete of color.

Summary

In a critique of children's novels with multicultural texts, Bishop (1992) argued that books are mirrors because they allow readers to see reflections of themselves (and others) that reaffirm or challenge their realities. The novels in our study did precisely what Bishop points out: They reaffirmed, modified, and challenged cultural assumptions about race and gender. Though few in number, girls of color in White dominant/novels challenged the notion that African Americans are only from a particular economic class, or only able to excel in certain sports. These novels also showed awareness of, and sensitivity to, an increasingly multiracial society. For example, the portrayal of Monica Hales reflects the widening access racial minority groups have to traditionally "White-only" sports such as gymnastics. And finally, by avoiding a race + sport = upward mobility narrative, White/dominant novels provided an alternative vision to popularly held beliefs about the role of sport in the lives of people of color.[6]

On the other hand, White/dominant novels confirmed widespread cultural assumptions about race by emphasizing a "people are people" narrative. This contributed to an oversimplified and sanitized view of racial relations in three important ways. First, by portraying the participation of middle-class girls of color in swimming and gymnastics as an unproblematic, taken-for-granted reality, White/dominant novels obscured a very different kind of reality: That increasingly large numbers of people of color (particularly women and children) live in poverty (McDonald, 1996), and that African American women continue to be significantly underrepresented in these types of sports (Smith, 1992). Second, by ignoring the deleterious effects of racism, White/dominant novels obliterated the realities of people of color within and across class lines. Both Rosa Gonzalez and Monica Hales reaffirmed the steadfast belief that sport serves as a meritocracy whereby "individuals who work hard and possess the right stuff will always prevail" (Birrell, 1989, p. 213). Their characterizations seem to suggest that once people of color have "prevailed," they will no longer experience racism because they have become, in effect, White and middle-class.

Closely related to notions of sport-as-meritocracy were narratives that reinforced an assimilationist paradigm. This was the third way in which White/dominant novels simplified race and racial relations. Birrell (1989) points out that assimilationist theories have traditionally assumed a voluntary and orderly desire by "minority" groups to take on dominant cultural values. Viewed from this perspective, assimilationist models bear a striking resemblance to the "people are people" narratives that served as cornerstones for White/dominant novels. While these narratives clearly intend positive outcomes, they not only elide racial difference, but also, as Cornel West (1990) explains, subordinate "Black" particularity to a false universalism. We certainly do not accuse the authors (the majority of whom we assume to be White) of conscious use of, or collusion with, racist discourse. Rather we emphasize that their writings unwittingly reflect dominant Eurocentric ideologies that overlook and ignore cultural authenticity.[7]

In discussing the effects of assimilation, Birrell (1989) also argued that groups who have not been assimilated are "seen as culturally deprived" (p. 217). This is precisely how one could read diversity/dominant novels. A central component of the "ghetto to glory" narrative is an "up and out" assimilationist mind-set. In addition, one obvious (though we assume unintended) message of diversity/dominant novels is that whenever you have a critical mass of people of color, you get, by definition, an "underprivileged" environment. In spite of these shortcomings, it should be recalled that diversity/dominant novels provided a breath-of-reality approach that was in stark contrast to the Leave-it-to-Beaver fantasies of White/dominant novels.

Carrington (1998) and Messner (1992) have argued that sport is an important cultural site where subordinate groups can challenge and resist the established order. Tomlinson (1982) made much the same argument about the importance of sports fiction. We would suggest that the same is true for YASF. Because a middle school age population is particularly impressionable (Duncan & Sayaovong, 1990), the authors of YASF have a special responsibility (not to mention opportunity) to create characters that reflect and reaffirm the complexities of girls' lives. Books are not only mirrors, but windows through which these girls—whether White or of color, gay or straight—learn not only about themselves, but about "the lives of people whose culture and life experiences are different from their own" (Bishop, 1992, pp. 34–35). Such is the potential and the power of young adult sports fiction.

Notes

1. A few of the novels in the two earlier studies had some characters who were younger than fourteen, but the bulk of the adolescent population was late- to mid-high school.

2. The 1990s have witnessed the launching of two new professional basketball leagues, unparalleled success for U.S. women's team sports at the Olympic Games, and an explosion of corporate and media interest.

3. One measure of influence—readership—is difficult to determine, in part, because of definitional problems. However, one indirect measure comes from the United States Department of Education (1994), who reported that young adults account for 23 percent of public library patronage.

4. Though our analysis is confined to deconstructing authors' preferred readings, other types of critical textual analysis focus on the production of texts (e.g., who the publishers are), as well as how the intended readers may interpret the texts (e.g., even texts with traditional narratives may still be read oppositionally by some young girls). A more detailed discussion of these types of textual analysis can be found in Davis (1997) and Duncan and Messner (1998).

5. "Mrs. D." refers to Mrs. Del Rio, the girls' basketball coach. This character of color is described in very stereotypical ways throughout the novel as in she had a "temper to match [her] bullhorn voice" (p. 24), and she wore "chandelier earrings" (p. 69).

6. Even though White/dominant novels did not construct "ghetto to glory" narratives, minor variations of that theme did arise for Monica Hales and for the "Awesome Keisha." As mentioned, Monica resolves to use gymnastics as a way to get a scholarship to go to college. Keisha tells Michelle that the reason she needs to play basketball in two leagues is because she "has to be visible. Coach says if you want a scholarship, you gotta work" (p. 119).

7. Although we could not always determine the author's race, we do know that both diversity/dominant books were written by White authors (one female and one male). Ten of the books were written by females. A more detailed discussion of the race and sex of the authors—and how those factors relate to particular types of narratives—is beyond the scope of this study.

References

Andrews, D. L. (1996). Deconstructing Michael Jordan: Reconstructing postindustrial America. *Sociology of Sport Journal, 13,* 315–318.

Birrell, S. (1989). Racial relations theories and sport: Suggestions for a more critical analysis. *Sociology of Sport Journal, 6,* 212–227.

Birrell, S., & Theberge, N. (1994a). Feminist resistance and transformation in sport. In D. M. Costa & S. R. Guthrie (Eds.), *Women and sport: Interdisciplinary perspectives* (pp. 361–376). Champaign, IL: Human Kinetics.

Birrell, S., & Theberge, N. (1994b). Ideological control of women in sport. In D. M. Costa & S. R. Guthrie (Eds.), *Women and sport: Interdisciplinary perspectives* (pp. 341–359). Champaign, IL: Human Kinetics.

Bishop, R. S. (1992). Children's books in a multicultural world: A view from the USA. In E. Evans (Ed.), *Reading against racisms* (pp. 19–38). Buckinghamshire, England: Open University Press.

Carrington, B. (1998). Sport, masculinity, and black cultural resistance. *Journal of Sport & Social Issues, 22,* 275–298.

Charbonnet, G. (1996). *Competition fever.* New York: Bantam Books

Charbonnet, G. (1996). *Split decision.* New York: Bantam Books.

Charbonnet, G. (1996). *The bully coach.* New York: Bantam Books.

Coakley, J. J. (1998). *Sport in society: Issues & controversies* (6th ed.). New York: WCB/McGraw-Hill.

Collins, P. H. (1990). *Black feminist thought: Knowledge, consciousness, and the politics of empowerment.* London: Harper Collins.

Copeland, J. S., & Lomax, E. D. (Eds.) (1992). *Contemporary issues in young adult literature* (2d ed.). Needham Heights, MA: Ginn Press.

Davis, L. R. (1993). Critical analysis of the popular media and the concept of the ideal subject position: *Sports Illustrated* as a case study. *Quest, 45,* 165–181.

Davis, L. R. (1997). *The swimsuit issue and sport: Hegemonic masculinity in Sports Illustrated.* Albany: State University of New York Press.

Davis, L. R., & Harris, O. (1998). Race and ethnicity in US sports media. In L. Wenner (Ed.), *MediaSport: Cultural sensibilities and sport in the media age* (pp. 154–169). London: Routledge.

Donelson, K. L., & Nilsen, A. P. (1989). *Literature for today's young adults* (3rd ed.). Glenview, IL: Scott, Foresman, and Company.

Duncan, M. C. (1990). Sports photographs and sexual difference: Images of women and men in the 1984 and 1988 Olympic Games. *Sociology of Sport Journal, 7,* 22–43.

Duncan, M. C., & Messner, M. A. (1998). The media images of sport and gender. In L. Wenner (Ed.), *MediaSport: Cultural sensibilities and sport in the media age* (pp. 170–185). London: Routledge.

Duncan, M. C., & Sayaovong, A. (1990). Photographic images and gender in *Sports Illustrated for Kids. Play & Culture, 3,* 91–116.

Dworkin, S. L., & Wachs, F. L. (1998). "Disciplining the body": HIV-positive male athletes, media surveillance, and the policing of sexuality. *Sociology of Sport Journal, 15,* 1–20.

Early, G. (1998, August). Performance and reality: Race, sports and the modern world. *Nation,* 11–20.

Forrest, L. A. (1993, Fall). Young adult fantasy and the search for gender-fair genres. *Youth Services in Libraries,* 37–43.

Goldberg, D. T. (1990). *Anatomy of racism*. Minneapolis: University of Minnesota Press.

Griffin, P. S. (1985). R. R. Knudson's sport fiction: A feminist critique. *Arete,* 3–10.

Hall, S. (1980a). Introduction to media studies at the Centre. In S. Hall et al. (Eds.), *Culture, media, language* (pp. 117–121). London: Hutchinson.

Hall, S. (1980b). Encoding/decoding. In S. Hall (Ed.), *Culture, media, language* (pp. 128–138). London: Hutchinson.

Jackson, A. (1993). *Blowing bubbles with the enemy.* New York: Dutton Children's Books.

Jackson, D. (1989, January 22). Calling the plays in black and white. *Boston Globe,* A30–A33.

Kane, M. J. (1995). Resistance/transformation of the oppositional binary: Exposing sport as a continuum. *Journal of Sport and Social Issues, 19,* 191–218.

Kane, M. J. (1996). Media coverage of the post Title-IX female athlete: A feminist analysis of sport, gender, and power. *Duke Journal of Gender Law & Public Policy, 3,* 95–127.

Kane, M. J. (1998). Fictional denials of female empowerment: A feminist analysis of young adult sports fiction. *Sociology of Sport Journal, 15,* 231–262.

Kane, M. J., & Disch, L. J. (1993). Sexual violence and the reproduction of male power in the locker room: The "Lisa Olson incident." *Sociology of Sport Journal, 10,* 331–352.

Kane, M. J., & Lenskyj, H. (1998). Media treatment of female athletes: Issues of gender and sexualities. In L. Wenner (Ed.), *MediaSport: Cultural sensibilities and sport in the media age* (pp. 186–201). London: Routledge.

Kriegh, L. A. (1996). A novel idea: Portrayals of female athletes in young adult sports fiction of the 1970s, 1980s, and 1990s. Unpublished master's thesis, University of Minnesota.

Kriegh, L. A., & Kane, M. J. (1997). A novel idea: Portrayals of lesbians in young adult sports fiction. *Women in Sports and Physical Activity Journal, 6* (2), 23–62.

Levy, M. (1996). *Run for your life.* Boston: Houghton.

Mathewson, A. D. (1996). Black women, gender equity and the function at the junction. *Marquette Sports Law Journal, 6* (2), 239–266.

McDonald, M. G. (1996). Michael Jordan's family values: Marketing, meaning and post-Reagan America. *Sociology of Sport Journal, 13,* 344–365.

Messner, M. A. (1992). *Power at play: Sports and the problem of masculinity.* Boston: Beacon.

Moore, F. (1994). *Who let girls in the boys' locker room?* New York: Troll Communications.

Newfield, D. (1992). Reading against racism in South Africa. In E. Evans (Ed.), *Reading against racisms* (pp. 39–63). Buckingham: Open University Press.

Rueth-Brandner, T. (1991, June). Sports fiction for young women: Not enough of a good thing. *Voices of Youth Advocates,* 89–90.

Ryan, J. (1995). *Little girls in pretty boxes: The making and breaking of elite gymnasts and figure skaters.* New York: Doubleday.

Smith, Y. R. (1992). Women of color in society and sport. *Quest, 44,* 228–250.

Sullivan, A. (1992). *Molly Maguire: Wide receiver.* New York: Avon Books.

Tomlinson, A. (1982, September). Sports fiction as critique: The novelistic challenge to the ideology of masculinity. In *Sporting Fictions: Proceedings of the University of Birmingham Department of Physical Education and the Centre for Contemporary Cultural Studies, September 1981* (pp. 249–275). Birmingham, West Midlands, England: University of Birmingham.

Tuggle, C. A. (1997). Differences in television sports reporting of men's and women's athletics: ESPN SportsCenter and CNN Sports Tonight. *Journal of Broadcasting & Electronic Media, 41,* 14–24.

U.S. Department of Education, National Center for Educational Statistics, Fast Response Survey System (1994). *Surveys of library services for children and young adults in public libraries,* FRSS, 47.

Wallace, B. (1993). *Never say quit.* New York: Holiday House.

Wenner, L. (1995). The good, the bad, and the ugly: Race, sport, and the public eye. *Journal of Sport and Social Issues, 19,* 227–231.

West, C. (1990). The new cultural politics of difference. In R. Ferguson, M. Gever, T. T. Minh-Ha, & C. West (Eds.), *Out there: Marginalization and contemporary cultures* (pp. 19–36). New York: New Museum of Contemporary Art and Cambridge: Massachusetts Institute of Technology.

Wyeth, S. D. (1996). *Swimmers in deep water.* New York: Bantam Books.

FIVE

We Got Next

Negotiating Race and Gender
in Professional Basketball

SARAH BANET-WEISER

The date June 21, 1997, marked the inaugural season of the Women's
National Basketball Association (WNBA). Although a century of
women's basketball—including some unsuccessful professional leagues—
preceded the WNBA, this time promised to be different. The official slogan
of the WNBA, We Got Next, assured basketball fans of not only a televised
team sports league during the lagging summer off-season of the National
Basketball Association (NBA), but also a future for women's basketball,
complete with high-powered demonstrations of athletic skill and competition. As *Newsweek* magazine put it, "Jammed into the nexus of prime-time
sports and gender politics, the WNBA offers an untested combination of
old and new, a game of naked female aggression played below the rim"
(Leland, Rosenberg, Van Boven, & Gegax, 1997, p. 57).

It is precisely this "naked female aggression" that has simultaneously
legitimated and delegitimated the WNBA in terms of both players and fans.
The action shots of strong, sweaty female bodies, simply by their sheer cor-
poreality, challenge dominant masculine conventions involving sport.
However, these bodies pose a threat to the clearly male-dominated realm of
team sports, and complicated cultural negotiations are required by both the
league and its sponsors in order to establish that professional women's basketball is a legitimate sport. The WNBA has also attempted to assuage
sponsors and fans that their sport, while professional and athletic, was not
overly "masculine," which is to say, not lesbian "occupied." In other
words, the WNBA has strategically represented itself in such a way as to

93

counteract the American public's fears about the players—and thus, by association, the sport—being homosexual. Fans and sponsors are encouraged to see basketball as a sport where not only those women labeled as *deviant* by dominant ideology could play, but as a game played by those who followed normative conventions of femininity.

Notwithstanding these formidable obstacles, in the first two years since its founding, the WNBA has managed to situate itself, if only precariously, as a legitimate professional league and challenge to the hypermasculine NBA. In fact, it is the connection with the NBA that shapes the media discourse that surrounds coverage of the WNBA: the NBA owns the WNBA, and in terms of its own marketing, clearly sees the league as a way to extend the merchandising network of the NBA throughout the year. And, although there was an outpouring of media criticism about the apparent substandard athletic abilities displayed when the WNBA was first organized as a league, more recently the league has received more favorable reviews—often in comparison with the NBA.

At a time in sports history when the NBA players are increasingly offered more money and marketing opportunities than ever before in the history of the league, and are vigorously sought after as commodities, many of the players have also demonstrated more "bad boy" behavior on and off the court. Hailed as "poor sports," "prima donnas," and even "thugs," NBA players such as Dennis Rodman, Charles Barkley, and Latrell Sprewell seem to conjure cultural stereotypes and narratives about the violent and dangerous Black male body, and are understood as "damaging" the all-American, morally upright reputations of players such as Magic Johnson and Michael Jordan. The players of the WNBA enter media discourse at this juncture and are positioned by the social constructions of race and gender. In these discourses, the Black male body is positioned as subversive and dangerous even while it has also been the site of terrific profit. By contrast, the players in the WNBA are increasingly seen as *returning to the game,* rather than being individuals. In a curious reversal of the way in which women's bodies have historically been commodified and objectified, Black male bodies in the NBA have become reified and objectified, while the WNBA players are seen as less jaded, less distracted, less corrupted by monetary success, and therefore more able to play the game of basketball the way it should be played.

The Quest for Legitimation

"Here Come the Women!" the ad reads, implicitly arguing that there is, in fact, a place for a professional women's basketball league (*Newsweek,* September 1, 1997). Since its debut, the WNBA has been consistently compared with the NBA and almost as consistently, it has been found lacking in the areas of particular kinds of athletic skill. Yes, they were terrific athletes, but could they *play* like the NBA players—could they attract fans with their rebounding skills, their "hang time" abilities, their slam dunks? Again and again, the press lamented that the female players were simply not as exciting, not as aggressive, not as entertaining as professional male basketball players. In the words of one especially critical (and obviously threatened) columnist, "The WNBA is to the NBA as the Special Olympics is to the Olympics. . . . The game they play bears only superficial resemblance to basketball as it is played by men, even at the larger high school level" (Wilson, 1997). Clearly, transgressing the boundaries of professional male team sports is an enormously challenging task. Even with the implicit approval of the NBA, the WNBA athletes have had to "prove" to the fans and their sponsors that they are "worthy" of the game. Part of their strategy has been to challenge the rules of the game: the WNBA plays with a smaller ball than the NBA, the lanes are narrower, the three-point distance is shorter, and they play in twenty-minute halves rather than in twelve-minute quarters. These rule changes have produced a somewhat different game, played in terms of passing and handling the ball. This may have the effect of delegitimating the sport, because changing the rules of the game—and thus ostensibly lowering the standards of the game—functions to infantalize the female players. Paradoxically, though, in the case of the WNBA it has simultaneously worked to *legiti mate* the game: the fact that the WNBA players do not perform the exaggerated moves and jumps of the NBA has worked to emphasize team camaraderie rather than the showboating and scene-stealing of the NBA players. The camaraderie of the women works to situate the WNBA as a "different" women's sport, different from the kinds of sports toward which women have been traditionally tracked.

The American public's fascination with female athletes has almost always centered on individual athletes—tennis players, professional golfers, figure skaters, and gymnasts. These sports demonstrate the agility and elegance "natural" to women and, although athleticism is clearly a major aspect of these sports, the individual stars are known, culturally at least, more for their "feminine" attributes: self-sacrifice, glamour, and grace. Indeed, the public recognition of individual female athletes attends much more to their feminine beauty and objectified status as particular kinds of commodities than to their athletic skill. And, if individual women athletes are not naturalized as sexual, feminine beings, it is usually because they are not, in fact, women at all, but rather little girls. In the last decade, sports such as tennis, figure skating, and gymnastics can hardly be called "women's" sports: Tara Lipinski won the Olympic gold medal in figure

skating when she was 14 years old, there was not a single individual over
the age of 16 on the entire American Olympic team of female gymnasts,
and tennis superstar Martina Hingis is 17 years old (see Chisholm, 1999,
for an intriguing discussion of women's gymnastics). But the WNBA is not
only a team sport, it is a team sport for *women*—the players are required
to complete their college eligibility or be 21 years old. Hence, they can
acquire their status as role models *for* little girls—an important feature of
professional team sports in the United States—precisely because, unlike
Lipinski or gymnast Kerri Strugg, they are *not* little girls.

But because the masculinist assumptions of team sports challenge the
individualist and moralist ideology that constructs sports such as figure
skating and gymnastics, the women athletes in the WNBA have had to
manage a contradictory set of cultural images. Strategies are needed to
reassure fans that although they are not dancing gracefully over the ice in
designer outfits, professional female basketball players are in fact feminine
beings. For example, on the official Website of the WNBA, alongside features that list game schedules, highlights from previous games, and new
sponsorship partners, there is a section called "WNBA Unveils Uniform."
This section claims that the WNBA "injects fresh perspective into the creation of its basketball uniforms," and there is information about the decisions made for the official WNBA uniforms: Should they wear dresses?
Tunics over shorts? Unitards? Or "skorts" (skirts/shorts)? There is also
detailed information about the materials and colors used for the final
choice of uniforms (which, incidentally, was shirts and shorts). Finally,
there is a section where fans can vote on their favorite uniform, with pictures of both the home and away uniforms. Clearly, this particular section
of the Website contributes to a dominant ideology that women are overly
concerned with clothing and fashion. There is no comparable section on
the Website of the NBA, and, while not surprising, the presence of this feature tells us something about the various ways in which the players and the
institution of the WNBA function to shore up dominant notions and ideologies about the construction of womanhood. Given the threat that is
posed by paying women to play basketball and thus recognizing them as
professionals, naturalizing them as "true women" is a predictable strategy.

Compulsory Heterosexuality and the WNBA

The threat of women participating in the sporting world is by no means a
new one. Susan Cahn has argued that the stereotype of the mannish, lesbian athlete has worked to shape not only female competitors themselves,
but also sports organizations, funding sources, and the overall popularity
of women's sports. The most common strategy employed by athletic orga-

nizations to overcome this stereotype is to reassure audiences and fans that women involved in sports are indeed "women"—meaning, of course, that they are heterosexual. As Cahn (1998) points out, "The lesbian stereotype exert[s] pressure on athletes to demonstrate their femininity and hetero-sexuality, viewed as one and the same" (p. 76). Not surprisingly, it is in those sports that most resemble masculinized athletics (e.g., softball or hockey), and those that have the greatest need to attract a paying audience that the fear of, and anxiety over, lesbianism are most prominent. Because these sports are culturally defined as masculine, and because there is an easy cultural slippage between "masculine women" and lesbian identity, strategies are needed by the players in order to redefine and recast the sport as feminine or womanly. For example, "flex appeal" is translated as "sex appeal" in the context of female body building, female tennis players are often depicted as "playing for" their love interest in the stands, and female professional basketball players are shown as fashion models and mothers.

Intriguingly, stories about the lesbian following of the WNBA have shaped the media discourse and promotion strategies of the league. As Leland, Rosenberg, Van Boven, and Gegax put it in *Newsweek* in September of 1997, the first season of the WNBA, "The league also has another, less trumpeted core constituency. Though TV broadcasts pan moms with their kids, plenty of women come on their own. Says Sarah Pettit, editor of *Out* magazine, 'Next to the 'Ellen' episode, this is the biggest news in the lesbian community all year long. If there's one thing lesbians are talking about, it's who's on the bench and who's on the floor'" (p. 57). Not sur-prisingly, the WNBA does not acknowledge any gay following; Rick Welts, chief marketing officer for both the NBA and the WNBA, replied when asked about a lesbian audience, "I'm not aware of that. . . . We don't take attendance that way. The league does not discriminate" (Leland et al., 1997, p. 57).

Balancing Baby with Basketball

While Welts uses antidiscriminatory rhetoric as a slick way to deflect ques-tions about the public awareness of a lesbian following of the WNBA, a more successful strategy to reassure fans of the players' heterosexuality has been to focus on maternity. When WNBA star Sheryl Swoopes of the Hous-ton Comets became pregnant the first season of the league, it proved to be a great advantage to her as a player, and a golden marketing opportunity for the league. When asked about Swoopes, Welts said, "We embrace maternity" (Leland et al., 1997, p. 57). Her pregnancy became a press bonanza, with soft news stories about maternity in general, balancing baby with basketball, and the generous sacrifice of Swoopes's husband, Eric

Jackson, to stay home with the baby. When Swoopes plays, the camera continually returns to shots of the sideline where the baby and father watch the game. And, on the official WNBA Website, where there is a section called "Ask Olympia" that allows visitors to the Website to write in questions to Utah's Olympia Scott-Richardson, a full three fourths of these questions asked about the player's recent pregnant status, what sex the baby would be, what her name would be, and whether or not Scott-Richardson would take her baby on tour with her (WNBA, 1999). This focus on maternity resonates with another dominant cultural assumption about women: that they are, above all, interested in becoming mothers. Not only do these kinds of media strategies provide what seems to be iron-clad evidence of the players' heterosexuality, they also establish the WNBA as a family-oriented, moral game, or as *Newsweek* puts it, the WNBA is "the good apple in the increasingly rotting barrel of professional sports" (Leland et al., 1997, p. 57).

Establishing the WNBA as a sporting event for the family is an important discursive move. The league is often lauded as a "hoop dream come true for millions of American girls," and is explicitly marketed as a sport the whole family can watch together. Moreover, the long-held dominant ideology that women are "morally superior" to men finds its way to the WNBA in the way that the women athletes are seen as less corrupted, whether by power or money, than NBA athletes. In turn, the wholesome quality of the WNBA is both constituted and bolstered by the increasing public disapproval of "bad boy" behavior in the NBA. As one columnist put it, "For women's basketball to become a major sport in America, as opposed to a profitable one like arena football, something is going to have to be offered other than just pure skill. That something should be, and in fact will have to be, a different attitude, a purer sense of the sport, than the men deliver" (Kallam, 1999). This "different attitude" resides in the bodies of the female players, indeed, *is* the bodies of the players, bodies that are more moral, more pure, less likely to succumb to temptation, and less corrupt than male bodies. This comparison with professional male basketball players serves a particular purpose: the "moral" feminine bodies of the WNBA players perform the cultural work of restabilizing the racial bodies of NBA players. In other words, media portrayals of the defiant, "bad" behavior of professional male basketball players situates the WNBA as a positive alternative, a sport that emphasizes a kind of feminine behavior and attitude that contains the unruliness of the NBA.

Although clearly the feminine body of the WNBA player is naturalized through a variety of discourses and strategies, it is also the case that the players are not objectified in the way that women's bodies have been objectified traditionally. They are constantly referred to in the press as "mature women," and the play itself shapes the bodies of the players as active subjects rather than as passive objects, team players rather than prima donnas. Ann Meyers, a former all-American basketball player and currently a coach, has pointed out, "Basketball is basketball, regardless of gender, race, or age. . . . The women's edge is they do the fundamentals. It's a great game. The men's game has gotten out of hand a little bit. They carry the ball, they travel. They've gotten away from fundamentals. The taunting, the fights, the trash talking. I don't think there's any place for it in the game" (Salter, 1996, p. 110). Characterizing the NBA as a realm where "taunting" and "trash talking" works to solidify the purity of the WNBA, even as it also functions to construct the NBA implicitly in terms of race politics.

Trash Talking vs. Collaboration

The dominant understanding of the bodies of Black athletes works to both commodify and naturalize these bodies. The image of Michael Jordan, placed on everything from cologne to long-distance companies to hamburgers, stands in stark contrast to the image of Dennis Rodman, draped naked over a motorcycle. Where Jordan is used to confirm the successful use of the Black athlete as a commodity, Rodman both affirms and disrupts assumptions about the naturalized Black body. (For more on Jordan, see Dyson, 1993.) In much the same way as the "unruly" racial politics of the NBA function to solidify the moral status of the gender politics that shape the WNBA, Rodman, through his defiance, stabilizes the image of Jordan and serves to contain the potential threat of his Black body. This shaping of Black male athletes into objects dilutes the potential threat that they carry simply by *being* Black male bodies. It is clear in the media that more recently other players in the NBA, through their challenge to authority and defiance, have "needed" precisely this kind of domestication.

The rhetoric of "poor sportsmanship" that shapes the media discourse of the NBA, along with "bad boy" behavior, the violence and aggression that is increasingly part of the game, and the presence of cultural bodily markings such as tattoos and body piercing signify Blackness and menace. The underlying subtext of the "ego problems" of the NBA players, often young men straight out of high school who are made instant millionaires, is that these are men from the *inner cities* (another code word for race in U.S. cultural politics), and that they are both natural athletes and natural thugs. When Sprewell attempts to choke his coach, or when the news reported that Portland Trail Blazer Shawn Kemp has fathered seven children by seven different women, or that Sacramento King Chris Webber associates with "questionable" people, dominant narratives that naturalize Black men as sexual menaces, physically violent, and defiant are affirmed.[1] Though still immensely popular with fans and sponsors, the NBA has also been reinvented as a site of potential violence, with an implicit assumption that the "cause" for the violence is the presence of unrefined, "uncivilized" Black men. In order to assuage the threat posed by some NBA players, the marketing and manufacturing networks have worked assiduously to construct the more well-known athletes as commodities. The threat that players such as Webber and Sprewell pose is diluted by their commodification, by making them into things that one can buy or observe. However, this kind of marketing is precarious, because players such as Spreewell and Rodman are explicitly *needed* by the NBA as particular kinds of commodities—players such as these offer an attractive "edge" for youth marketing. Hence, the threat posed by unruly players must be balanced in a way that maintains the public titillation caused by the defiant Black male body while not disrupting the broad marketability of the league.

Interestingly, the positioning of the Black male athlete as a commodity—and thus as a passive object—is a curious reversal of the way in which women's bodies have been traditionally objectified. As bell hooks (1994) comments, "it has taken contemporary commodification of Blackness to teach the world that this perceived threat, whether real or symbolic, can be diffused by a process of fetishization that renders the Black masculine 'menace' feminine through a process of patriarchal objectification" (p. 110). The cultural fear of the Black male body is diluted by shaping Black male athletes as commodities, even as this fear is legitimated by what is ostensibly seen and experienced on the court.

The racist discourse that shapes the media construction of the NBA works, ironically, to offer a more positive picture of the WNBA. In media portrayals of the WNBA, *gender* is the central category of analysis, despite the overwhelming African American presence in the league. Of course, the same discourses that shape conventions of Black masculinity have also constructed damaging representations of Black women. However, at present the WNBA has been characterized more in terms of normative femininity—maternal, moral, and collaborative—than according to dominant representations of Black women, which in other arenas have emphasized sexuality and amorality. In other words, while it can be argued that the figure of the trash-talking "bad boy" in the NBA has a specific cultural purpose, there is no racialized "bad girl" equivalent in the WNBA—at least not yet. The racial politics of the NBA that represent the Black male body as naturalized and dangerous also serve as the negative screen against which the WNBA creates its positive gender commodity image.

In an interesting discursive move, the naturalized bodies of the female athletes of the WNBA have been reframed to represent values more often associated with masculinist team sports, allowing talent to reign over glamour. The athletes of the NBA, on the other hand, are increasingly objectified, shaped as individual stars, their bodies transformed into objects through their relentless commodification. The WNBA and the NBA can thus be interpreted as cultural realms that construct categories of race and gender as mutually constituitive. The media portrayals of the NBA represent the Black players as potentially dangerous and menacing, allowing for the WNBA to construct itself in positive opposition to these racial politics. And, in the women's league, dominant conventions of gender function on the surface to threaten the NBA, but these politics implicitly serve to contain the unruly Blackness of the NBA, stabilizing the league by helping to police the "greed" and the bodies of unruly Black men of the NBA. With the racial and gender boundaries tightened and clarified, the safely domesticated Black male bodies can become the symbols that advertisers want, and the female players emerge as appropriate role model spokespersons for the league.

Despite the various ways in which the WNBA normalizes conventional notions of femininity, the league, and the politics of gender that both surround and shape it, present an opportunity for a disruption of these conventions. In only its second year, the WNBA has already been hailed as a cultural realm that offers new conditions of possibilities for both girls and women. The hip 90s adage Girl Power has been applied to the WNBA, and though this slogan has a clear transparency to it (after all, it was coined by The Spice Girls) the association of power with girls, whatever the source, deserves at least some critical attention. The major sponsors of the WNBA, Nike and Reebok, have adopted explicit liberal feminist rhetoric into their advertisements, and while obviously using this language as a lucrative avenue for selling products, it nonetheless shapes the dominant construction of women athletes. Clearly the last decade of the twentieth century marked a moment where dominant norms of gender and race are negotiated in interesting and complex ways, and the WNBA is situated at the center of these negotiations.

Notes

I would like to thank Marita Sturken, Val Hartouni, Dana Polan, and Michael Messner for their helpful comments on this chapter.

1. I am grateful to Titus Levi for his suggestions and insights about NBA players.

References

Cahn, S. K. (1998). From the "Muscle Moll" to the "Butch" ballplayer: Mannishness, lesbianism, and homophobia in U.S. women's sports.

In R. Weitz (Ed.), *The politics of women's bodies: Sexuality, appearance, and behavior.* New York: Oxford University Press.

Chisholm, A. (1999). Defending the nation: National bodies, U.S. borders, and the 1996 U.S. Olympics gymnastics team. *Journal of Sport and Social Issues, 23,* 126–139.

Dyson, M. E. (1993). "Be Like Mike." In M. E. Dyson (Ed.), *Reflecting Black: African-American cultural criticism.* Minneapolis: University of Minnesota Press.

hooks, b. (1994). Feminism inside: Toward a Black body politic. In T. Golden (Ed.), *Black male: Representations of masculinity in contemporary American art.* New York: Whitney Museum of American Art.

Kallam, C. (1999, March). Will power corrupt female athletes? Available: *http://fullcourtpress.com.*

Leland, J., with Rosenberg, D., Van Boven, S., & Gegax, T. T. (1997, September 1). Up in the air. *Newsweek, 57.*

Salter, D. F. (1996). *Crashing the old boy's network: The tragedies and triumphs of girls and women in sports.* New York: Praeger.

Wilson, B. (1997, December). The WNBA: Another liberal feminist program. *The Ethical Spectacle.* Available: http://www.spectacle.org.

Women's National Basketball Association (1999, March). Available: *http://WNBA.com.*

SIX

Teaching Against the Grain

A Learner-Centered, Media-Based, and Profeminist Approach to Gender and Nonviolence in Sport

JIM McKAY

> Perhaps no single institution in American culture has influenced our sense of masculinity more than sport.
> —N. Trujillo,
> "Hegemonic Masculinity on the Mound"

In this chapter I present some pedagogical strategies that I have found useful in getting *some* university students to demystify commonsense understandings of the links among sport, violence, the media, and *hegemonic masculinity*. The latter term refers to a "culturally idealized form of masculine character," which associates masculinity with "toughness and competitiveness," the "subordination of women," and "the marginalization of gay men" (Connell, 1990, pp. 83, 94). Since many of my students at the University of Queensland are enrolled in vocational degrees such as journalism, physical education (PE), coaching, and sports administration, my approach tries to encourage them to conceive of practical alternatives that they can institute in both their professional practices and interpersonal relations. For instance, it is unlikely that prospective PE teachers are going to be able to inform their students how to be critical of media representations of gender and sport if they have not been educated about this topic themselves.

My approach should not be interpreted as a formula that can be transplanted unmodified into other contexts. The interaction between my background (a relatively privileged, heterosexual, middle-aged, White male) and my students' characteristics (relatively privileged, young Whites)

103

would make any such inference both presumptuous and dangerous. Moreover, the techniques are an idiosyncratic bricolage of principles derived from profeminism, peace education, critical media studies, critical sociology of sport, and learner-centered-learning (see fig. 6.1). However, it is hoped that some of the generic strategies will be relevant to teachers who are attempting to change both hegemonic masculinity and sport.

Basic Pedagogical Principles

I use a learner-centered-learning (LCL) approach (see figure 6.1) in all of my undergraduate sociology courses, which have enrollments ranging from 50 to 200. In each course students are exposed to conventional sociological motifs such as debunking, cultural relativity, micro-macro links, anthropological and historical sensitivities, and the importance of empirical evidence (Berger, 1963, 1992; Giddens, 1982; Mills, 1970). Whereas teacher-centered-learning (TCL) tends to reproduce passive and dependent learning and only extracts surface knowledge, LCL affords greater opportunities for fostering active, independent, and deep learning (Ramsden, 1992). LCL is also conducive for developing communication skills, especially learning how to resolve group tensions. All courses are divided into the following sections: (1) an A/V "trigger" (e.g., a clip of a football match or excerpts from *Hoop Dreams,* a documentary about the harsh material and cultural realities that confront two African American high school boys who are trying to obtain athletic scholarships, and *Any Given Sunday,* a film that critically examines gender, racism, and violence in American professional football, (2) 10–15 minutes of group discussions of exam study questions related to the clip, (3) 10–15 minutes of group reports to the entire class, (4) a 10-minute minilecture, (5) a 10-minute break, and (6) 100–120 minutes of work on group projects.

In this chapter I will restrict my comments to the media components of my course "Sport, Culture, & Society," which investigates social inequalities, social problems, and social justice in contemporary sport. About half of the students take the course as the required part of an Applied Science degree in PE or exercise management, while the rest take it as an elective in vocational degrees such as education, social work, journalism, occupational therapy, and physiotherapy, and in a variety of traditional arts, humanities, and social sciences programs. My university has an enrollment of approximately 20,000 undergraduate and 5,000 graduate students. Although the federal government funds virtually all Australian universities, a disproportionate number of students come from elite, private secondary schools.

Figure 6.1
Pedagogical Bases of "Sport, Culture & Society"

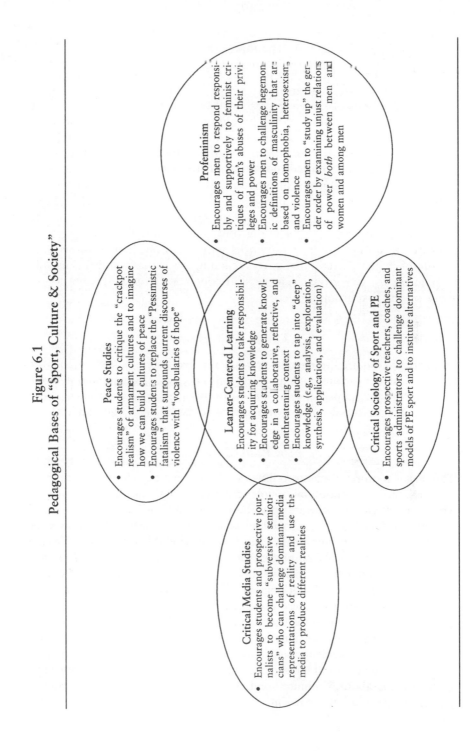

Profeminism

- Encourages men to respond responsibly and supportively to feminist critiques of men's abuses of their privileges and power
- Encourages men to challenge hegemonic definitions of masculinity that are based on homophobia, heterosexism, and violence
- Encourages men to "study up" the gender order by examining unjust relations of power *both* between men and women and among men

Peace Studies

- Encourages students to critique the "crackpot realism" of armament cultures and to imagine how we can build cultures of peace
- Encourages students to replace the "Pessimistic fatalism" that surrounds current discourses of violence with "vocabularies of hope"

Learner-Centered Learning

- Encourages students to take responsibility for acquiring knowledge
- Encourages students to generate knowledge in a collaborative, reflective, and nonthreatening context
- Encourages students to tap into "deep" knowledge (e.g., analysis, exploration, synthesis, application, and evaluation)

Critical Sociology of Sport and PE

- Encourages prospective teachers, coaches, and sports administrators to challenge dominant models of PE sport and to institute alternatives

Critical Media Studies

- Encourages students and prospective journalists to become "subversive semioticians" who can challenge dominant media representations of reality and use the media to produce different realities

The First Day

On the first day students form groups of five on the basis of topics they have selected for the first group assignment. This way groups are established on the basis of shared interests rather than random allocation. The students then engage in some "ice-breaking" activities that allow them to get acquainted and discuss their motivations. It is stressed that the decision to form a group entails a commitment that is somewhat different from the normal requirement to attend lectures and tutorials. As an indication of this obligation, each group member is asked to complete a contract in which they consent (morally if not legally) to attend every weekly three-hour session and to ensure that everyone else participates equally in the researching and writing of the two group assignments. Each group is then allocated to a "facilitator" who works with them on the two projects. A *facilitator* (a generic term that covers teaching assistants and me) is usually responsible for five groups. The session concludes with the facilitation of work on the first group project.

Group Projects

Students are required to complete two group projects: a poster on how the media construct various social problems in sport and a content and semiotic analysis of newspaper coverage of sportswomen and sportsmen. Both assignments are supplemented with extensive reading lists and minilectures.

The Poster Project

The poster requires students to illustrate how the media frame social problems related to homophobia, violence, and sexual harassment in sport. They then must demonstrate how the media's definition of a given social problem differs from how sociologists view the situation and how they would investigate it empirically using social research methods. Although the poster receives only 20 percent of the overall grade, I allow four sessions for its completion. I believe this amount of time is justified, because the students are not only working on unfamiliar tasks, but are also coming to terms with what is involved in functioning as a successful team.

The presentation of the posters in the fifth week stands as a landmark in the course and I devote an entire session just to this. Each group's poster is exhibited on the walls of the lecture theater and the students spend up to 30 minutes "viewing" the results of everyone's labors. Subsequently, each group spends about 5 minutes explaining to the entire class the rationale for the poster and the particular features they have incorporated. This opportunity for students to judge their own efforts in relation to those of others is a salutary experience. In general terms, I view the outcome of the poster presentation session as one of group consolidation and confidence building. Even the most well-organized and harmonious groups may have entertained doubts about their abilities and the reassurance they gain from viewing their achievements in a collective context is obvious. The second project is invariably completed with far less group angst.

The Media Analysis Project

The second project involves analyzing a large file of newspaper articles about male and female athletes that I have lodged in the university library. The students must first demonstrate their knowledge about the codes, frames, and ideologies by which the articles construct commonsense ideas about gender differences in sport. They then must explain the how these everyday conventions are intertwined with broader economic and political hierarchies of power between men and women. Finally, they are asked to describe how they would convince an editor to let them write countersexist articles about sportswomen if they were sports journalists.

Wrap-Up

I conclude these two assignments with a minilecture which stresses that (1) the media are simply part of a larger process by which *a* highly selective masculine model of sport gets naturalized as the *only* imaginable mode of sporting practice, and (2) how this makes it difficult for us to comprehend that what appears to be universal and eternal is actually socially constructed. I emphasize that this does not make us "cultural dopes" or victims of "false consciousness," but simply makes us unaware of how both the explicit and covert interests of a male-dominated nexus of big business and the media set the agenda with respect to what is defined as "real" sport. I note that this simultaneously constrains our capacity to envision alternatives to dominant sporting practices. Thus in the final segment of the course the students are asked to discuss how they would design a media kit for a high school PE syllabus that provides an alternative to "malestream" curricular material, including items such as (1) Messner and Sabo's (1994) 11–point strategy for changing men through changing sports; (2) robust affirmative action principles (McKay, 1997); (3) Lenskyj's (1991, 1992) checklist on sexual harassment for coaches and athletes and strategies for combating homophobia in sport; (4) Katz's (1995) "mentors in violence project" with male athletes; (5) the participatory principles of the Gay Games; and (6) the profeminist philosophies of groups like the National Organization of Men Against Sexism, and the White Ribbon Campaign, an international, grass-roots, pro-feminist movement that encourages men to become involved in eliminating violence against women.

Discussion

Student Evaluations

Students usually evaluate the course above the university mean, with over 80 percent giving it an overall rating of 5 or better on a 7–point scale. Over 90 percent of the students agree that the video triggers contribute to their understanding of the subject, and the vast majority agree that they (1) learn to think critically, (2) reconsider many of their former viewpoints, (3) learn to feel responsible for their own learning, and (4) gain a solid understanding of the field. Although students generally have reacted favorably toward my LCL courses, the approach poses some key difficulties for both students and teachers. These relate to planning, student resistance, and the high level of energy required from facilitators.

Planning

LCL requires an enormous amount of preparation, especially the first time it is offered. Writing a Study Guide, which is seventy pages long for the course described in this chapter, is a particularly demanding task, as it covers items such as (1) course format and objectives, (2) details of assessment items, (3) details of topics covered, (4) glossary of key concepts, and (5) management of student-led groups.

The A/V triggers and readings need to be chosen very carefully, as they must stimulate discussions of sociological concepts. Fortunately, my university has a superb A/V library, so I can draw on a wide array of pertinent programs (e.g., news and current affairs, documentaries, and advertisements), and I also monitor TV programs in order to use up-to-date material. Having an appropriate venue also is vital. It is imperative that students have access to rooms with movable chairs and/or large desks where they can lay out their work and where the facilitators can easily move in and out of groups.

Student Resistance

It is often difficult to eliminate the tenacious student belief that the role of a teacher, even in the more egalitarian guise of facilitator, should be to provide "the right answers" (see fig. 6.2). This resistance to LCL is com-

Figure 6.2
Consensual and Contradictory Patterns of
Learner-Centered-Learning (LCL) and
Teacher-Centered-Learning (TCL) Contexts

		TEACHER'S GOAL:	
		To spoon-feed (TCL)	To develop independent learning (LCL)
STUDENT'S GOAL:	To be spoon-fed (TCL)	+ + (Consensual)	− + (Contradictory)
	To become an independent learner (LCL)	+ − (Contradictory)	+ + (Consensual)

pounded by how I approach sociology. In my opinion sociology *ought* to help "all kinds of people (fellow experts, policy makers, fledgling graduate students, novice undergraduates, well-informed citizens) gain a critical understanding of the society in which they live" (Baker & Rau, 1990, p. 183). My experience has been that students come to sociology expecting it to be a "soft option" and that there is a resulting hostility to sociological concepts. The argument goes something like this: "I live in society; I get along quite well and can see what's happening around me—why should I have to learn these unnecessary words and ideas?" Even when students learn the limitations of this viewpoint, many are perturbed, because sociology challenges "sacred cows" and cherished values. Since there are no straightforward "answers" to the ethical issues and social problems that we examine, and sociology, as I teach it, does not rely on rote learning, many students initially are apprehensive about what they perceive to be its impracticality and intellectually subversive motifs. This is particularly true for intending PE teachers, who generally have been successful at sport so have extremely positive and uncritical views of it.

Furthermore, I believe that students should "do" sociology by investigating the empirical links between biography and history, and their intersections within society (Giddens, 1982; Mills, 1970). One way I encourage students to make these connections is by getting them to specify a range of quantitative and qualitative research methods they would use to analyze social issues and problems that are relevant to the sporting media's portrayals of violence. This can serve as an antidote to the apprehensions many students have about handling data and seeing research as some eso-teric activity that is beyond their reach.

Resistance is particularly strident from those men who see profemi-nism as irrelevant or against their self-interest, who protest that they have never harassed or raped a woman, or who dismiss rapists as psychopaths. In introducing profeminist precepts, I emphasize that men and women are not monolithic categories, but divided by social class, age, sexuality, and ethnic/racial backgrounds. I also stress that since profeminism involves a male-positive position, it is important not to posit an "us versus them" research agenda in which "Men are reduced to a gender with no redeem-ing qualities and women [are] regarded as blameless in the maintenance of gender-stratified societies" (Davis, 1994, p. 236). Thus I emphasize that although a given man may not be a rapist, all of us live in a *rape culture,* which is constituted by a constellation of signs, ideologies, and images that legitimize men's violence against women (Sanday, 1996). I provide data showing that the overwhelming majority of sexual assaults are perpetrated by men, most of whom are friends or relatives of their victims, Thus, I stress that widespread misogyny, homophobia, sexual assault, and violence are not the random acts of psychopathic individuals, but the "normal" behavior of men who accept aggression, intimidation, and violence as a rightful and necessary aspect of their relationships with women (Breines, Connell, & Eide, 2000)." As Brod (1987) puts it,

> What then emerges is a picture of considerable socialization *towards* violence. Whether learned in gangs, sports, the mili-tary, at the hands (often literally) of older males, or in simple acceptance that "boys will be boys" when they fight, attitudes are conveyed to young males ranging from tolerance to approval of violence as an appropriate vehicle for conflict reso-lution, perhaps even the most manly means of conflict resolu-tion. From this perspective, violent men are *over* conformers, men who have responded all too fully to a particular aspect of male socialization. (p. 51)

One way I illustrate this point is by screening three video items. The first is *Crossing the Line,* an investigative documentary of the sexual abuse and harassment of Canadian female rowers, swimmers, and volleyball players by their male coaches (Hall, 1997). The second is a clip about a Canadian junior ice hockey coach who in 1997 was sentenced to three and a half years for sexually assaulting two of his players. I next get male stu-dents to discuss the implications these events have for members of their families and friends. I then get all of the students to discuss some global and local statistics that demonstrate the incidence of violence against women by men and the enormous economic and social disparities between men and women. This exercise is also useful in countering the increasingly prominent conventional wisdom that men are "oppressed" by women (McKay & Ogilvie, 1999). Finally, I conclude with a clip on a media campaign in Australia that involved high-profile male athletes speaking out against violence against women, in order to show that men from all walks of life have a role to play in encouraging other men to be nonviolent.

I also provide examples of privileged groups who have used their positions to assist oppressed people in obtaining justice (e.g., White men and women who formed antislavery organizations, worked for liberation movements like the African National Congress, support the American civil rights movement, and teach counterracist curricula in their classrooms). Students are also introduced to the pedagogical concepts of educators like Paulo Friere, who work with indigenous people or oppressed groups in developing countries, the political stance of academics who have mobilized against powerful groups (e.g., Scientists Against Nuclear Arms), and the individual and collective support that some men have given to the women's movement (Kimmel, 1992; Messner, 1997). I also use the analogy of racism by suggesting that although individual White men and women may not be racists, they nevertheless live in a racist culture. And just as White people have a fundamental role to play in eliminating racism, men have the capacity to eradicate sexism. This is also an apposite point at which to introduce how the media use the subtle practices of "enlightened racism" and "celebrity feminism" to represent Black sportsmen and sportswomen (Andrews, 1996; Andrews & Cole, 2000; Cole & Hribar, 1995; Cole & King, 1998; Dworkin & Messner, 1999; Lafrance, 1998; McKay, 1995; Wilson, 1997; Wilson & Sparks, 1996).

I have found these strategies to be useful in stressing that from the perspective of profeminism, masculinity per se is not the problem, but rather the fact that *a* very restrictive way of being a man is idealized as *the* way that *all* men should act. For instance, Connell (1983) correctly argues that masculinity is not, as some critics would have it, an impoverished phenomenon but a "plenitude." However, he goes on to argue that "the specific richness of hegemonic masculinity is oppressive, being founded on, and enforcing, the subordination of women" (p. 22). We can add the oppression of gay men to this observation. Similarly, Messner and Sabo (1994) argue that there is nothing inherent in sport that makes male athletes rape women. Rather, the way in which sports are organized to glorify violence and devalue and objectify women produces the male "groupthink" that so often rewards male athletes for their abusive and violent behavior.

As pressure begins to mount from peers, some students' rationalizations gradually lose credibility; a few students simply retreat and become even more rigid in their outlook; some change their views and become more reflective; many change what they say, or what they think facilitators want to hear, without altering their sexist, racist, and classist values; a handful transform their beliefs quite dramatically

Emotional Energy Required from Teachers

Acquiring a sociological imagination can result in what Berger (1961) calls "the precarious vision." This involves a loss of innocence about the nature of social reality, because one's taken-for-granted view of the world is destabilized. As Berger and Berger (1972) put it, sociology "seems to shake the very ground on which one is standing" (p. 364). Consequently, students often experience a form of "culture shock" due to being strangers in their own land (Berger, 1963; Berger & Kellner, 1981; McGee, 1972; Natanson, 1963). Like some other teachers, I have discovered that some students are profoundly disturbed when this happens (Davis, 1994; Neitz, 1985). Incredulity, frustration, hostility, despair, paralysis, cynicism, nihilism, and outrage are some of the reactions that I have observed, especially in the early stages. Although the severity of some responses causes some discomfort, discussing the objectives of the course can usually alleviate these feelings.

Given this scenario, it is clear that just as LCL is not for all students, it also does not suit every teacher. LCL is both emotionally and physically demanding. I would discourage teachers from using LCL unless they are energetic, enthusiastic, attentive to verbal and nonverbal behavior, able to mediate group tensions, and, above all else, capable of thinking quickly on their feet. LCL is definitely not for "control-freaks," as teachers must both relinquish the high degree of control that they usually wield and be willing to receive as well as generate passionate and critical responses from students (Greene, 1984a, 1984b, 1986; Passmore, 1975).

I have found that LCL works best with a team-teaching approach, whereby all team members attend every session, participate in regular meetings, and comark assessment items. Unless the facilitators demonstrate to students that they work as a team, then the latter are unlikely to operate cohesively. I have found that LCL is an effective, efficient, and rewarding way to teach. Working with a highly motivated teaching team is thoroughly exhilarating, and I delight in seeing scores of students laughing and debating and *generating* knowledge, instead of attempting to *transfer* it to their notebooks from a professor's lips. I frequently observe deep learning patterns that are rare even in conventional tutorial settings, and marvel at the insights that some students make when given the opportunity to reflect, discuss, and write collectively. In addition to these pedagogical spin-offs, another important benefit of LCL is that it can ameliorate some of the impersonality of university life. Many groups establish strong friendships and support networks. Some students have maintained the same group for all of my courses, because they enjoy the camaraderie as much as the subject matter.

I have not entirely abandoned traditional lecturing techniques in my teaching, but in the majority of cases I have also adopted some form of LCL in addition to any individually based forms of assessment. I know some teachers have who have mounted LCL courses in which 100 percent of the grade is based on group work that the students assess themselves. This suggests that LCL can be implemented to varying degrees at different levels in the undergraduate curriculum. Perhaps this chapter might encourage other teachers to relinquish some aspects of TCL and to take the plunge into LCL.

The pedagogical strategy of encouraging students to think critically for themselves in groups usually proves to be a novel and frightening experience in the early stages, especially for younger students. Consequently, I devote a huge amount of time and energy getting students to realize that a sociological imagination is not acquired *immediately*. However, once students get over the initial dismay of having to be responsible for much of their own learning, they generally respond favorably to (1) the liberation of their minds from the limits of common sense, (2) the satisfaction that comes from gaining a new way of looking at themselves and their society, and (3) the experience that rigorous learning can be a satisfying goal *in itself*.

Pedagogical Caveat

Although I believe that the time and energy invested in LCL is well spent, teachers have to consider the costs and benefits of using it. For instance, ask yourself how often you have heard the phrase *publish or perish*. Now think about how often you have heard the term *teach or perish*. The fact that you probably have never even heard the latter expression signifies teaching's subordinate status to research in many universities. According to Smith (1991), it is because of the "publish or perish" syndrome that American higher education is perishing. Similarly, McNaught and Anwyl (1992) claim that many academics perceive being labeled a good teacher as a *kiss of death* to their research image. Like these authors, I have seen little evidence that excellent teachers have been being rewarded via promotion and tenure, despite rhetoric from politicians and university administrators about the significance of teaching quality. So, if there is resistance to LCL among some students, there is also opposition from some teachers and administrators. This network of resistance by both students and teachers is one reason why most undergraduate "teaching" and "learning" resembles the upper-left-hand cell of figure 6.2. Smith (1991) aptly describes this situation as the "cult of lecturing dully." Thus, prospective users of LCL must be motivated by an intrinsic commitment to improving their students' learning. For me, the best reason for using LCL is probably summarized by the maxim that "If people cannot think for themselves, then others will do their thinking for them."

Summary

It sounds animalistic, but I got such a rush I was slobbering. That's the game. It might be crazy, but it goes back to Pop Warner football. At every level, the harder you hit, the more you get patted on the back and the happier you are.
—Los Angeles Ram Fred Stokes,
describing how he felt after hitting an opponent
(King, 1994, p. 29)

If we're going to be an exemplary community, if we're going to teach the society at large, we need to confront issues of racism, ageism and sexism that still plague us. The primary purpose of sport should be self-fulfilment, but athletics can also be a powerful medium for social change.
—The late Dr. Tom Waddell, Olympic
athlete and founder of the Gay Games
(Messner & Sabo, 1994, p. 119)

I have asserted that part of the struggle to change the links among violence, men, sport, and the media involves teaching students to be "subversive semioticians" regarding the media and proactive with respect to implementing gender equity in their personal and professional lives. This is part of what Aronowitz and Giroux (1985) refer to as making "the pedagogical more political and the political more pedagogical." However, this project can only be done if it is based on a theory and practice in which we, as teachers, make "hope practical rather than despair convincing" (Williams, 1985, p. 240; also see Hutchinson, 1996).

I am not saying that encouraging future PE teachers and coaches to write better lesson plans and coaching manuals will result in some magical transformation of the media, sport, and hegemonic masculinity or eradicate violence from the sporting arena. I am arguing, however, that *in conjunction with* other modes of political action, the hegemonic forms of both masculinity and the media can be challenged, politicized, and transformed. What Giroux (1983) says about education applies to all cultural forms:

[Educators] will not change society, but we can create in [students] pockets of resistance that provide pedagogical models for new forms of learning and social relations—forms which can be used in other spheres more directly concerned in the struggle for a new morality and view of social justice. (p. 292)

Progressive intellectuals have a small but important role to play in the project of democratizing sport. Sport is not an immutable, monolithic entity—it is a montage of dominant, emergent, and residual practices, characterized by inconsistencies and tensions, and thus can be challenged and transformed. It is also a particularly fertile ground on which to challenge myths about media constructions of gender and violence (McKay, Messner & Sabo, 1999; Messner, & Sabo, 1994). I would not argue that sport is the most important element in mobilizing democratic and peaceful forms of popular culture. But sport's global popularity makes it too important to be *explained away* by terms such as *false consciousness, opiate of the masses,* or *bread and circuses.* Moreover, if progressive intellectuals dismiss sport as being irrelevant to changing men, then conservative academics will simply continue using it to glorify hegemonic masculinity (Hargreaves, 1986).

As fathers, partners, workers, lovers, and political activists, men have an indispensable role to play in supporting women's struggle for full equality by attempting to transform hegemonic masculinity. I have argued in this chapter that this is something they can also do in their classrooms.

References

Andrews, D. (1996). The fact(s) of Michael Jordan's Blackness: Excavating a floating racial signifier. *Sociology of Sport Journal, 13,* 125–158.

Andrews, D., & Cole, C.L. (2000). America's new son: Tiger Woods and America's multiculturalism. In N. K. Denzin (Ed.), *Cultural studies: A research annual.* (Vol. 5) (pp. 109–124). Stamford, CT: JAI Press.

Aronowitz, S., & Giroux, H. (1985). *Education under siege.* Boston: Bergin & Garvey.

Baker, P., & Rau, W. (1990). The cultural contradictions of teaching sociology. In H. Gans (Ed.), *Sociology in America.* London: Sage.

Berger, P. (1961). *The precarious vision.* New York: Doubleday.

Berger, P. (1963). *Invitation to sociology: A humanistic perspective.* New York: Doubleday.

Berger, P. (1992). Sociology: A disinvitation? *Society, 36* (1), 10–18.

Berger, P., & Berger, B. (1972). *Sociology: A biographical approach.* New York: Basic.

Berger, P., & Kellner, H. (1981). *Sociology reinterpreted: An essay on method and vocation.* New York: Doubleday.

Breines, I., Connell, R. W, & Eide I. (Eds) (2000). *Male roles, masculinities and violence: A culture of peace perspective.* Paris: UNESCO Publications.

Brod, H. (1987). The case for men's studies. In H. Brod (Ed.), *The making of masculinities: The new men's studies.* Boston: Allen & Unwin.

Cole, C., & Hribar, A. (1995). Celebrity feminism: Nike style, post-Fordism, transcendence, and' consumer power, *Sociology of Sport Journal, 12,* 347–369.

Cole, C. L., & King, S. (1998). Representing Black masculinity and urban possibilities: Racism, realism and "Hoop Dreams." In G. Rail (Ed.), *Sport and postmodern times* (pp. 49–86). Albany: State University of New York Press.

Connell, R. W. (1983). *Which way is up?* Sydney: George Allen & Unwin.

Connell, R. W. (1990). An iron man: The body and some contradictions of hegemonic masculinity. In M. Messner & D. Sabo (Eds.), *Sport, men, and the gender order: Critical feminist perspectives.* Champaign, IL: Human Kinetics Press.

Davis, N. (1994). Teaching about inequality: Student resistance, paralysis, and rage. *Teaching Sociology, 20,* 232–238.

Dworkin, S., & Messner, M. (1999). 'Just do—what? Sport, bodies, gender. In M. M. Ferree, J. Lorber, & B. Hess (Eds.), *Revisioning gender.* Thousands Oaks, CA: Sage.

Giddens, A. (1982). *Sociology: A brief but critical introduction.* London: Macmillan.

Giroux, H. (1983). Theories of reproduction in the new sociology of education. *Harvard Educational Review, 63* (3), 257–293.

Greene, M. (1984a). "Excellence," meanings and multiplicity. *Teachers College Record, 86,* 55–67.

Greene, M. (1984b). How do we think about our craft? *Teachers College Record, 86,* 283–297.

Greene, M. (1986). Reflection and passion in teaching. *Journal of Curriculum and Supervision, 2* (1), 68–81.

Hall, M. A. (1997). Review of "Crossing the Line." *International Review for the Sociology of Sport, 32,* 307–309.

Hargreaves, J. (1986). Where's the virtue? Where's the grace? A discussion of social production of gender relations in and through sport. *Theory, Culture and Society, 3,* 109–121.

Hutchinson, F. (1996). *Educating beyond violent futures.* New York: Routledge.

Katz, J. (1995). Reconstructing masculinity in the locker room: The Mentors in Violence Project. *Harvard Educational Review, 65,* 163–174.

Kimmel, M. (1992). *Against the tide: Pro-feminist men in the United States 1776–1990. A documentary history.* Boston: Beacon

King, P. (1994, December). Halt the head-hunting. *Sports Illustrated, 37,* 27–30.

Lafrance, M. (1998). Colonizing the feminine: Nike's intersections of post-feminism and hyperconsumption. In G. Rail (Ed.), *Sport and post-modern times.* Albany: State University of New York Press.

Lenskyj, H. (1991). Combating homophobia in sport and physical education. *Sociology of Sport Journal, 8,* 61–69.

Lenskyj, H. (1992). Sexual harassment: Female athletes' experiences and coaches responsibilities. *Science Periodical on Research and Technology in Sport, 12* (6), 1–5.

McGee, R. (1972). *Points of departure: Basic concepts in sociology.* Hinsdale, IL: Dryden Press.

McKay, J. (1995). "Just Do It": Corporate sports slogans and the political economy of "enlightened racism." *Discourse: Studies in the Cultural Politics of Education, 16,* 191–201.

McKay J. (1997). *Managing gender: Affirmative action and organizational power in Australian, Canadian, and New Zealand Sport.* Albany: State University of New York Press.

McKay, J., Messner, M., & Sabo, D. (1999). *Men, masculinities, and sport.* Thousand Oaks, CA: Sage.

McKay, J., & Ogilvie, E. (1999). New age—Same old men: Constructing the "New Man" in the Australian Media. *Mattoid, 54,* 18–35.

McNaught, C., & Anwyl, J. (1992). Awards for teaching excellence at Australian universities. *Higher Education Review, 25,* 31–44.

Messner, M. (1997). *Politics of masculinities: Men in movements.* Thousand Oaks, CA: Sage.

Messner, M., & Sabo, D. (1994). *Sex, violence and power in sports: Rethinking masculinity.* Freedom, CA: Crossing Press.

Mills, C. W. (1970). *The sociological imagination.* London: Oxford University Press.

Natanson, M. (1963). Introduction. In M. Natanson (Ed.), *Philosophy of the social sciences: A reader.* New York: Random.

Neitz, M. J. (1985). Resistance to feminist analysis. *Teaching Sociology, 12,* 285–298.

Passmore, J. (1975). On teaching to be critical. In R. Dearden, P. Hirst, & R. Peters (Eds.), *Education and the development of reason.* London: Routledge & Kegan Paul.

Ramsden, P. (1992). *Learning to teach in higher education.* London: Routledge.

Sanday, P. R. (1996). Rape-prone versus rape-free campus cultures. *Violence Against Women, 2,* 148–162.

Smith, P. (1991). *Killing the spirit: Higher education in America.* New York: Viking.

Trujillo, N. (1991). Hegemonic masculinity on the mound: Media representations of Nolan Ryan and American sports culture. *Critical Studies in Mass Communication, 8,* 290–308.

Williams, R. (1985). *Towards 2000.* Harmondsworth, England: Penguin.

Wilson, B. (1997). "Good Blacks" and "Bad Blacks": Media constructions of African-American athletes in Canadian basketball. *International Review for the Sociology of Sport, 32,* 177–189.

Wilson, B., & Sparks, R. (1996)."It's Gotta be the Shoes": Youth, race, and sneaker commercials. *Sociology of Sport Journal, 13,* 398–427.

SEVEN

Blowing Whistles

The Sports Violence Profile

LAWRENCE A. WENNER

W histle-blowing is a powerful concept. As critics, academics often blow whistles on social problems from the safety of the ivory tower. Here, a cacophony of whistles blow, so many and so discordant, that orchestrated movement is inevitably muted. Inside organizations, whistle-blowers can upset apple carts in dramatic ways. This kind of whistle-blowing calls attention to nefarious, institutionalized practices and can accelerate policy changes. Whistle-blowing occurs in other ways. In sports, referees blow whistles to signal different kinds of calls: personal fouls, team fouls, technical fouls, and time-outs. In this chapter, I would like to suggest a way to publicly blow whistles on mediated sports violence.

Academics and sports activists can create an annual stocktaking that might be called "The Sports Violence Profile." The Sports Violence Profile would take the form of an annual report issued to the media. More important would be its function in naming a series of nominees and award winners across a variety of sports violence categories. Each year we would recognize leagues, organizing bodies, teams, coaches, athletes, and media for performances that have contributed to making violence in association with sport either greater or more socially acceptable.

Now, some people might cringe at the idea of going public and mounting this kind of Bad Sport Awards. Indeed, some good arguments may be made for issuing Good Sport Awards for good "sportspersonship" to balance the Bad Sport Awards. But there are plenty of "good" sports awards already, and in watered-down form, the Sport Violence Profile will

119

lose some teeth. Even so, it makes sense to recognize organizations, teams, and media for improvements in their violence profile or in their coverage of sports violence.

Comfort levels aside, I think it is important to learn a lesson from our efforts in media violence research. Here the mounting ifs, ands, and buts undercut a tonnage of social science data gathered in experimental, survey, and natural settings. We should recognize that the findings concerning intervention strategies have been far more clear. The evidence suggests that real inroads can be made in moderating the effects of media violence through learning how violence is harmful, inappropriate, and how it will encounter negative sanction. In making the Sports Violence Profile and its Bad Sport Awards an annual media event, we can change the climate of the debate over violence in sports. Through negative reinforcement and public recognition, this profile can put pressure on the world of sport to rethink the value of violence. And certainly a yearly report can serve as a baseline that can guide educational and intervention strategies aimed at youth participating in sport.

Who might organize such a Sports Violence Profile? I would hope it would be an interorganizational effort. We might start with some of the sponsors underwriting the conference that fueled this book. Organizations such as the Amateur Athletic Foundation of Los Angeles, the National Institutes of Health, the University of Southern California's Steering Committee for the Study of Sport in Society, and Northeastern University's Center for the Study of Sport in Society (that already puts out an annual Racial Report Card on sports) would all be good sponsors. A broad organizational coalition including the Women's Sports Foundation, the North American Society for the Sociology of Sport, the North American Society for Sport Management, and the National Association for Sport and Physical Education would likely want to be on the "right" side of this issue. Compelling reasons might persuade the professional leagues, amateur organizing bodies, and major sport sponsors to join a coalition committed to making sport a safer place. The professional players' unions, in particular, would have a very personal interest in moving toward a safer work environment.

What might the categories be for the Bad Sport Awards and how would they be determined? One set of awards could be named by expert boards. Each year, we could name nominees and winners in diverse categories such as Most Dangerous Practice Allowed by Current Rulemaking; this award would pressure leagues and organizing bodies to change dangerous but legitimate practices. We could identify individuals and teams who committed the year's Most Violent Incidents Receiving a Penalty or Fine, and the Most Violent Incidents Not Receiving a Penalty or Fine. We could identify individuals and teams who committed the most number of on-field violent infractions.

To make sure that these awards did not avoid the superstars, I would suggest making equivalent Superstar Bad Sport awards to remind sponsors about fair play in awarding lucrative endorsement contacts. We need to be able to operationalize the basketball star Charles Barkley's "I am not a role model" pronouncement and make it felt in the pocketbook when athletes flaunt this responsibility through their violent acts.

I would also suggest team and individual awards for off-the-field violence and "most interceptions" by the criminal justice system. Again, by taking stock here, we can begin to apply public relations pressure to the wallets of the teams and individuals that implicitly condone violence and criminal activity off the field. The Dallas Cowboys would have probably been recent award winners in the team category.

It also seems to me that we can use the endless slew of statistics and record keeping in our award process. Granting special recognition to teams and individuals for the most personal or technical fouls would make "roughhousing" as an organizational or individual strategy subject to public scrutiny and enable the mounting of boycotts to the products related to teams, players, and manufacturers.

If we enter into making such Bad Sport Awards, there are dangers. If we concentrate too much on individual athletes and their violent actions, we may subvert our efforts to induce real structural change in sport. Elite athletes, after all, are workers in an institutional system not of their own making. It is important that we be vigilant in our recognition of organizational, institutional, and social strategies that fuel individual actions by athletes, normalizing and condoning violence in the process.

Because the media is a key institutional player in normalizing the culture of violence that surrounds sport, a series of media awards need to be featured center stage. Awards such as an Exploitation of Sports Violence Award could go to the most explicit and graphically overdone coverage of sport violence. A Sport Violence as Humor Award could be awarded to reporters who make jokes in the context of the reporting incidents of sports violence. We need to remind the sports media that in sports violence is not cartoonish and real people are harmed.

These are only a few of the possibilities for recognizing implicit and explicit support for violence in the context of sports. We need to think about how we can put the pressure on and keep it on. While we need to recognize organizations and individuals who make improvements, sports violence is one of those things where improvement is always possible. The average level of civility in sport can be improved, but first we will need to change public tolerances for the organizations and individuals in sports who use violence systematically, strategically, and too often, effectively.

"Let's Face It"

A Conversation with David Davis
on Sports Journalism

A staff writer and editor for several years with the LA Weekly, David Davis is now a freelance writer who is widely admired for the way his features illuminate social issues related to sport. He is a contributing writer for Los Angeles Magazine; he has written for Sports Illustrated, the Los Angeles Times, and the New York Times Book Review. His 1995 feature story about boxer Jerry Quarry, "The 13th Round," won several journalism awards.

Ed.: What are the advantages or disadvantages of working as a freelance or "alternative" sportswriter, rather than as a reporter for a daily? Do you have a particular vantage point?

DD: In the daily grind of sports journalism, a reporter is concerned very much with the nuts and bolts. Who won the game? How many points Joe Blow scored. Who got traded to whom? Those type of issues. Their main fare is to feed the public what the public wants. How are the Lakers doing? How are the Kings doing? That type of thing. The advantage for me is I don't have to worry about that sort of thing. I don't have to worry about, for instance, how's [L.A. Dodgers pitcher] Kevin Brown's arm feeling? Which, while it's important today, in the big scheme of things, is *not* important. What might be important for me about Kevin Brown is not how his arm is, or whether he went eighteen and eight, or if he's going to lead you to the World Series, but what does his huge contract represent? What does it mean for him to be moving from the small market, San Diego Padres to the big market, Rupert Murdoch-owned Dodgers? What are the implications of that? The dailies might get to that a bit, but their main concern is, Are the Dodgers going to win the pennant now?

Ed.: But haven't mainstream sports journalists begun to tackle more social issues in their coverage in recent years?

DD: Lately, I think my "turf" has been tread upon by the mainstream media. What that means is I have to work harder to find stories. No doubt about it. And I have to do a better job of looking at the mainstream media and critiquing them, criticizing when needed, and pointing out when they're not covering the right things or not covering certain issues well. Women's sports is a good example: If you read the papers today, you would not know that there is a women's golf tournament in Glendale this weekend. And there *was* an article in the *Times* today on the men's tournament in Torrey Pines, which is way outside L.A. I don't even know where Torrey Pines *is!* There's a dozen stories you could do in preparation for a major LPGA [Ladies Professional Golf Association] event. For instance, here we are in southern California where there's a huge Asian population. A great story would be the proliferation of Asian women golfers on the LPGA tour.

Ed.: When I talk with reporters and TV people about the lack of coverage of women's sports, the usual response is, "We're doing a little better than before, but, frankly, people don't want to watch women's sports." Some media scholars have been arguing for years that media doesn't simply just respond to what people want. They help create what people want by promoting and building interest for certain kinds of stories. What's your sense of what the responsibility of the media is or should be?

DD: They're a business, so they need to take care of the Lakers and the Kings. That's bread and butter. But I do think they have a responsibility to do more to use their vast resources. That sort of bothers me, as someone who worked in the alternative media where we have to count our paper clips at the end of the day: when you have corporate media resources behind you, it seems to me you have a responsibility to go out and find stories that don't necessarily translate into advertising dollars. To go after women's sports. OK, maybe you're not going to sell fourteen more pages of advertising, but you're certainly doing a better job of being a *journalist,* of covering stories.

Let's face it: The people in sports teams and organizations don't look at the *LA Times* or other major forms of media as, "Oh, these guys are covering us 'as journalists'." No, this is a form of free advertising. That's the way it's always been. It has nothing to do with the fact that they give media passes to journalists. That's a courtesy. But why do we have to cover every Laker game? Well, the Lakers are pretty happy about it! *That's* what it's all about. The earliest innovators in sports recognized that relationship between media and sports. It's always been a little bit cozy. Another example: for several years, *Sports Illustrated* has been a sponsor, or an advertising partner, with the Olympics. In other words, *Sports Illustrated* does the program for the Olympics, and yet they cover it! There's a potential conflict of interest. Now, I would say that for the most part *Sports Illustrated* has done a pretty good job. *But,* bottom line, they're a *partner* with the Olympics! It's in their interest to have the Olympics thrive and then cover it and sell it and so on. That's the way it's been, that type of relationship.

Ed.: It seems especially that televised sports media have found that highlighting violence seems to really sell. On TV news, instead of showing the goals that were scored, they show the fights during the hockey match; instead of showing the winning car at the finish line of the Indianapolis 500, they show the car exploding on the twelfth lap, and the big hits in the football game. How does that trend affect print sports coverage?

DD: Televised sports has changed the way we cover sports in the print media. In the mid-eighties, ESPN [an all-sports cable TV station] started to really come to the fore and SportsCenter became sort of the Bible. The whole sports industry watches ESPN SportsCenter like Hollywood people read *Variety.* You have to do it, OK? That changed the way *Sports Illustrated* covered things. The managing editor said to me in an interview, "That's our competition now." Imagine that, a weekly magazine looking at a nightly TV highlight show and saying, "That's my major competition." He recognized that this is where people were getting the basic information. So now they had to change. They had to do personality-driven pieces, shorter articles, different types, more graphics, more photos, bigger photos, more in-your-face photos.

Ed.: A lot of parents and some scholars are concerned with the effects on children who watch sports violence. What do sports media people think about this issue?

DD: I cover boxing, a sport that is all about violence, and yet interestingly enough, because it is so transparently about the violence, there's never really any thought to the question of, "Is this a bad influence?" Because that's what it is. It is what it is. Which is a way of saying that other forms are maybe a little more insidious because they're not *supposed* to be about violence. Hockey's supposed to be hockey, this thing played on ice with beautiful motions and passing. I think, as a matter of fact, that the *Village Voice* does a running column of the best fights. And I know there are tapes that go around of the best hockey fights. I don't know if I have an explanation for that or what it means to kids to watch that because I haven't done studies on that. I haven't written about that, per se. I just know that it's popular.

Ed.: Larry Wenner has suggested in chapter 7 that scholars develop what he calls a "Sports Violence Profile." His idea is that every year some panel of scholars measure how much violence is shown by sports media and how it's portrayed and then give out some sort of awards at the end of the year, for instance, to the people who are the worst at sensationalizing violence. Maybe the *Village Voice* would be contending for such a prize. What do you think about that idea?

DD: Academics sort of come in and observe, which is why you pick up on things that most people don't notice. Sports media people are there every night. They're watching hockey every night. They see the fights, and they become so accustomed to it, inured to it, immune to the effects of it. I don't even think they really think about it that much. Or if you did talk to them, they'd say, "Oh, it's just part of the game. You gotta have a fight or two." And you know what? They're right about that. Most of the beat writers don't mention fighting in the context of a game story. They're not going to say, "Oh, and then there was a great fight in the third period!" That doesn't really happen. Every once in awhile you'll get a profile on some enforcer guy. "Hey, he's a great thug, but you know he's got a great wife and kids, and isn't that nice?" That's sort of how they like to cover it, like "Surprise! He doesn't beat up everybody off the ice." However, every once in awhile there'll be somebody investigating a story on athletes and violence. I think the *LA Times* did a very good story on the recent arrests and convictions of athletes.

Ed.: Yes, a reporter who worked on that story told me that they had initially planned to run a head shot of each of these guys—professional and college athletes—who was arrested in 1995. But when they laid it out they realized that almost all the guys were Black and they just thought it would look too bad to have all those photos. So they pulled most of the pictures and just ran the names and the stories, including an article (White & Reid, 1995) about race. Is this story a good indicator of how sports media today deal with race issues compared with say, ten to twenty years ago?

DD: It's improved. I think they do a better job, and I would point to stories about the lack of African American coaches in the NFL, for instance—That story you read now all the time. "Why isn't so-and-so being hired?" That's a positive. I think the story, like you mentioned, about violence where more of the athletes were Black than White—we're only now getting to more of the subtle stories like that. Similar was *Sports Illustrated*'s [SI] cover story last year about all of the children born out of wedlock to athletes. I think you could see in that story, sort of reading between the lines a little bit, you could see that, yeah, the majority of these players that they talked about happened to be Black, they were in the NBA, but you could see *SI* making sure that they wrote about White athletes because that had happened with them, too. And yet the image with that we're left with was of a young Black kid on the cover going, "Where's my daddy?" I think as we talk about the sort of the nuts and bolts story, which are Black coaches and Black managers, hopefully that will make us be more sensitive when we have stories like violence among athletes. If it happens to be that it's more Black athletes than Whites, well, you have to report that. Maybe *that's* the story, as opposed to just the sheer numbers, and maybe that's something that people will start investigating, not to just go, "Well, there's more Blacks than Whites who are violent." Well, why? How? Where does that come from? There happens to be more Black athletes in pro sports. So, percentage-wise, you would imagine that would hold to form on other issues outside of sports.

Another encouraging sign is I think more media people are aware that there's a lack of minority sportswriters and sports editors. That's more of a shameful contradiction or statistic than what you have in NFL head coaches. Count the number of Black sports editors on major metropolitan dailies. You don't have to use very many of your fingers, you know? Yet that's not an article you'll necessarily read. So the hope is that mainstream editors will start recognizing this and will bring in, recruit, Black journalists.

Ed.: What's the significance of the lack of African Americans and/or women on TV or newspaper sports desks in terms of what gets covered, and how?

DD: I think diversity is so important in a newsroom, and in any part of the media. Not just because you want to reflect the reality of the world that you're covering, but hopefully diversity is going to bring other ideas and perspectives—people with different backgrounds might know a little bit more about a subject than I would.

Ed.: Sarah Banet-Weiser's analysis of the WNBA in chapter 5 suggests that sports media are now presenting women's basketball as "pure" and unadulterated basketball, in contrast to the tarnished NBA—which is viewed as a bunch of spoiled, rich millionaires.

DD: Right. And I think that stereotype is going to come back and bite people in the butt, because let's face it: we haven't even begun to go into some very interesting controversial aspects of women's sports. They are going to come up.

Ed.: Some women journalists like Joan Ryan of the *San Francisco Chronicle* and freelance writer Mariah Burton Nelson have illuminated some of the heavy stuff like sexual abuse of girls by coaches, and anorexia among young gymnasts. Their work does get noticed some in the mainstream media, but it doesn't seem necessarily to affect the ongoing coverage of women's or men's sports.

DD: Right. I mean, it gets noticed when they need a quote or something. "Oh, how do you explain this? Well, let's bring in our designated women's sportsperson: Mariah Burton Nelson or Joan Ryan." But at this point the mainstream hasn't quite caught that there's going to be some interesting stories coming down the line. I think they're doing better covering things like what Joan Ryan would cover, like anorexia in gymnastics and ice skating. But we haven't read a lot about, for instance, unwanted pregnancies among athletes. I think there's some interest in stories about young girl athletes, some of the figure skaters, and their coaches and/or their managers, and manipulations thereof. You don't read about some of that sort of stuff. Let's face it, most of the people covering this are male writers. How do you cover this? Those sorts of issues are going to be out there.

Ed.: When independent journalists like yourself have covered something that mainstream media might not have thought to touch, sometimes it eventually works its way into their coverage. For instance, the profile you did on [former boxer] Jerry Quarry in 1995 seemed, as far as I was concerned, to come out of nowhere. I hadn't thought about Jerry Quarry for a long time, and it was a deeply powerful and moving piece that raised fundamental questions about the human costs of boxing. Not long after that, I started seeing features about Quarry on TV and in major print media. Was there a correlation there, direct or indirect?

DD: I think on that one you can see a direct correlation, and it speaks to the copycat element where if somebody sees an article on their beat, they'd better go get that article.

Ed.: Don't you think there's a little more to it than that? You were speaking earlier about the writers on the boxing beat for the major dailies. In the past, the Jerry Quarrys were so easy to just ignore and forget. It's convenient for boxing reporters—given their symbiotic relationship to the sport—to forget about the victims of boxing.

DD: I think you're right. I think there's definitely an element of that. Probably those guys—and I'm not defending them or condemning them—but they've read a half dozen stories on down-and-out boxers, and it just didn't register, whereas for me, because I was very new to the scene of boxing, this was a fascinating story. I had to do it. Sometimes the stories that are right in front of us, we don't see. I think, quite frankly, that's one of the reasons why I like to read and look at what academics write about sports.

Ed.: Because we come in from the outside? . . .

DD: Exactly. And it's sort of like what I was talking about with, say, the violence in hockey. If you're there every night, what's the big story?

Ed.: If it's clear the advantage that academics have in looking at sports more as outsiders, what do we miss?

DD: Well, you do miss the day-to-day. I've never worked on a daily, but I can tell you from knowing people who do—that it's an incredibly tough job to be a beat writer for, let's say, the LA Lakers, where you're going to cover them for the whole season. You're going to travel with them. You're going to be on the same airplane. You're going to be in the same hotels, that sort of thing. You've got to keep a relationship with these people! Yes, you can say, "he had an off day," and this happened and this happened, but you don't want to burn a player so that he'll never talk to you, and the same with the coach. That form of relationship, it's so subtle and it's so difficult to explain to people who ask, "Why don't you just write that Del Harris [coach of the Lakers] can't coach his way out of a paper bag?" Well, you've got to go to him for a quote every night and he reads what you write every night! And a lot of people don't see that. I'm very glad I don't do that, because I would not want to lose any sort of "edge" I have from being a little bit of an outsider.

Reference

White, L., & Reid, J. (1995, December 27). Time of turmoil. *Los Angeles Times,* C5.

PART III

Racial Inequality and Intergroup Contact

R ace is often implicit in discussions of youth and sport. When sport is proposed as a way of reaching at-risk youth in order to prevent their getting into trouble, the term *at-risk youth* is often a coded phrase for non-White youth. When sport is touted as an avenue for upward social mobility, it is predominantly African American males who are the imagined beneficiaries. When professional athletes are held up as role models to help motivate youth, often the exemplars are African American, usually male. In turn, when commentators decry the negative behavior of collegiate and professional athletes, the focus is often on an African American male athlete. In order to move beyond coded phrases and unexamined assumptions, in this section of the book, race becomes an explicit topic. Two issues are highlighted: athletes as role models and the implications of sport as a context for intergroup contact. As in other sections of the book, this section too brings together different voices, so that the reader hears from athletes, from researchers, and from scholars who were also athletes.

In chapter 8, Kenneth L. Shropshire discusses the issue of role models, in particular the disproportionate expectation placed on African American star athletes that they should be more than athletes. Associated with this tendency is media emphasis on those athletes who are poor role models, primarily by virtue of their behaviors off the court or off the field. The athlete is determined—not by himself—to be a role model, then blamed for failing to live up to expectations. At the conclusion of the section, Terrence Barnum provides an athlete's perspective on how it feels to be placed in this position and to be the receptacle of the assumptions of others about one's background. Shropshire's recommendation is that a broader array of role models must be made available to youth. Both he and Barnum urge that

coaches, sports agents, and administrators of intercollegiate athletic programs can help to direct the attention of youth to other influential leaders.

More than many institutions, sport is a venue that cuts across race.
Teams are comprised of athletes of different racial and ethnic groups. Spectators too are diverse. Sometimes race becomes a tension; other times, it is
seemingly incorporated as part of the context. The researchers Patricia M.
Greenfield, Helen M. Davis, Lalita K. Suzuki, and Ioakim P. Boutakidis in
chapter 9; James S. Jackson, Shelley Keiper, Kendrick T. Brown, Tony N.
Brown, and Warde Manuel in chapter 10; and Barnum all suggest that
sport participation should be regarded as a unique interracial situation.
Social psychological theory (Brewer & Miller, 1988) has indicated conditions under which prejudice can be reduced:

- There should be sufficient numbers of individuals from both
  groups.
- Members of the two groups should have contact with one
  another under conditions of equal status.
- The situation should require that members of the two
  groups must cooperate toward achieving a common goal.
- Contact and cooperation between the groups should be
  sanctioned by authorities.

Using quite distinct methodologies, Greenfield and Jackson both
address the use of sport to reduce prejudice and intergroup conflict. Their
findings illustrate how these principles can predict either reduced intergroup prejudice or increased conflict, according to the conditions that are
in place. Using newly available national survey data, Jackson and his colleagues found that, for White male freshman collegiate student-athletes,
having had greater interracial contact on their high school sports teams
was related to more positive attitudes toward Blacks. Greenfield and her
colleagues observed boys' and girls' multiethnic high school sports teams in
order to see what sorts of intergroup encounters typically take place. The
research team also collected data about how the boys and girls participating in sports view others on their team, including those from the same or
different ethnic groups. One basketball team illustrated how intergroup
conflict can arise when there is not equal status. A challenge for coaches is
to promote equal status and cooperation when there are real differences in
skill. Greenfield and her colleagues' other observation was that differences
in cultural values—whether the young athlete tended to hold an individualistic perspective or a collectivistic perspective—were another factor in
understanding harmony and conflict. Because certain value orientations are
more often associated with different ethnic groups, value conflicts may
sometimes appear to be ethnic conflicts. These concerns have international

implications, because racial, ethnic, and religious divides can be found around the globe. For example, the question whether sport can serve as a unifier has also been raised in Northern Ireland (Gallagher, 1997) and in South Africa (Ogle, 1997).

In chapter 11, Robert M. Sellers, Tabbye M. Chavous, and Tony N. Brown focus on intercollegiate athletics as a potential avenue for upward mobility for African Americans. That avenue has become more difficult with the reform movement in the National Collegiate Athletic Association. New rules have made it more difficult academically for high school students to obtain athletic scholarships to attend college or university. Sellers and his colleagues argue that the reform movement is based on assumptions that student-athletes lack sufficient academic motivation, assumptions that primarily place the burden on the athlete. The authors offer evidence that these assumptions are flawed, and they propose that structural barriers are a better explanation than lack of motivation for the poor academic preparation of many African American student-athletes. Like Jackson, Sellers focuses on collegiate student-athletes, but uses this group to discuss high school experiences.

Finally, Jackson and his colleagues bring survey data to bear on the pivotal question of the relationship between aggression on the field and aggression off the field. Despite expectations that African American males are the problem group, the data showed that it was White student-athletes, both male and female, who showed a correlation between on-the-field and off-the-field likelihood of using aggression in romantic relationships.

The reader of this section should take away a desire for more study of sport and race and an appreciation for the complexity of using sports to motivate youth or introducing star athletes as role models.

References

Brewer, M. B., & Miller, N. (1988). Contact and cooperation: When do they work? In D. A. Taylor & P. A. Katz (Eds.), *Eliminating racism: Profiles in controversy. Perspectives in social psychology* (pp. 315–326). New York: Plenum Press.

Gallagher, A. M. (1997). Sport and community background. In J. Kremer, K. Trew, & S. Ogle (Eds.), *Young people's involvement in sport* (pp. 114–125). London: Routledge.

Ogle, S. (1997). International perspectives on public policy and the development of sport for young people. In J. Kremer, K. Trew, & S. Ogle (Eds.), *Young people's involvement in sport* (pp. 211–231). London: Routledge.

EIGHT

Race, Youth, Athletes, and Role Models

KENNETH L. SHROPSHIRE

If the Negro could abandon the idea of leadership and instead stimulate a larger number of the race to take up definite tasks and sacrifice their time and energy in doing these things efficiently, the race might accomplish something.

—Carter G. Woodson,
The Mis-education of the Negro

When the basketball star Charles Barkley asserted on behalf of Nike that he was not a role model, most paused to think. In the advertisement Barkley asserted, "I am not a role model. I am not paid to be a role model. I am paid to wreak havoc on the basketball court. Parents should be role models. Just because I dunk a basketball doesn't mean I should raise your kids" (Gribeaut, 1997). Since then many, including the United States Supreme Court, have taken sides on the issue as it relates to athletes. One factor that seems clear is that there is much more focus on role models as it relates to African Americans than any other group. It appears to be the exception, for example, when the role model status and qualifications of White males is the focus of public discourse. The issue of the reality of the athlete as role model is certainly an appropriate one for further exploration. The disproportionate focus on African Americans and role models reveals something more. What does such a disparity tell us about popular American culture?

The status given to African American athletes by the American media is fascinating. It also serves to perpetuate Woodson's assertion, that there is the need, or even the requirement, for standout individuals in the African American community. Absent such a figure or figures there is some perceived inadequacy in the community. With this aura constantly present, the anointing of role models and leaders occurs with hyperfrequency as well. A colleague related to me his dismay on a recent Monday morning as he explained how he had rushed home from church the day before to hear "experts" discuss with the distinguished commentator Bob Costas the problems of welfare reform, crime, and drug addiction. He was perplexed when those *Meet the Press* experts were professional basketball players Charles Barkley, Grant Hill, and Michael Jordan. "At least include one White athlete," he told me in trying to lessen the racial edge of the event.

Barkley's proclamation is, of course, much more complex than it seems on its face. No one could argue in earnest that America's youth do not look up to athletes. The merchandise sales, fashion, language, and other style imitations are clear indicators of this. The wake-up call of the statement is that parents, media, and others look up to athletes for more than they should. This being the point, Barkley's view seems to be, "if there is a vacuum in the raising of your children you must fill it, not us." The assumption of the role model discourse is that the off-the-playing-venue influence of these athletes is powerful, particularly toward African American young men. The assumption further reads that, certainly if you wear your logo cap backward you are being influenced inside of your head in broader ways as well. It is clear that if you are an African American athlete, you carry a greater burden than your White counterparts. There was a time when the appropriate phrasing would be: you must be *a credit to your race.*

A credit to your race is a phrase that has probably never been used in reference to a White man. For example, in the Bill Clinton White House scandal regarding the alleged affair with the intern Monica Lewinsky, Clinton is not viewed popularly as a *discredit* to his race. Similarly, there was no overt racial connotation to Mark McGwire's 1998 drive toward Roger Maris's home run record. Jung (1986) has captured the conundrum through pointing out implicit acceptance that majority group members do not need role models in the same way as minorities. Thus we have little role model discourse focusing on majority group members.

Those who have heard the phrase *a credit to your race* before are generally not sure where they first heard it. At some point the statement was probably meant to be both complimentary and instructive. It is much like the usage of the term *role model* in today's popular culture. To be a role model is to be something exceptional. This too was the case with being a credit to your race. The intermediate phrasings have been a bit more straightforward and now are almost as taboo as the "credit to your race" discourse: "I don't think of you as Black," or "You're not like other Blacks." But, occasionally the negative phrasing or variations are still used. Gen. Colin Powell reflects in his autobiography that during his early years in the military he was instructed by one individual to be a good "Negro." In the initial instance when this instruction was given, Powell (1995) recalls, "I do not remember being upset at what he said. He meant well" (p. 38). The designation of certain athletes as "good" role models and others as "bad" is presumably well-intentioned, too.

The initial use of the phrase *role model* can be traced to psychology and sociology literature of the 1950s (Addis, 1996). The murkiness in the role model discussion lies in what exactly someone means when the phrase is uttered. There is certainly the complete emulation versus task distinction. The broader issue is the difference between role model as defined by those two and the two closely related terms, *mentor* and *hero*. There is another interpretation, which in relation to people such as General Powell is relevant—*spokesperson* or *leader*. This was certainly Woodson's concern in the cited epigraph. In sports the hero and emulation models are probably the most relevant. As a credit to all, athletes usually level off as role models— although lofty; rarely are they trusted further. Even Major League Baseball star Ken Griffey Jr. apparently asked that the Nike advertisements touting him as a presidential candidate be curtailed in 1996—this on the heels of a reporter seriously querying regarding his views on abortion. The 1998 incident when the football star Reggie White stumbled in a speech with politically incorrect views on the races and homosexuality is an example of an athlete overstepping this role model as hero boundary.

There are, to be sure, certainly other uses of the term *role model* that fall short of the emulation of the entire person. Prof. Adeno Addis (1996) observes two models. In summarizing the view of other scholars—the "Role Imitation View" and the "Comprehensive View." The Role Imitation View is a precise form of emulation. In this view the individual focuses on limited elements of the role model, for example, Barkley's style of defense on the basketball court. The Comprehensive View is much broader, and, according to Addis, role models in this context possess a degree of power over emulators in areas where the role models have no expertise. Few would argue that this comprehensive view should be encouraged with regard to athletes at all. This is the concern, for example, with the off the court problems of National Basketball Association star Allen Iverson and National Football League star Michael Irvin. The in the ring antics of the boxer Mike Tyson biting an opponent's ear and then San Francisco Warrior star Latrell Sprewell choking his coach at practice are more related to the athletic activity, and possibly more legitimately issues to be concerned about possible emulation.

Needless to say, the role model phrasing, although disproportionately, is not solely focused on African Americans. When White heavyweight boxer Tommy Morrison held a press conference acknowledging that he had contracted the AIDS virus, he said,

> I ask that you no longer see me as a role model, but see me as
> an individual who had an opportunity to be a role model and
> blew it. Blew it with irresponsible, irrational, immature deci-
> sions that will one day cost me my life. (Romano, 1996, p. A1)

A good number of Morrison's fans, and presumably those he was addressing, were largely White. In a bit of irony, following an hour long telephone
conversation with the African American basketball player Magic Johnson,
Morrison proclaimed of his fellow HIV-positive athlete, "He's a great role
model" (Wieberg, 1996, p. 3C).

It is not difficult to understand why this overblown focus on role models is made on what represents a subset of only 12 percent of the population
of the United States. The images on the evening news are (once again, disproportionately) filled with young African American men involved in crime.
The broad presentation is that there is no solution to the problem in sight,
so why not present, or place on a pedestal, the appropriate way to "act."
Those who someone, generally not African Americans, have anointed as a
credit to their race. There is an irony to this focus, particularly in 1998 when
there has been a rash of school yard murders, mainly by White youths.
Oddly too, arguably the most notorious assassins, such as Lee Harvey
Oswald, James Earl Ray, and Sirhan Sirhan, and mass murderers such as
Charles Manson and Ted Bundy, have seemingly been predominantly White.

The role model focus, however, remains on African Americans. Jack
Johnson was a bad one. The first Black heavyweight champion of the
world broke the law, partied hard, and married White women. Even
Muhammed Ali *was* a bad role model. Joe Louis and Jackie Robinson were
ideal. Grant Hill of the Detroit Pistons (now Orlando Magic) seems like a
fine young man. Why not be like him? That Michael Jordan. Well, for a
while *maybe* not, the gambling thing, but now, he's fully back in favor.
That *Space Jam* was a wonderful film. To be a positive role model one must
not only be a stellar athlete, but largely apolitical and "raceless" as well.
Both were shortcomings of Ali in his prime. The list of "bad" sports role
models, however, seems to overwhelm the underpublicized "good guys."
For example, one must look to the not so readily available *Chronicle of
Philanthropy* for a detailed account of the National Basketball Association's Steve Smith's pledge of $2.5 million to his alma mater for an acade-
mic support center (Blum, 1997).

It is not the popular press alone that is guilty of believing that these
athletes are important for more than their athletic ability. In this regard,
U.S. courts are guilty as well. Arguably much approval comes about in
society when the Supreme Court says it is so or that the time has come for
a societal transition. This occurred with school desegregation in the 1950s.

Those decisions made it publicly all right to question the value of affirmative action in the 1990s. In 1995 the Court said that athletes *should* be treated as role models. (115 S.Ct. 2386 [1995]) The Court held that athletes *should* be treated differently. In that case, *Veronia School District v. Acton,* Justice Antonin Scalia wrote, "It seems to us self-evident that a drug problem largely fueled by the 'role model' effect of athletes' drug use, and of particular danger to athletes, is effectively addressed by making sure that athletes do not do drugs." In this case the Court essentially argued that on this issue, because of the "role model effect" the privacy rights against search enjoyed by all citizens could not be enjoyed by athletes. For those in search of it, this is a major instance where a court could not be accused of giving athletes preferential treatment.

For what it's worth, I believe that in the end Barkley is right. He is even more correct if, in fact, the representation in the media is such that African Americans, more than anyone else, are receiving this misguided focus on athletes. No one needs to be like an athlete. We do not know them. As NBA star Chris Webber told us on ESPN one evening, we do not know about most of the good they do. The Toronto Raptors' Carlos Rogers's decision to donate a kidney to his ailing sister—at the risk of ending his athletic career—was news for but a day. Commit a Michael Irvin, Mike Tyson, or O. J. Simpson type crime and the news will never go away.

What we learn from these athletes is how to throw or hit a curve, how to shoot a jumper, or, from Tiger Woods, how to drive a golf ball, but in general not much more. Our youth should clearly be discouraged from any further emulation. Some studies indicate that our youth are wiser than we seem to believe. They look to athletes for those athletic moves and rappers for raps (MEE, 1992). Not much else. But when there is a roundup for role models and spokespersons, and finger-pointing for serving as poor role models, athletes are wrongly placed at the top of the heap.

We should recognize that the push for this athlete-role model positioning is disproportionately directed at African Americans. A more valuable push might be toward providing appropriate role models for those athletes, including positively influential African American sports agents, coaches, administrators, college presidents, and team owners. It is these young people who need the guidance, not to be involuntarily pushed into positions of leadership for which they are not prepared. Any focus beyond the athletic skills of an athlete should be the exception.

Holding an individual such as Powell up as a role model is not without its problems, but such a move is more sensible than the similar elevation of the majority of professional athletes. This reminds me of the interview with a high school coach in Louisiana in 1968. He told *Sports Illustrated,*

A White kid tries to become President of the United States, and all the skills and knowledge he picks up on the way can be used in a thousand different jobs. A Black kid tries to become Willie Mays, and all the tools he picks up on the way are useless to him if he doesn't become Willie Mays. (Johnson, 1991, p. 41)

It may oversimplify matters to state that we all need role models of the right type. Certainly not just African Americans and certainly not overwhelmingly celebrities. Simple but apparently not understood by all, particularly some representatives of the media and the courts. The most poignant telling of this came from the near death baseball star Mickey Mantle who in acknowledging years of alcohol abuse stated, "Don't be like me . . ." (Anderson, 1995, p. B9).

References

Addis, A. (1996). Role models and the politics of recognition, *University of Pennsylvania Law Review, 144* (4), 1377–1468.

Anderson, D. (1995, July 12). I'll try to make up for stuff. *New York Times,* B9.

Blum, D. E. (1997, March 6). Basketball player makes charitable giving part of his game plan, *Chronicle of Philanthropy,* 10.

Gribeaut, J. (1997, August). Who's raising the kids? Parents are supposed to be role models. With many receiving failing grades in that department, lawmakers are cracking down on teens with curfews and dress codes, *ABA Journal, 83,* 62.

Johnson, W. O. (1991, August). How far have we come? *Sports Illustrated,* 41.

Jung, J. (1986), How useful is the concept of a role model? A critical analysis, *Journal of Social Behavior and Personality, 1,* 525–536.

The MEE Report: Researching the Hip-Hop Generation (1992). Research Division of MEE Productions, for the Robert Wood Johnson Foundation.

Powell, C. (1995), *My American Journey.* New York: Random House.

Romano, L. (1996, February 16). Remorse from a heavyweight; Morrison grieves over lifestyle that led to HIV. *Washington Post,* A1.

Wieberg, S. (1996, February 16), Magic offers Morrison advice about HIV situation, *USA Today,* 3C.

Woodson, C. G. (1990), *The Mis-education of the Negro.* Trenton NJ: Africa World Press (original edition, Associated Publishers, 1933).

NINE

Understanding Intercultural Relations on Multiethnic High School Sports Teams

PATRICIA M. GREENFIELD, HELEN M. DAVIS,
LALITA K. SUZUKI, AND IOAKIM P. BOUTAKIDIS

O ur study utilizes the context of multiethnic high school sports teams to understand the sources of intergroup conflict. Teams are one of the few contexts in which multiethnic youth come together under conditions social psychology has found favorable for the reduction of prejudice: these conditions are, "equal status contact between . . . groups in the pursuit of common goals" (Allport, 1954/1958). In theory, the members of a sports team are defined as having equal status and working together for a common goal. Indeed, Allport uses the multiethnic sports team to exemplify his principle: "Here the goal is all-important; the ethnic composition of the team is irrelevant. It is the cooperative striving for the goal that engenders solidarity" (Allport, 1958, p. 264).

However, the theoretical potential of team sports for equal status contact in the service of a common goal may not always be realized in practice. Under certain conditions, a dominance hierarchy of socially constructed ethnic groups (Sidanius, Levin, Rabinowitz, & Federico, 1999) can form within the team. This was an unexpected finding of our research.

Nonetheless, even when the conditions of equal status contact in the service of a common goal are obtained on a team, these conditions are, according to our theoretical framework, *necessary* but *not sufficient* for intergroup harmony. Our notion was that even equal status contact and a common goal cannot eradicate the difference between two very basic, yet unspoken value frameworks: individualism and collectivism. We hypothesized that this difference in values lies at the root of much inter-group conflict among youth in general, and on sports teams in particular.

Individualism and collectivism are cultural models both for generating behavior and for interpreting the behavior of others. Mainstream culture in the United States is generally viewed as individualistic, encouraging independence, self-reliance, individual achievement, and personal self-esteem as important goals of development (Markus & Kitayama, 1991). However, many groups come to the United States bringing a collectivistic value system from their ancestral culture into our highly individualistic society (Greenfield & Cocking, 1994). Collectivism is a cultural value orientation that emphasizes interdependence (Markus & Kitayama, 1991), group needs and goals, and personal modesty (Boutakidis, Davis, Suzuki, Greenfield, & Baidoo, 1997). This situation sets the stage for intergroup conflict, particularly between Euro-Americans or African Americans and members of non-Western immigrant minorities. The conflict that can arise from differences in value systems is subtle and often goes unrecognized as being culturally based.

In sum, divergent value frameworks, as well as attitudes of group dominance or superiority, disrupt the ideal conditions of sports teams: equal status and common goals. In this chapter, we describe how and why intercultural conflict occurs. In line with our theoretical framework and findings, we have two foci: (1) value differences and (2) the presence of hierarchically arranged ethnic subgroups within a team. Both conditions lead to intergroup misunderstanding and conflict.

Value Differences

Players bring differing value lenses into the team sport situation. Different players then see the same behaviors through the different cultural lenses of individualism and collectivism, and interpret the meaning of the behaviors in ways that may contrast with another's interpretation. In particular, we look at differing cultural approaches on the themes of (1) self-enhancement (individualistic) versus self-deprecation (collectivistic) (Kitayama, Markus, Matsumoto, & Norasakkunkit, 1997); and (2) the role of a team member as an individual achiever (individualistic) versus as a supporting player (collectivistic). *Conflict occurs when the behavior valued in one perspective is negatively evaluated through the lens of the other perspective.*

These issues of value difference were particularly salient in our analysis of conflict on a girls' high school volleyball team. For a boys' high school basketball team, these issues were also present. However, they did not seem to lead to the escalation of conflict as much as did problems of in-group/out-group definition and the formation of a dominance hierarchy composed of different ethnic groups, our next topic of discussion.

A Hierarchy of Ethnic Groups

For the boys' basketball team, we found it necessary to examine the disruption of equal status team membership by the formation of an ethnically defined social dominance hierarchy (Sidanius, Levin, Rabinowitz, Federico, & Pratto, 1999). In this case, the team fractionated into a racially constructed dominance hierarchy with an ethnically defined in-group in the dominant position (Black-identified players). The divisive issues were an attitude of Black superiority at basketball and coach favoritism toward the Black players. In line with the model of Gaertner, Dovidio, Nier, Ward, and Banker (1999), we concluded that this process of ethnic fission was a function of these divisive issues; which, in turn, led to negative intergroup attitudes and to a high level of conflict, including some physical aggression. On this team, an ethnically defined dominance hierarchy went side-by-side with value differences as sources of conflict.

Subjects and Context

The research presented here is part of a larger study involving multiethnic high school basketball and volleyball teams, both girls' and boys', in two schools in Los Angeles County. Our study of value perspectives and conflict on these teams includes players, coaches, and parents as subjects. In this chapter, we will present data from two multiethnic teams to illustrate how cultural value conflict can motivate both subtle and blatant conflict in the context of high school sports. Conflict abounded on both teams, but on the second team, conflict also led to physical aggression.

The first team we will discuss is a girls' high school volleyball team from a suburb east of downtown Los Angeles. This varsity team contained Asian-Americans, Euro-Americans, Latinas, and mixed-race players and had many instances of interethnic conflict. The second team was a varsity boys' basketball team comprised of African Americans, Asian-Americans, Euramericans, Latinos, and mixed-race players from the same school as the girls' team. This boys' team was the only one in which player conflict led to physical aggression among team members.

Methods

The work presented in this chapter is based on ethnographic data and player journals. An important feature of our methodology is the multivocal ethnography, an ethnography composed of many voices. We investigated conflict not only from the researchers' points of view, but also from the points of view of our subjects. Our research team was multiethnic in order to provide varying cultural interpretations of the same observed events at team practices, games, and team gatherings; and the multiethnic high school players kept journals concerning their personal experiences of harmony and conflict with their teammates. Player opinions and ideas in the journal entries showed us the players' thoughts in their own voices. In this way, we analyzed the interpretations of multiple observers and multiple journal writers to understand conflict from multiple perspectives.

At the end of each sports season, we also administered two individualism/collectivism assessments to each player. We assumed that these assessments were stable over the length of a sports season and therefore reflected the values each player brought into the team situation. One assessment was based on Likert-scale items assembled by Singelis, Triandis, Bhawuk, & Gelfand (1995, pp. 255–266). This assessment allows one to measure individualism and collectivism as two separate and independent dimensions.[1] We also gave participants our own scenario measure of individualism and collectivism. In this measure, participants try to resolve social dilemmas that have both individualistic and collectivistic solutions (see Raeff, Greenfield, and Quiroz [2000] for sample dilemmas and responses). This instrument assesses the extent to which individualism or collectivism is prioritized in choice situations; it therefore yields a single dimension with individualism at one pole and collectivism at the other.

Our analysis is primarily qualitative. Although we derived quantitative scores from our assessments, we use them on the individual rather than the group level. For example, we tried to connect the values that pairs of individual players bring into the team situation with the interaction of the pair. For example, would a player who scored in the assessments as more collectivistic take the collectivistic position in a conflict with a teammate assessed as less collectivistic? We use pseudonyms when presenting individual data from researcher observations, journal entries, and individualism-collectivism assssments.

The Issue of Cultural Essence

Note first that we are not assuming that a particular value system constitutes a cultural essence (cf., Miller & Prentice, 1999) for all members of a given ethnic group. Instead, we are measuring values on the individual level and relating these values to interactive behavior in specific conflict situations. To avoid stereotyping ethnic groups, we focused on differences in player values and in conflict behavior rather than on ethnic labels. The connection between ethnicity and values or between ethnicity and conflict behavior then became empirical questions. Thus, as a second stage in the analysis, we looked to see whether particular values and particular conflict behaviors are associated with particular ethnic groups.

Secondly, we are not assuming that a given score on the Individualism-Collectivism Scale will always be associated with the same type of behavior in a conflict situation. Instead, we see value conflicts as interactional constructions; the context provided by the other person in a particular conflict is crucial to the construction process. Thus, we look at the *relationship* between the individualism and collectivism scores of two parties, in order to understand the positions each has taken in a given conflict. In short, it is the *relationship* between the values of the two parties—value differences—that instigate the value conflict process.

We tested our hypothesis—that the most salient issues of conflict in a multiethnic group setting can be traced to differences in individualist and collectivist values—with a microanalysis of players' underlying values and their interactive behavior in several cases of observed team conflicts. We then related this behavior to individual assessments of collectivism and individualism; this was done in order to understand more fully the relationship between player values and interactional behavior.

Findings

Girls' Volleyball

The first case of conflict comes from the girls' volleyball team and shows how value differences can animate subtle interpersonal conflict. The heart of this conflict stems from a contrast between the individualistic emphasis on *self-esteem and the protection of self-esteem in front of others* (self-enhancement) versus the collectivistic emphasis on *promoting personal modesty* (self-deprecation).

First, we will highlight examples showing self-esteem and modesty as contrasting values. We will then demonstrate how each value system provides a lens for negatively evaluating behavior stemming from the other framework.

On this particular team, both of our individualism/collectivism assessments indicated that two players (Molly and Julia) were relatively more collectivistic and relatively less individualistic than another player (Arlene). These differences on our questionnaire measures were reflected in attitudes and behavior on the playing field. A member of our research team noted that when the more individualistic player, Arlene, made a good play, she looked at the coach for approval and praise; for example, she made a "kill" (a very desirable play in volleyball) and looked toward Coach Landford, who cheered. On the other hand, when she made a mistake, she was quick to explain the reasons and circumstances for the error. For example, Arlene and another player were talking when a ball came to them, and they missed it. Coach Landford said "You can talk later." Arlene replied with a reason for talking: "We're talking about approaches."

In contrast, when Molly, one of the more collectivistic players, made a good play and her teammates hi-fived and cheered, "Yay, Molly!" Molly hid her face in her shirt to hide a smile and pretended to wipe sweat. Also, when Molly made a mistake, she dropped her head down saying, "my fault." Whereas the more individualistic girl sought praise and shied away from blame, the more collectivistic girl sought modesty, shied away from praise, and was quick to assume personal responsibility for the error.

While promoting one's self-esteem is seen as beneficial from an individualistic perspective, this may be seen as undesirable egotism from a collectivistic perspective. On the other hand, while modesty and self-deference are seen as behavioral ideals in collectivistic societies, such behavior may be interpreted as a lack of self-assertion in individualistic societies. It is these negative interpretations of the positive values of the other framework that provides a potential for intergroup conflict and misunderstanding.

These contrasting approaches to accepting/deflecting praise and responsibility for error led to subtle forms of conflict and misunderstanding between the players. Molly, relatively collectivistic and the cocaptain of this volleyball team, wrote in her journal, "It gets me mad when I see Coach being easy on Arlene and sticks up for Arlene by saying 'It's okay, it wasn't your fault.'" (Arlene is the more individualistic player.) "Coach saying things like that just keeps Arlene playing the same way instead of trying to push herself to correct it." Molly is upset that Coach Landford deflects criticism from her more individualistic teammate rather than instigating a change in her teammate's skills.

The fact that Arlene, the individualist, deflects criticism from herself also upsets Julia, another player who scores as a relative collectivist. In her journal, Julia writes of Arlene, "She gets very defensive when you try and tell her something and she is always making excuses. I confronted her before about it and she said, 'There is always an excuse for everything.'" For her part, Arlene, the relative individualist, resents Julia's criticism, writing, "It pisses me off big time." Arlene also expresses love for the head coach ("I love her to death."), who was observed to protect her from criticism. On the other hand, Arlene expresses hatred for the assistant coach, because, she writes in her journal, "he always tells me that I don't even try or I need to try harder. " She dismisses this criticism as "complete bull*–?!."

As prior research has indicated (Greenfield & Suzuki, 1998), the individualistic goal of creating and maintaining self-esteem and presenting a strong image of self-esteem to others is linked to an emphasis on praise as a feedback mechanism. In this framework, admission of error may be considered a threat to one's self-esteem. However, Arlene's consistent defense of her own self-esteem is interpreted by Molly, in her journal, as "her big ego." This is because the collectivistic emphasis is on personal modesty. Associated with the positive value of modesty is the positive value of self-criticism and criticism by others. In this value framework, criticism of error is seen in a more benign light, as a feedback mode for improvement. This kind of conflict, rooted in deep-seated value differences, tends to go on and on without resolution because the players do not recognize the conflicting values.

Analysis of this case supports our hypothesized relationship between value frameworks and interactive behavior. Here we see the same behaviors—praise and criticism, self-defense, and self-blame—evaluated differently by different players. This differential evaluation leads to interpersonal tension and conflict because each party to the conflict takes her own perspective for granted: the journals indicate a complete lack of awareness of alternative value orientations, or even comprehension that values are at issue. We also found that the values expressed in the journals were corroborated by individual value assessments on two different measures, the Singelis et al. questionnaire and our scenario measure.

Additionally, the value frameworks represented by the positions taken in the conflict correspond with the expected ethnic groups: Arlene, the player who scored the most individualistically of the three, is Euramerican. Molly, the more collectivistic cocaptain, is the daughter of Korean immigrants and was raised in Korea and the United States. Julia, the other more collectivistic player, is a Latina immigrant. The head coach (also Euro-American) is liked by the Euro-American player because the coach deflects blame and is disliked by the collectivistic players for the same reason. The assistant coach (who is disliked by the individualistic, Euro-American player because he told her to try harder) is a Mexican immigrant.

Boys Basketball

The second case of team conflict comes from a multiethnic boys' basketball team and shows the conditions for aggressive conflict. A different source of conflict was salient for this team. It had a racial basis. The societal domination of basketball in the United States by African Americans was reflected in a racially-labeled hierarchy of players on this team. Although there was some conflict based on value differences in the dimensions of individualism and collectivism, these were subordinated to and structured by a racial divide.

Racially constructed dominance hierarchy. One theme that frequently arose on the boys' team concerned the relationship between African Americans and basketball. There was a feeling that the African American players felt they were the superior players and received preferential treatment by the coach. The perceived unequal status of the players on the team broke down Allport's conditions for the reduction of prejudice on the team and led to conflict and racial tension.

African American basketball superiority: The end of equal status team membership. The following journal excerpts show how a status hierarchy among the players on the team contributed to intergroup ill will. The first journal excerpt was written by Jay. He says of Stewart and Kenny, the two African American players on the team,

> Sometimes I feel Kenny and Stewart think they are special because they are black. They think being black makes them superior to everyone else and they are so wrong. I heard them make a comment that isn't it a coincidence that the two best players on the team are black. For 1, Kenny isn't even in the top 4 best players on the team and for 2, so what if they are black?

The journal entries on "Blackness" and playing ability were not limited to this comment. In fact, at least one member of every non-African American group commented on this fact. Erron, a Euro-American player, wrote,

> Nobody passed me the ball. It was almost as I didn't exist anymore. It was all because of Kenny. He figured since he is "black," and Stewart is "black," that only they should shoot the ball.

In this way, it appears that the players on the team sensed a hierarchy within the team. This hierarchy is in accord with Sidanius and Pratto's social dominance theory (e.g., Sidanius, 1993; Sidanius & Pratto, 1993); the African American players on the team were socially constructed as being of a higher status than the rest of the team members. This led to many instances of tension between team members.

Cooperative activity: In-group and out-group patterns. There is another condition recognized by Allport as favorable to good intergroup relations that is violated here: Working together cooperatively (see also Sherif & Sherif, 1953). We see in this example ("No one passed me the ball. It was almost as I didn't exist anymore.") that the fissioning of the team into a dominance hierarchy of racially defined subgroups was also manifest in the absence of cross-ethnic cooperative play.

At the top of the dominance hierarchy, Kenny and Stewart, the two African American players, were close friends and functioned as an "in-group." In an informal interview, Kenny told a researcher that Stewart was his "cousin," and that if anything happened to him, he would have to help out no matter what. This is an interesting statement, since it is probable that Kenny and Stewart are not related by blood. (Kenny had earlier stated that he had no relatives in Los Angeles except his mother and sister.) Kenny had created a symbolic kinship with Stewart that implicitly excludes "unrelated" others. This attitude was confirmed behaviorally: a researcher observed a situation where Kenny was fouled by an opposing player. After the play, the fouler pushed Kenny with his body. Stewart saw this and immediately walked up to the other player and glared at him, his body so close that it touched the body of the fouler.

Yet the dominant in-group was not simply defined along racial lines. According to a mother, Mrs. Rose, Joshua, another player, said he was Black in order to get the ball passed to him (in fact Joshua is Euro-American and Filipino). While the other members of the team were angry, the fact that Joshua seems to be the non-African American teammate that gets along the best with Stewart and Kenny indicates that, under some conditions, symbolic group identification is more important than "racial" group membership.

In line with Allport's conditions for positive intergroup relations, however, the functional in-group needed to be expanded to include the team as a whole. Indeed, a number of player journals noted that they were not functioning as a team. In fact, there was a suggestion in Kenny's journal that he wished he could expand his in-group to include the team as a whole. He wrote, "A team is supposed to be people you can go to. But my team is like being out on the streets." Here we see that Kenny longs for a team where people will help him, but instead, he feels that playing on the team provides no more help than being out on the streets.

Bearing in mind the ethnically defined ingroup symbolically constituted by the African American players, we can understand the connection between behavior, attitudes, and values in the individualism/collectivism conflict, to be presented next.

Individualism and collectivism: Team member as individual achiever or supporting player? In this particular case, interpersonal conflict, involving physical aggression between two players, was long-term. The conflict was repeated and escalated over a period of a month. There were two central characters in the conflict, Stewart, whom we have met previously, and Jay, who self-identifies as Costa Rican, French, and Mexican. It became evident from observer comments and journal entries that the conflicts between Jay and Stewart were ongoing. After a practice during which a member of our research team observed physical aggression on and off the court between Jay and Stewart, the researcher was invited to observe a peacekeeping meeting between the two players and the coach. The researcher made the following observation:

> The coach asks Stewart and Jay, who had exchanged apparently angry words . . . into his office after practice. The conflict was between Jay and Stewart over Jay's perception that Stewart was 1) overly aggressive on the court during practice, i.e., throwing elbows, pushing, grabbing were particularly mentioned; and 2) was far too vocally critical of the other players when they made mistakes. Specifically, Jay stated that Stewart was acting like a "punk" and that he was *"not supportive"* of the team. Jay stated that he really did not want to "play with someone who acted like that." Stewart's retort was that he probably would have fought with Jay if Jay had called him a punk off the court; that he *"didn't care" how anyone felt about his behavior during practice; and that it was how he "pumped himself up."* Stewart also stated that *the important thing was winning,* and the team needed to get "angrier" if they were to win. (Italics added by the researchers for emphasis.)

A few days later, Jay wrote in his journal, "It is clear that Stewart isn't going to lift his grudge that he has on me. That's fine with me as long as he knows that *he is hurting the team, not me."* (Italics added by the researchers for emphasis.)

This example shows a classic conflict between individualism and collectivism. The individualist values his own achievement, which bolsters self-esteem, and considers personal achievement to be his contribution to the group. Stewart reflects the individual player mentality: An individual player leads the other players in skills. Stewart voiced his needs as an individual achiever and his lack of concern for others' opinions of him. Stewart's comments in the meeting reflect his perspective that he had a responsibility to be the best he could. Stewart was very upset by Jay's criticisms and plainly did not understand Jay's position.

In contrast, the collectivist prefers to subjugate individual achievement in favor of supporting the others in the group in order to further the group's joint achievement. Jay presents the group player mentality: He voices the interests of the group and identifies more with team goals than with personal goals. Jay's main point was that Stewart did not play as a supportive team player. Jay was critical of how Stewart emphasized his own feelings and motivations, an attitude that Jay felt was neglecting the team's goals.

From this analysis of the conflict, we would expect Stewart's assessed value preferences to be more individualistic than Jay's, and this is the case for the Singelis et al. individualism measure. We would also expect Jay to be higher on collectivism, but, in fact, Stewart scores higher. We think this has something to do with the in-group/out-group structure just presented.

The data presented so far indicate that Stewart was probably thinking of his ethnic group (including family) rather than his team as his in-group. For example, on the Singelis et al. Likert-scale measure of collectivism, Stewart indicated the strongest possible agreement (a score of 9 out of a possible 9) with "I hate to disagree with others in my group." This makes sense if "group" refers to African Americans; it flies in the face of reality if "group" refers to the team. The only other "9" Stewart assigned for a collectivism item was "If a relative were in financial difficulty, I would help within my means." This item refers explicitly to family and excludes team as a relevant ingroup for this question. Hence, as these items show, by defining ingroup as African Americans, Stewart could logically score high on collectivism and yet act individualistically vis-a-vis the team. Hence, we see that behavioral expressions of individualism and collectivism are relative to particular definitions of in-group and out-group (Iyengar, Lepper, & Ross, 1999).

The relationship of this example to individualism and collectivism is further elucidated by Markus and Lin (1999):

> Conceptions of the self in African American contexts reflect mainstream models of the autonomous agentic self, but they also reflect interdependent understandings of group identity and belongingness. . . . This type of interdependence may be a legacy of African notions of personhood and/or a continuing legacy of involuntary immigration, slavery, discrimination, poverty, and minority status, or some combination of all of these. (pp. 324–325)

Under this analysis, it is not surprising that an African American player should be assessed both as more individualistic and more collectivistic than his partner in conflict.

This combination of individualism and collectivism is also seen in the African American approach to conflict (Markus & Lin, 1999). Markus and Lin write:

> In African American cultural contexts, the meaning of conflict may be simultaneously individual and relational . . . the participants in a conflict are often expected to formulate personal positions on an issue and present those positions as advocates. . . .

This style of conflict may reflect the cultural value placed on movement, expressive individualism, and affect in many African American contexts (Boykin & Toms, 1985). . . . One goal of conflict in African American contexts is to work toward resolving the problem that initially caused the disagreement by representing personal views in an impassioned confrontation. . . . By forcefully but credibly making a case for their own point of view, people engaged in African American contexts in conflict may persuade others of their position and thereby re-establish interpersonal harmony. (Markus & Lin, pp. 325–326)

This description applies extremely well to Stewart's behavior in the conflict described above: an impassioned confrontation in which he tries to persuade the others of a heartfelt case. The "Black mode," as Kochman (1981) calls it, "is often animated, interpersonal, emotional, and confrontational. In many African American cultural contexts, being animated or energetic is entirely appropriate in a dispute or conflict" (Markus & Lin, 1999, p. 222).

Leadership norms: Coach favoritism. Coach favoritism solidified the unofficial status hierarchy among the players, increasing the tension between ethnic groups. Allport's (1954/1958) theory of prejudice presented another element that he considered a secondary factor in reducing prejudice. He stated that the effect of equal status contact between groups in pursuit of common goals "is greatly enhanced if this contact is sanctioned by institutional supports (i.e., by law, custom or local atmosphere)" (Allport, 1958, p. 267). Considering coach leadership as the most immediate institutional support, we found that perceived coach favoritism implicitly undermined equal status contact among players.

The following examples show that some players and at least one parent claimed that the coaches gave preferential treatment to the African Americans. Players felt that the coaches, who were Euramerican, treated the African American players with a different standard, allowing them to miss more practices and have more playing time in games.

Alvin, an Asian-American team captain, wrote,

Every year since my freshman year I've had to work my butt off for playing time. . . . Maybe every player feels like that, but I think I've really had to work harder than others have had to. Sometimes maybe because I'm too short or not fast enough or whatever, but I felt that a few times it was because I wasn't black. Not to be racial or anything, because I love all the guys, but people have told me that one of my past coaches was biased toward the black guys and the people who told me this are very qualified people.

In this excerpt, Alvin alluded to the fact that even coaches tend to favor African American players over others. Alvin's perceptions that the coaches were biased in favor of the African American players was echoed by other non-African American players as well. This idea was echoed by at least one parent.

In contrast, Kenny's perspective on his relationship with the coach showed that he was deeply grateful for the coach's attention. At the end of the season, the coach tragically died. In a moving eulogy at his funeral, Kenny acknowledged the special off-court help the coach had given to him. The other African American player, Stewart, was reported to be disappointed that there would be no one else to help him find college scholarships.

Racism. The intergroup conflict that developed from unequal status among the players also erupted into racial tension. While the previous journal excerpts described the feelings surrounding a status differential, the following excerpts address perceived racism by the African American players. Player Greg noted the following in his journal:

> Stewart got pissed off at Penn because Penn said something very stupid. He said "these people . . ." then Stewart said "What do you mean these People, are you talking about Black People." Then Penn said, "No just you and Kenny." Stewart and Kenny are the only two Black people on the team. This was the first time that the race card has been dealt during a practice.

Here we see clear racial tension between the African American players and Penn, whose mother is Euro-American and whose father is Samoan. From the African American perspective, Penn's comment was racist and highly inappropriate. It is interesting, however, to learn more about other players' reactions to this situation. Alvin, an Asian-American, witnesses this incident and writes in his journal,

> I guess Stewart took it as a racist comment, since coincidentally, Kenny and Stewart are the only 2 African Americans on the team. I think Stewart was in a bad mood, and that's why he took it so personal. I had noticed earlier during the play run-throughs that Stewart looked a little irritated for some reason and I guess Penn's comment was misinterpreted by him.

While many of the non-African Americans did not perceive Penn's "these people" comment as racist, Kenny and Stewart obviously did. Very clearly, there are two perspectives in conflict, producing intergroup tension.

Summary

An important point is that values that each person brings into an interaction strongly influence the nature of disagreement or conflict. Importantly, it is value *differences* that shape the nature of disagreements and the positions of each participant in the disagreement.

These teams' experiences of conflict and misunderstanding reflect the misunderstandings that occur in society as a whole. The different perspectives that were heard by means of our multivocal methodology provide us with solid evidence of the players' perceptions of intergroup and interpersonal issues in their own words. This allows us to provide a more in-depth and objective interpretation of what people are really thinking about each other. Our method of multivocal ethnography has been successful in revealing different cultural voices in situations of interpersonal conflict.

First, we identified misunderstandings that occur due to differences between an individualistic and a collectivistic value system. These value conflicts, of which a sample has been presented in this chapter, were at the center of the problems experienced by the girls' volleyball team. Although they were not central to the boys' basketball team, they were also present.

Second, we were able to measure individualism and collectivism in each individual, and, using these scores, were successful in most cases in postdicting the roles and interpretations players had taken in real-world misunderstandings and conflicts. Where scores did not relate to behavior and attitudes on the playing field, it was because the collectivity specified in the instrument or assumed by the respondent was their family or ethnic group rather than their team. In such a case, collectivism assessed on the questionnaire did not match behavior and attitudes vis-a-vis the player's team. An important theoretical and methodological point is that the operational measurement of collectivism must include specification of a particular collectivity with which the respondent identifies (cf. Iyengar, Lepper, and Ross, 1999).

Third, on the boys' basketball team only, we found attitudes of racial superiority supported by perceived Black favoritism on the part of the coach. In line with the theoretical formulation of Gaertner, Dovidio, Nier, Ward, and Banker (1999), these conditions led to a fissioning of the team into a racially and culturally defined dominance hierarchy, with African Americans at the center of the top group. Also in line with Gaertner and his colleagues' model, the fissioned groups were associated with perceived racism and physical aggression. Note that this dominance hierarchy was specific to the basketball court and does not necessarily reflect the dominance hierarchy of ethnic groups in society as a whole.

In conclusion, as this team actually functioned, it did *not* contain the prerequisites for good intergroup relations delineated by Allport (1954/1958):

All members were *not* perceived as having equal status and working together for a common goal. Moreover, higher and lower status were identified with ethnic group membership. These are just the conditions that social psychology has shown to be *unfavorable* to positive intergroup relations. In line with this theoretical formulation, this team had the worst intergroup relations of all eight teams studied: it was the only one in which physical aggression became an issue and the only one in which racist remarks were noted. Thus, we see that theoretical definitions concerning the nature of a team and how it functions must be supported by internal dynamics. Otherwise, the potential of multiethnic sports teams to create positive intergroup relations will be squandered.

Notes

We are indebted to our research team: Blanca Quiroz, NanaEfua Baidoo, Nattu Coleman, German Hercules, Adrienne Isaac, Cacilia Kim, Kiahnna Patton, Alissa Taylor, Dawn Vo, and Nicole Weekes. We very much appreciate the participation of the teams and coaches who participated in our research. Finally, we acknowledge the generous support of the Carnegie Corporation of New York and the Russell Sage Foundation. The statements made and views expressed are solely the views of the authors.

1. For our purposes, we did not use the authors' horizontal/vertical dimension.

References

Allport, G. (1954/1958). *The nature of prejudice.* Palo Alto, CA: Addison-Wesley, 1954 (abridged version published by Doubleday Anchor in 1958).

Boutakidis, I. P., Davis, H., Suzuki, L. K., Greenfield, P. M., & Baidoo, N. (1997, June). *Cultural sources of intergroup conflict: Collectivism vs. individualism.* Poster presented at the 27th annual symposium of the Jean Piaget Society, Santa Monica, CA.

Boykin, A. W. & Toms, F. D. (1985). Black child socialization: A conceptual framework. In H. P. McAdoo & J. L. McAdoo (Eds.), *Black children: Social, educational, and parental environments* (pp. 33–52). Beverly Hills, CA: Sage.

Gaertner, S. L., Dovidio, J. F., Nier, J. A., Ward, C. M., & Banker, B. S. (1999). Across cultural divides: The value of a superordinate identity. In D. A. Prentice & D. T. Miller (Eds.), *Cultural divides: Understanding and overcoming group conflict* (pp. 173–212). NY: Russell Sage.

Greenfield, P. M. & Cocking, R.R. (Eds.) (1994). *Cross-cultural roots of minority child development.* Hillsdale, NJ: Erlbaum.

Greenfield, P. M., & Suzuki, L. K. (1998). Culture and human development: Implications for parenting, education, pediatrics, and mental health. In W. Damon, I. E. Sigel & K. A. Renninger (Eds.), *Handbook of child psychology* (5th ed.). *Child Psychology in Practice* (Vol. 4) (pp. 1059–1077). New York: Wiley.

Iyengar, S. S.. Lepper, M. R., & Ross, L. (1999). Independence from whom? Interdependence with whom? Cultural perspectives on ingroups versus outgroups. In D. A. Prentice & D. T. Miller (Eds.), *Cultural divides: Understanding and overcoming group conflict* (pp. 273–301). NY: Russell Sage.

Kitayama, S., Markus, H. R., Matsumoto, H, & Norasakkunkit, V. (1997). Individual and collective processes in the construction of the self: Self-enhancement in the United States and self-criticism in Japan. *Journal of Personality and Social Psychology, 72,* 1245–1267.

Kochman, T. (1981). *Black and white styles in conflict.* Chicago: University of Chicago Press.

Markus, H. R., & Kitayama, S. (1991). Culture and the self: Implications for cognition, emotion, and motivation. *Psychological Review, 98,* 224–253.

Markus, H. R. & Lin, L. R. (1999). Conflictways: Cultural diversity in the meanings and practices of conflict. In D. A. Prentice & D. T. Miller (Eds.), *Cultural divides: Understanding and overcoming group conflict* (pp. 302–333). NY: Russell Sage.

Miller, D. T. & Prentice, D. A. (1999). Some consequences of a belief in group essence: The category divide hypothesis. In D. A. Prentice & D. T. Miller (Eds.), *Cultural divides: Understanding and overcoming group conflict* (pp. 213-238). NY: Russell Sage.

Raeff, C., Greenfield, P. M., & Quiroz, B. (2000). Conceptualizing interpersonal relationships in the cultural contexts of individualism and collectivism. In S. Harkness, C. Raeff, & C. M. Super (Eds.), *Variability in the social construction of the child, New Directions for Child and Adolescent Development, 87,* 59–74. San Francisco: Jossey-Bass.

Sherif, M., & Sherif, C. W. (1953). *Groups in harmony and tension.* New York: Harper and Row.

Sidanius, J. (1993). The psychology of group conflict and the dynamics of oppression: A social dominance perspective. In S. Iyegnar & W. McGuire (Eds.), *Explorations in political psychology* (pp. 183–219). Durham, NC: Duke University Press.

Sidanius, J., Levin, S., Rabinowitz, J. L., & Federico, C. M. (1999). Peering into the jaws of the beast: The integrative dynamics of social identity, symbolic racism, and social dominance. In D. A. Prentice & D. T. Miller (Eds.), *Cultural divides: Understanding and overcoming group conflict* (pp. 80–132). NY: Russell Sage.

Sidanius, J., & Pratto, F. (1993). The inevitability of oppression and the dynamics of social dominance. In P. Sniderman & P. Tetlock (Eds.), *Prejudice, politics, and the American dilemma* (pp. 173–211). Stanford, CA: Stanford University Press.

Singelis, T. M., Triandis, H. C., Bhawuk, D.P.S., & Gelfand, M. J. (1995). Horizontal and vertical dimensions of individualism and collectivism: A theoretical and measurement refinement. *Cross-Cultural Research, 29,* 240–275.

TEN

Athletic Identity, Racial Attitudes, and Aggression in First-Year Black and White Intercollegiate Athletes

JAMES S. JACKSON, SHELLEY KEIPER, KENDRICK T. BROWN,
TONY N. BROWN, AND WARDE MANUEL

Our study uses questionnaire responses from first year collegiate athletes to explore potential relationships among athletic identity, racial identity, interracial contact, and interpersonal aggression. A significant number of college students are influenced through their direct participation in intercollegiate athletics. Whether by forging self-identities as athletes (MacClancy, 1996); interacting with and working toward mutual goals with teammates of different racial or ethnic backgrounds (Hanrahan & Gallois, 1993; Widmeyer, Carron, & Brawley, 1993); or competing against opponents, the athletic arena is one in which participating students come to develop normative attitudes, beliefs, and behaviors in a wide range of social areas (MacClancy, 1996). This chapter examines empirically how the backgrounds and prior experiences of first-year Black and White, male and female, scholarship athletes are related to the nature of their athletic and racial identities, their interracial attitudes and contacts, their perceived interpersonal aggression both on the field, and the nature of beliefs about their interpersonal relationships.

The Intersection of Athletic and Racial Identities

Students' perceptions of themselves and of society are heavily influenced by their athletic and racial identities. White and African American student-athletes' sense of racial identity may be minimized or overshadowed by

159

their athletic identity. Because winning on any sports team depends upon cooperation and cohesion among members of the team (Carron, 1982; Widmeyer, Carron, & Brawley, 1993; Williams & Widmeyer, 1991), coaches and advisors seek to downplay intergroup differences and diversity. Distinctions between sports team members based upon students' racial centrality, or sense of belonging to their racial group, may hinder such cohesion and interfere with the superordinate goals of the team. Consequently, the competing nature of athletic and racial group social identities may have an influence upon how students react to and perceive racial discrimination in the larger society. Because their racial identities are strongly socialized to be preempted by their athletic identities, issues of race and racial discrimination may be less salient to college athletes. The positive and equal interracial contact experienced on the playing field may minimize issues of race and racial discrimination that would ordinarily be of more concern to members of student-athletes' respective racial groups.

The Influence of Interracial Contact

Interracial contact on the playing field may play a large role in affecting student-athletes' racial attitudes. Based upon one of the basic tenets of the intergroup contact hypothesis (Pettigrew, 1998), we hypothesized that socially sanctioned, proximate, and cooperative interaction on an equalized basis between members of different, hierarchically defined racial groups may be one of the key mechanisms in minimizing prejudice among ethnically and racially different athletic team members. The athletic arena is a domain that requires positive group-based interactions in order for team members to experience success, and in fact is one of the few realms in which all of the essential conditions for reducing prejudice are met (Allport, 1954; Pettigrew, 1998). Specifically, the contact occurs between individuals with equalized status in the situation, the contact entails purposeful activity toward common goals fostering interdependence, the contact is cooperative, and the contact is socially sanctioned. Student-athletes train and practice with members of other racial and ethnic groups and are dependent upon them for personal and team success. This interdependence emphasizes norms of cooperation and fair play that would be undermined by racial and ethnic antagonisms. Athletes are socialized to see beyond race and color; they are instructed instead to see only opponents and teammates.

Interpersonal Aggression On and Off the Playing Field

Although cooperative interracial contact and the predominance of athletic identity over racial identity may decrease the likelihood of racial and ethnic conflicts, the potential for discord on and off the playing field remains a reality (Eitzen, 1993). One additional domain in which it is important to assess the development of students' normative behaviors is by evaluating the nature of their interactions with those with whom they share close personal relationships. One recurring theme in the relationships of athletes, both with teammates and with romantic partners, is aggression or violence (Thirer, 1993). A number of both scholarly publications and popular media have explored the idea that sports provide a relatively healthy outlet for natural male aggression (Melnick, 1992; Messner, 1992; Messner & Sabo, 1994; Toufexis, 1990). Apparently, however, men are not alone in behaving in an aggressive manner; women too have been found to participate in violence against their partners (Riggs, O'Leary, & Breslin, 1990). Thus, it is important to assess the link between sports and aggression on and off the field, for both genders. Aggression in either direction on the playing field (either toward others, or from others) may be related to aggression in close personal relationships. Aggression on the field toward others may contribute to aggressiveness off the field, including aggressiveness toward a romantic partner. If a student-athlete receives aggression from others on the field, perhaps they seek control in their personal lives by displaying aggression toward their significant others. These behaviors may manifest themselves in spite of professed norms about interpersonal interactions that are contrary to these actions.

The Empirical Study

We explored many of the potential social contributors to athletic identity, racial attitudes, and beliefs about athletic and interpersonal aggression in student-athletes by surveying all incoming (freshman) intercollegiate athletes on full and partial scholarships at twenty-four universities and colleges in the United States. The project was funded through the National Collegiate Athletic Association (NCAA). Student-athletes completed the Progress in College/Social and Group Experiences (PIC-SAGE) questionnaire that focused on academic skills, academic attitudes and achievement orientations, and social and group experiences before college and during the first year. Cooperation among the athletes was very positive, since athletic counselors at the respective universities and colleges administered the questionnaire in groups during mandatory skills assessment sessions.

The sample size for the 1996 PIC-SAGE was 533. About 0.6% of the sample respondents were Asian-American, 4.0% were Latino/Hispanic Americans, 75.3% were White/Caucasian, 18.3% were Black/African American, and 2% were self-identified as Other. The remaining 6.6% of student-athletes had missing data on racial status. Sample sizes were not adequate within each of these categories for statistical analysis by each group; therefore the analyses were limited to those student-athletes who self-identified as White/Caucasian or Black/African American. Men constituted 54.8% of the sample. There was little variation in age and education because the respondents were college freshmen surveyed near the beginning of their first year of college. A wide range of sports for both men and women were represented.

Empirical Results

Athletic Identity

In light of the fact that high athletic identity tends to somewhat diminish the strength of one's racial identity, we anticipated that student-athletes with high athletic identity would be less likely to have a high racial centrality or identity and would be more likely to perceive that racial discrimination is no longer a problem in the United States, than would students with low athletic identity. Despite the effects of high athletic identity, however, we also expected that White student-athletes would be more likely than Black/African American student-athletes to state that racial discrimination is no longer a problem in the United States.

Athletic identity was measured using a subset of items from the Athletic Identity Measurement Scale (AIMS) developed by Brewer, Van Raalte, and Lander (1993). A scale encompassing the extent to which the respondent agreed that "my main sport is the most important thing in my life," "I spend more time thinking about my sport than anything else," "other people see me mainly as an athlete," "I need to participate in sports to feel good about myself," and "I would be very depressed if I were injured and could not compete in my sport" was constructed. For each item, higher scores on the 6-point scale equaled higher levels of athletic identity. A measure of internal consistency, the coefficient alpha for the reliability of additive items for the entire sample was .75, for White student-athletes it was equal to .75, and for African American student-athletes it was equal to .69. The arithmetic mean of the five items was used in the subsequent analyses.

The centrality of racial identity was assessed by a single item: "In general belonging to my ethnic or racial group is an important part of my self-image." Higher scores on the scale corresponded to higher racial centrality. Student-athletes were also asked the degree to which they agreed or disagreed with the following statement: "Discrimination against people of different racial or ethnic groups is no longer a problem in the United States." This measure was used to operationalize the perception that racial discrimination has real-life consequences for racial and ethnic groups in the

United States. Higher scores on the scale indicated less of a tendency to perceive discrimination. Demographic background variables included parents' education, importance of religious beliefs, sport classification (whether on the first team in terms of playing time or position on the roster), and experience of racial conflict. The latter was assessed by a single question, "Have you ever been involved in any conflicts involving someone of a different race or ethnic group?"

Table 10.1 shows descriptive statistics for the major athletic identity and demographic background variables by racial status and gender. Overall, levels of parental education were fairly similar for all the athlete groups and Black male and female athletes attached more importance to religious beliefs. Female and White male athletes were more likely to report being on the first teams in their respective sports, a finding that may reflect the larger concentration of Black athletes in football. All athletes generally believed that racial discrimination was still a problem in the United States. Both Black and White female first-year athletes, however, felt more strongly than male athletes that discrimination was still a problem. Black athletes attached greater importance to racial group membership than did White athletes, while the reverse was true for athletic identity. Finally, both Black male and female athletes reported experiencing more racial conflict (about 50%) than did either White male (29%) or female (22%) athletes.

It was hypothesized that student-athletes with higher athletic identities would be less likely to perceive race as central to their own identities, and less likely to perceive racial discrimination. In White male student-athletes, those with higher athletic identity were more likely to identify with their racial group r (181) = .27, p < .01, while for African American male student-athletes, those with higher athletic identity were less likely to identify with their racial group r (67) = −.28, p < .05. Higher athletic identity was not significantly related to the tendency to perceive racial discrimination for either White male student-athletes r (181) = .06 or for African American male student-athletes r (67) = .24. For White female student-athletes there were no significant relationships between athletic identity and either racial identification r (190) = .08 or the tendency to perceive racial discrimination r (190) = .04. There were also no significant relationships for African American female student-athletes between athletic identity and either racial identification r (19) = .25 or the tendency to perceive discrimination r (19) = .21.

Thus, African American male student-athletes with high athletic identities were less likely to say that membership in their racial group was an important part of their self-image, consistent with the hypothesis; but White male student-athletes with high athletic identity were more likely to say that membership in their racial group was an important part of their

Table 10.1
Distribution of Athletic Identity Variables by Race and Gender

	Black/ African American Male (N = 69)	Black/ African American Female (N = 22)	White/ Caucasian Male (N = 183)	White/ Caucasian Female (N = 192)
	Mean (Std Dev)	Mean (Std Dev)	Mean (Std Dev)	Mean (Std Dev)
Athletic Identity Measurement Scale (1 = low, 6 = high)	3.64 (1.11)	3.35 (.91)	3.88 (1.11)	3.78 (.98)
Importance of racial group (1 = strongly disagree, 6 = strongly agree)	4.24 (1.59)	4.55 (1.74)	3.10 (1.49)	2.94 (1.67)
Discrimination no longer a problem (1 = strongly disagree, 6 = strongly agree)	2.07 (1.30)	1.23 (.87)	2.21 (1.28)	1.82 (1.04)
Parents' highest level of education (1 = junior high school or less, 8 = doctoral)	4.41 (1.59)	4.53 (1.41)	4.83 (1.25)	5.03 (1.48)
Sport classification (% on first team)	24.6%	59.1%	43.7%	60.9%
Racial conflict (% ever involved)	50.7%	50.0%	29.0%	21.9%
Importance of religious beliefs (1 = not import, 6 = of great importance)	4.79 (1.44)	5.10 (1.22)	4.08 (1.54)	4.01 (1.53)

self-image. There was no relationship between athletic identity and the tendency to perceive racial discrimination among any of the student-athletes in the sample.

Racial Attitudes

As discussed earlier, because the athletic arena is a domain that may satisfy the essential conditions for reducing prejudice, we anticipated that White student-athletes who have had contact with African Americans on their high school sports teams would be more likely than those who have not to display reduced prejudicial attitudes and increased policy support and positive affect towards African Americans.

There were four measures of racial outcomes. The first assessed the student-athletes' level of contemporary prejudice. A scale was constructed encompassing the extent to which the respondent agreed that "people of different races and ethnic groups can never really be comfortable with each other even if they are close friends," that "discrimination against people of different races and ethnic groups is no longer a problem in the United States," and that "over the past few years, members of racial and ethnic groups other than my own have gotten more than they deserve." Higher scores on the scale equaled greater contemporary prejudice. The index had a coefficient alpha of .62.

The second outcome assessed a dimension of social distance that can often be associated with traditional prejudice (Pettigrew, 1998). Respondents indicated their agreement with the statement that "I would be willing to date a person of a different race or ethnicity than me." Higher scores corresponded to greater willingness on the scale.

The third outcome focused on racial policy support. The policy item measured the extent to which respondents agreed that "the government should make every effort to improve the social and economic position of Blacks/African Americans living in the United States." Higher scores equaled greater endorsement on a 6-point scale.

The fourth variable is affect toward African Americans as a group. The affect dimension employed a feeling thermometer, with Blacks/African Americans as the target group, ranging from 0 representing "extremely cool" to 100 for "extremely warm."

The independent measure of interest was contact with African American teammates during high school. Contact was assessed by an item asking, "Including yourself, what percentage of people on your main high school athletic team were from each of the following groups?" We used the percentage for Black/African American teammates.

In addition to the independent measure, we utilized a number of other background measures to help interpret the relationship between contact and race-related outcomes. These included the estimated percentage of the athlete's parents' close friends of a different racial group, estimated percentage of Black/African American neighbors during most of the athlete's high school years, and estimated percentage of Black/African American students in the student-athlete's high school.

Table 10.2 shows descriptive statistics for the major variables by racial status and gender. While we hypothesized that contact between African Americans and Whites would affect the latter's racial attitudes, we also believed that Whites would report lower rates of cross-racial contact.

Table 10.2
Distribution of Racial Attitude Variables by Race and Gender

	Black/ African American Male (N = 69)	Black/ African American Female (N = 22)	White/ Caucasian Male (N = 183)	White/ Caucasian Female (N = 192)
	Mean (Std Dev)	Mean (Std Dev)	Mean (Std Dev)	Mean (Std Dev)
Contemporary prejudice index (1 = low, 6 = high)	2.40 (1.21)	1.89 (.97)	2.47 (.95)	1.85 (.74)
Willing to date person of different race/ethnicity (1 = strongly disagree, 6 = strongly agree)	4.09 (1.65)	4.00 (1.60)	3.53 (1.68)	3.84 (1.88)
Government should help Blacks (1 = strongly disagree, 6 = strongly agree)	5.21 (1.02)	5.50 (.91)	3.93 (1.46)	4.28 (1.34)
Feeling thermometer for Blacks (0 = very cool, 100 = very warm)	88.76 (18.96)	88.74 (16.34)	65.97 (22.99)	73.51 (20.72)
% Black athletes on main high school team	46.74 (35.80)	48.62 (38.93)	10.99 (18.87)	3.78 (10.62)
% Parents' close friends of different race/ethnicity	13.21 (16.33)	31.26 (26.44)	6.73 (11.50)	6.29 (10.86)
% Black neighbors during high school years	52.20 (33.58)	52.76 (34.69)	7.41 (11.29)	8.78 (13.24)
% Blacks in high school	35.17 (30.98)	36.38 (32.18)	12.75 (14.87)	11.89 (12.75)

As shown in table 10.2, White student-athletes report relatively low rates of contact for their parents' close friends of a different race, Black neighbors, and Black athletes on their main high school team. On average, both male and female White athletes were less likely than Black athletes, to be willing to date others of a different race, had higher prejudice scores, had less positive affect toward Blacks, and were less willing to agree that government should help Blacks.

It was hypothesized that greater contact by White student-athletes with African American student-athletes during high school would be related to less prejudice, more support for public policies, and more positive affect toward African Americans. Greater numbers of close friends of different races on the part of their parents was related to a greater willingness to date people of different races for both White males r (181) = .22, p < .01 and White females r (190) = .18, p < .05. Additionally, more parents' close friends of different races was related to more positive affect towards African Americans for White males r (181) = .25, p < .01, and was also related to higher levels of racial policy support for White females r (190) = .20, p < .01. Finally, greater numbers of African American student-athletes on their high school teams was also related to more positive affect toward African Americans for White males r (181) = .25, p < .01. Thus, greater contact by White student-athletes with African American student-athletes during high school was related to more positive affect toward African Americans. Other contact (e.g., with parents' close friends of different races) was related to a greater willingness to date African Americans, and higher levels of racial policy support and more positive affect toward African Americans.

Aggression

Because aggression on the playing field is related to aggression and norms regarding appropriate behavior in student-athletes' other close personal relationships, we anticipated that on-the-field aggression would be related to verbal/mental and physical abuse in romantic relationships.

The two main variables were based on responses to the following hypothetical situation: "If I were having a major fight or disagreement with the person I was in a serious relationship with, I would. . . ." Student-athletes were given a modified version of the Conflict Tactics Scale (Straus, Hamby, Boney-McCoy, & Sugerman, 1996). These variables factored into verbal/mental disrespect and physical mistreatment. The verbal/mental factor consisted of four items: insult or swear at my partner, stomp out of the room or house or yard, threaten to leave my partner, and shout or yell at my partner. A physical mistreatment scale was created using three of the remaining five items: grab my partner, push or shove my partner, and slap my partner. The coefficient alpha for the reliability of the verbal/mental disrespect scale was .78 and the reliability for the physical mistreatment scale was .79.

Other measures of interest were a relationship commitment scale, which assessed willingness to work out problems in a relationship, and the normative gender roles beliefs scale. Five items assessed student-athletes' sense of gender role equality: "both men and women should share equally in childcare and housework," "most women would not mind if a qualified woman was appointed as their boss," "both men's and women's collegiate athletic teams should receive the same amount of financial support," "after I leave college, I would not mind if a qualified woman was appointed as my boss," and "both men and women should have jobs to support the family," were summed into a composite measure. The coefficient alpha for the reliability of the normative gender roles beliefs scale was .73.

There were two additional variables. One was aggression toward others consisting of four items: "I have insulted or sworn at a member of my team while playing in a sporting event," "I have insulted or sworn at a member of another team while playing in a sporting event," "I have pushed or shoved a member of my team while playing in a sporting event," and "I have pushed or shoved a member of another team while playing in a sporting event." The second was aggression toward you, consisting of two items: "I have been insulted or sworn at by a member of my team while playing in a sporting event," and "I have been pushed or shoved by a member of my team while playing in a sporting event."

Finally, background variables included dating and participation in a contact sport. Participants were asked whether they were involved in a serious dating relationship. Football, men's and women's basketball, men's and women's soccer, wrestling, field hockey, and lacrosse were classified as contact sports; all others were considered noncontact.

Table 10.3 shows descriptive statistics for the major variables by racial status and gender. Men reported higher levels of aggression on the field than did women, both that they directed toward others, and that was directed toward them. Women, on the other hand, were more likely to report engaging in verbal and physical abuse directed toward their dating partners than were men. However, women also reported higher levels of commitment to working out relationship problems, and more egalitarian gender attitudes, than did men.

It was hypothesized that student-athletes who are more involved in aggression on the field would also be more likely to display aggression in their personal relationships off the field. In White male student-athletes, aggression directed toward others on the field was related to attitudes about verbal aggression in relationships r (181) = .25, $p < .01$, and aggression received from others on the field was related to attitudes about physical aggression in relationships r (181) = .16, $p < .05$. In White female student-athletes, aggression directed toward others on the field was related to attitudes about verbal aggression in relationships r (190) = .35, $p < .01$ and to attitudes about physical aggression in relationships r (190) = .39, $p < .01$. Also in White female student-athletes, aggression received from oth-

Table 10.3
Distribution of Aggression Variables by Race and Gender

	Black/ African American Male (N = 69)	Black/ African American Female (N = 22)	White/ Caucasian Male (N = 183)	White/ Caucasian Female (N = 192)
	Mean (Std Dev)	Mean (Std Dev)	Mean (Std Dev)	Mean (Std Dev)
Attitudes about relationships (verbal/mental disrespect) (1 = would not do this, 6 = would do this)	2.45 (.99)	3.10 (1.40)	2.45 (1.03)	2.79 (1.19)
Attitudes about relationships (physical mistreatment) (1 = would not do this, 6 = would do this)	1.57 (1.02)	1.86 (1.01)	1.38 (.69)	1.51 (.73)
Attitudes about relationships (commitment) (1 = would not do this, 6 = would do this)	4.72 (1.19)	4.83 (1.05)	4.91 (.84)	5.02 (.81)
Attitudes about gender roles (1 = strongly disagree, 6 = strongly agree)	4.55 (1.06)	5.42 (.61)	4.39 (.84)	5.31 (.63)
Active dating (% yes)	50.7%	40.9%	35.5%	36.5%
Participate in contact sport (% yes)	75.4%	40.9%	49.2%	39.6%
Aggression toward others on field (1 = never, 6 = usually)	2.96 (1.22)	2.25 (1.20)	2.69 (1.16)	2.03 (1.01)
Aggression toward you on field (1 = never, 6 = usually)	2.60 (1.34)	2.43 (1.49)	2.34 (1.15)	1.92 (1.03)

ers on the field was related to attitudes about verbal aggression in relationships $r(190) = .26$, $p < .01$, to attitudes about physical aggression in relationships $r(190) = .33$, $p < .01$, and to less egalitarian attitudes about gender roles $r(190) = -.16$, $p < .05$. For African American male student-athletes, however, there were no significant relationships between aggression on the field and attitudes toward verbal and physical aggression in relationships, and attitudes about gender roles $-.19 < rs(67) < .10$. There were also no significant relationships for African American female student-athletes between aggression on the field and attitudes toward verbal and physical aggression in relationships, and attitudes about gender roles –.01 < rs (19) < .30. Finally, participation in a contact sport was related to aggression on the field but not to attitudes toward abuse in personal relationships for either White or African American athletes. Thus, among White student-athletes, aggression on the field was related to aggression in their personal relationships off the field, but among African American student-athletes aggression on the field was not related to aggression in their personal relationships off the field.

Summary

These data provide a unique look at the attitudes, beliefs, and social behaviors of first-year intercollegiate athletes. The first wave of this longitudinal study provided us with an unprecedented opportunity to empirically assess student-athletes' backgrounds and current experiences, and how these influences are related to their development. Overall the results of these analyses indicate that prior background factors exert considerable influence on current racial attitudes, race policy positions, gender role beliefs, interpersonal aggression attitudes, and athletic identity. Some support was found for our hypothesized importance of athletic identity in decreasing the role of racial identity among African American students. It appears that social role identities may be subsumed to the development of a common athletic identity. If so, we would expect that this relationship should become even stronger as student-athletes progress through their academic programs. Similarly, we found support that prior racial contact on the playing field, neighborhood, and among parents, is related to more current positive policy attitudes by White students toward African Americans. Again, we would expect that these relationships should strengthen over time. Finally, among White but not African American student-athletes, we found that aggression on the field, both received and directed toward others, is related to reporting oneself more likely to use aggression in personal relationships.

In sum, these initial findings on first-year students suggests that in addition to academic preparation, a number of social and psychological factors may contribute to the nature of the interpersonal and social experiences of intercollegiate athletes. Among these are students' previous racial contact, racial attitudes, gender norms, and, athletic and racial identities. Students' high school experiences, which differ by race and gender, seem to play a large role in the development of attitudes, beliefs, and normative behaviors among these first-year Black and White student-athletes. Consequently, understanding the evolution of these attitudes, normative beliefs, and identity development in college, may permit a better understanding of how student-athletes participate in, and adjust to, their college, and subsequent, life experiences.

References

Allport, G. (1954). *The nature of prejudice.* New York: Anchor.

Brewer, B. W., Van Raalte, J. L., & Lander, D. E. (1993). Athletic identity: Hercules' achilles heel? *International Journal of Sport Psychology, 24* (2), 237–254.

Carron, A. V. (1982). Cohesiveness in sport groups: Interpretations and considerations. *Journal of Sport Psychology, 4,* 123–138.

Eitzen, D. S. (1993). Racism in college sports: Prospects for the year 2000. In D. Brooks & R. Althouse (Eds.), *Racism in college athletics: The African American athletic's experience* (pp. 269–285). Morgantown, WV: Fitness Information Technology.

Hanrahan, S., & Gallois, C. (1993). Social interactions. In R. N. Singer, M. Murphy, & L. K. Tennant (Eds.), *Handbook of Research on Sport Psychology* (pp. 623–646). New York: Macmillan.

MacClancy, J. (1996). Sport, identity and ethnicity. In J. MacClancy (Ed.), *Sport, identity and ethnicity* (pp. 1–20). London: Oxford International.

Melnick, M. (1992). Male athletes and sexual assault. *Journal of Physical Education, Recreation, and Dance, 63* (5), 32–55.

Messner, M. (1992). *Power at play: sports and the problems of masculinity.* Boston: Beacon.

Messner, M., & Sabo, D. (1994). *Sex, violence, and power in sports: Rethinking masculinity.* Freedom, CA: Crossing.

Murrell, A. J., & Gaertner, S. (1992). Cohesion and sport team effectiveness: The benefit of a common in-group identification. *Journal of Sport and Social Issues, 16,* 1–14.

Pettigrew, T. F. (1998). Intergroup contact theory. *Annual Review of Psychology, 49,* 63–85.

Riggs, D. S., O'Leary, K., & Breslin, F. C. (1990). Multiple correlates of physical aggression in dating couples. *Journal of Interpersonal Violence, 5,* 61–73.

Straus, M. A., Hamby, S. L., Boney-McCoy, S., & Sugerman, D. B. (1996). The revised Conflict Tactics Scales (CTS2): Development and preliminary psychometric data. *Journal of Family Issues, 17,* 283–316.

Thirer, J. (1993). Aggression. In R. N. Singer, M. Murphy, & L. K. Tennant (Eds.), *Handbook of Research on Sport Psychology* (pp. 365–378). New York: Macmillan.

Toufexis, A. (1990, August 6). Sex in the sporting life: Do athletic teams unwittingly promote assaults and rapes? *Time*, 76–77.

Widmeyer, W. N., Carron, A. V., & Brawley, L. R. (1993). Group cohesion in sport and exercise. In R. N. Singer, M. Murphy, & L. K. Tennant (Eds.), *Handbook of Research on Sport Psychology* (pp. 672–691). New York: Macmillan.

Williams, J., & Widmeyer, W. N. (1991). The cohesion-performance outcome relationship in a coacting sport. *Journal of Sport and Exercise Psychology, 13,* 364–371.

ELEVEN

Uneven Playing Field

The Impact of Structural Barriers on the Initial Eligibility of African American Student-Athletes

ROBERT M. SELLERS, TABBYE M. CHAVOUS, AND TONY N. BROWN

Historically, sports, along with entertainment, has been one of the few avenues of upward mobility in American society in which African Americans might hope to be judged on their ability instead of their skin color (Ashe, 1989; Edwards, 1979). Although African American males are underrepresented in just about every traditional venue for upward socioeconomic mobility in our society (e.g., education), they are significantly overrepresented in professional football, baseball, basketball, and boxing. While African Americans constitute 13% of the population and approximately 9% of the student population at National Collegiate Athletic Association (NCAA) Division I institutions (the most competitive level), they constitute about 25% of the student-athletes who are on scholarships at these institutions (NCAA, 1995a). Approximately 1 of every 9 African American males on the campuses of the 302 Division I universities are scholarship athletes (NCAA, 1995a). In contrast, only 1 of every 50 White male college students are scholarship athletes (NCAA, 1995a). Intercollegiate athletics clearly has become an important vehicle for higher educational attainment among African American males.

The Reform Movement in Intercollegiate Athletics

Over the past fifteen years, the approximately 300-member institutions that comprise the NCAA's Division I have been engaged in a reform movement

to restore academic integrity to intercollegiate athletics. The reform movement has been influenced, in part, by embarrassing and tragic incidents that
left big-time college athletics with a major image problem. Much of the
focus of the NCAA's reform efforts has been directed toward making incoming student-athletes as similar academically to the rest of the student body
as possible by increasing the precollege academic requirements for the initial eligibility of potential students. As a result, Proposition 48 was implemented in the fall of 1986. The legislation required that potential
student-athletes obtain a high school grade point average (GPA) of 2.0 in a
set of core courses as well as at least a 700 combined score on the SAT to
be eligible to participate in athletics during their first year. A potential student-athlete who met only one of the requirements was considered a partial
qualifier and was ruled ineligible to compete during their first year. However, the partial qualifier was allowed to receive an athletic scholarship. In
1989, the NCAA passed Proposition 42 that eliminated the partial qualifier.
This legislation meant that all student-athletes must meet both the SAT
requirement and the grade point average or they would lose the opportunity
to receive an athletic scholarship their first year in college as well as lose a
year of athletic eligibility. In 1996, the initial eligibility requirements were
raised, and a sliding scale was implemented to address some of the criticism
levied against the use of a single cutoff score for the SAT. Proposition 16
requires a potential student-athlete with a 2.0 high school core GPA to earn
a combined score of 1,010 on the recentered SAT in order to be eligible to
receive an athletic scholarship. A potential student-athlete with a combined
820 recentered SAT score (equivalent to 700 on the original SAT) needs at
least a 2.5 GPA in 13 core courses in order to be eligible.[1]

Recent evidence suggests that the increased initial eligibility requirements have been effective. The overall graduation rate for student-athletes
has steadily increased since the adoption of Proposition 48. The five-year
graduation rate for all student-athletes has grown from 45.7% in 1990 to
58% in 1995. African American male student-athletes also have exhibited
an improvement in their graduation rates. In 1991, the NCAA reported that
only 24.8% of the African American male student-athletes who entered
school in the fall of 1984 had graduated five years later (Lederman, 1991).
Four years later, the five-year graduation rate for African American male
student-athletes had climbed to 42% (NCAA, 1995b). Interestingly, African
American male student-athletes actually graduate at a significantly higher
rate than African American nonathletes, who graduate at a rate of 34%.

However, this rosy picture for African American male student-athletes is deceiving. There is growing evidence that African American male
student-athletes are excluded disproportionately as a result of the initial eligibility requirements. African American athletes enrolled before 1986 were

six times more likely than White student-athletes to fail to meet Proposition 48 (McArdle & Hamagami, 1994). Approximately 65% of the African American athletes who entered before Proposition 42 standards came into effect in 1990 would have been ineligible under those standards. Meanwhile, only 9% of the White male and female athletes would have suffered the same fate (NCAA, 1991). A 1993 NCAA report reveals that the percentage of African American male freshman athletes dropped significantly in the year immediately following the implementation of Proposition 48. Although the percentages of African American male athletes steadily increased over the next two years, they still did not reach the percentages witnessed in the pre-Proposition 48 year of 1984.

Other studies have reported evidence suggesting that many of the African American student-athletes who are excluded from full participation and scholarship opportunities by the initial eligibility requirements would actually graduate if they are given the chance. The NCAA (1984) reported findings regarding the graduation class of 1984, two years before Proposition 48 went into effect, that 54% of African American male athletes who attended and subsequently graduated from the surveyed institutions would have been disqualified from freshman eligibility by the standardized test requirement of Proposition 48 (NCAA, 1984). Similarly, Walter, Smith, Hoey, and Wilhelm (1987) reported that 60% of the African American football players at the University of Michigan from 1974 to 1983 would not have been eligible under Propositions 48 and 42. Yet, 87% of those African American football players who would have been excluded under Propositions 48 and 42 actually graduated.

The Motivational Argument

The NCAA reform movement's focus on increasing initial eligibility requirements has been based on the idea that the academic problems of student-athletes are motivational in nature. Four major assumptions underlie this motivation argument: (1) a large number of athletes undervalue academic achievement; (2) academic motivation is related to academic achievement for athletes; (3) taking away athletic opportunities will motivate student-athletes to work harder in the classroom; and (4) high schools are not motivated to prepare athletes academically, because there is no consequence for them not doing so. Specifically, the assumption has been that too many student-athletes place too much emphasis on athletics and not enough emphasis on academics. Thus, it is believed that the higher eligibility standards send the message to potential student-athletes in junior high school and high school that they must place a greater emphasis on academics if they plan to play sports in college. Furthermore, it is presumed that potential student-athletes' improved academic preparation at the secondary level will result in increases in the graduation rates once they reach college. Finally, some proponents believe that the initial eligibility requirements will send a message to high schools that they also must do a better job of preparing their athletes for the rigors of college work. The potential rejection of their underprepared athletes, therefore, will motivate schools to better prepare athletes academically.

With respect to the first assumption of the motivation argument, the research literature contradicts the premise that a significant number of student-athletes undervalue academics. In 1986, the NCAA commissioned the American Institutes for Research (AIR) to survey student-athletes at 42 Division I institutions about their academic, athletic, and social experiences. Overall, 95% of the student-athletes in football and basketball reported that getting a college degree was either important or of the greatest importance to them (Center for the Study of Athletics, 1988). In a report written specifically about African American athletes, AIR states that more than 82% of African American basketball and football players reported getting a college degree as being of the greatest importance (Center for the Study of Athletics, 1989). In both instances, student-athletes' reports of the importance of obtaining a degree were not significantly different from those of a comparison sample of college students who did not participate in intercollegiate athletics.

The second premise of the motivation argument, that academic motivation is related to academic performance for student-athletes, also is unsupported by the research literature. Surprisingly little research has examined the relationship between student-athletes' academic motivation and their academic performance. The little research on academic motivation that is available suggests that academic motivation is not a significant predictor of student-athletes' academic performance. Sellers (1992) found that neither effort (as measured by hours spent studying) nor aspirations (the importance of obtaining a degree) was a significant predictor of student-athletes' grade point average. In an AIR report focusing specifically on African American athletes, over one third of the African American football and basketball players who regarded earning a degree as being of the greatest importance had earned GPAs of less than 2.0 (Center for the Study of Athletics, 1989). Given such paradoxical findings, more research clearly is needed before definitive conclusions can be made regarding the role of academic motivation in the academic performance of student-athletes.

A third assumption underlying the motivation argument is that taking away the opportunity to compete at the intercollegiate level will motivate high school athletes to place more emphasis on their schoolwork. There is no research available that investigates the merits of this assumption directly.

However, high schools in many districts have adopted similar "no pass/ no play" policies in which students must meet a certain grade point require- ment in order to participate in extracurricular activities such as athletics. The research evaluating these policies at the high school level has been somewhat equivocal. Some school administers have lauded the "no pass/ no play" as an important motivating force for many athletes who were not tak- ing their academics seriously (cf. Morton, Richardson, & Vizoso, 1994). Proponents believe that the policy has improved some athletes' academic behaviors. Opponents of the policy concede that the "no pass/ no play" policies improve indicators of the teams' overall academic performance (e.g., Honea, 1987; Peterman, 1986). However, they argue that these poli- cies do so not by motivating academically weak students to work harder in the classroom, but by eliminating these students from the teams.

In addition to focusing on the personal motivation of the student-ath- lete, the motivation argument also assumes that initial eligibility require- ments will somehow boost the high schools' motivation to better prepare their athletes academically. The NCAA, of course, has neither funding nor regulatory powers over high schools. Yet, implicit in this final assumption of the motivation argument is the belief that high schools have the capacity to do a better job of preparing athletes but, for whatever reasons, are not motivated to do so. At present, there is no empirical evidence to support such an argument. Moreover, such a claim is simply illogical. If high schools are not already motivated to prepare their students as well as they possibly can, then it is doubtful that punishing these very same students by denying them access to an athletic scholarship will motivate the high schools. Fur- thermore, the school level factors that have been related to high school aca- demic performance (e.g., classroom size) do not suggest student motivation issues, but, rather, are tied to the level at which schools are funded.

In summary, student-athletes on average come to college less prepared than other nonathletic students (Center for the Study of Athletics, 1988; Sellers, Kuperminc, & Waddell, 1991). African American athletes come from poorer educational backgrounds than their White counterparts (Cen- ter for the Study of Athletics, 1989; Sellers, Kuperminc, & Waddell, 1991), and once in college, they perform less well academically (e.g., Ervin, Saun- ders, Gillis, & Hogrebe, 1985; Kiger & Lorentzen, 1986; Purdy, Eitzen, & Hufnagel, 1982; Sellers, 1992; Shapiro, 1984). The motivation argument would suggest that these differences in academic preparation are, in part, a function of differences in motivation. In essence, African American male student-athletes must suffer from lower academic aspirations or place less effort into their studies than their White counterparts. Interestingly, Sellers (1992) found no race differences in either aspirations or the amount of effort that student-athletes place on their schoolwork.

An Alternative Argument: The Structural Barrier Argument

A structural barrier argument may help explain the differences between the academic performance of African American collegiate athletes and White college athletes more accurately than the assumptions underlying the current motivation argument. The structural barrier argument suggests that those academic differences are a function of the *quality* of the educational experiences available to African American and White student-athletes at the secondary level. The quality of the public education available to a child in the United States varies greatly and is a function of the financial status of that child's family. People who live in communities that are more affluent have a greater tax base from which to finance their public schools and thus, have more money spent on their children's public education. For example, the public school system in Gary, Indiana, spends 38% less per student than is spent in the more affluent Evanston, Illinois, public school system. Even further, there is evidence that directly relates school funding to academic preparation. Hashway, Clark, Roberts, and Schnuth (1990) found a relationship between the amount of money that states spend on education and the average SAT scores of the students in the state, such that states that spent more money on education had students who scored higher on the SAT. It is not surprising, therefore, that the Chicago public school system has an overall dropout rate of about 40% compared to its neighbor to the north, Evanston, which has a dropout rate of approximately 3%. (The national high school dropout rate is approximately 12%.) Unfortunately, the present NCAA reform efforts consider the educational opportunities of students from the Gary and Chicago public school systems as being equal to the educational opportunities of students in the Evanston public school system.

A structural barrier argument would suggest that there are two main factors that have caused African American student-athletes to be affected disproportionately by the increased initial eligibility requirements. First, athletics has historically been and continues to be one of the most visible avenues for African American students from poor backgrounds to achieve upward mobility. Thus, athletics plays a much different role in the lives of poor African Americans than in any other group (including more affluent African Americans). Second, African Americans are overrepresented among the poor. As a result, African American student-athletes are the sole representatives on our college campuses of a growing number of African American high school students who, because they are not athletically gifted and are trapped in a deplorable educational system, have less access to higher education. For most such students, a college education is not a viable option.

African American student-athletes often come from different high schools and significantly poorer socioeconomic and educational backgrounds than even their African American nonathletic college classmates (Sellers, Kuperminc, & Waddell, 1991). Such differences are related to different admissions processes for the two groups. The football team and the admissions office do not recruit from the same place. The admissions office recruits African American students from schools that have strong academic reputations and whose graduates go onto college. Often, these schools have a disproportionately high number of African Americans from the upper levels of the socioeconomic stratum. Meanwhile, the football coach recruits from any school that has athletes with athletic talent. Since there is no evidence that athletic ability is causally related to socioeconomic status, the football team—more than the rest of the African Americans on campus—is representative of the African American population in terms of socioeconomic level. Unfortunately, many students from the same poor educational environment who do not possess superior athletic ability, but who have performed better academically than their athletic classmates, do not get the same opportunity for a higher education. Thus, excellence in athletics becomes one of the few keys that will open the door to higher education. As a result, African American student-athletes are often the only representatives of the inner-city educational system on many of the campuses of our most elite institutions of higher education.

Data released by the NCAA (1998) suggest that the increased initial eligibility requirements under Proposition 16 continue to have a disproportionately adverse impact on African American student-athletes' educational opportunities. Table 11.1 presents data on the race, income, and ineligibility status of high school seniors who were recruited by a Division I institution and who applied to the NCAA's clearinghouse for certification of their initial eligibility status. (All student-athletes who wish to compete at a Division I institution must have their transcripts and test scores certified by the NCAA Clearinghouse as meeting the requirements of Proposition 16 before they are eligible to compete.) An examination of table 11.1 demonstrates that African American seniors are disproportionately declared ineligible compared to White seniors; 21.4% of African Americans compared to 4.2% of Whites. The race difference in eligibility rates is due, in part, to the significant difference in the distribution of family income among African Americans and Whites. Whereas 37.2% of African American high school seniors who applied to the NCAA clearinghouse for a ruling on their initial eligibility reported family incomes of less than $30,000, only 8.5% of White high school seniors applying reported a similar level of income. Furthermore, even having higher income does not provide the same level of benefit to potential African American student-athletes as it does for potential White

Table 11.1
Percentage and Number of African American and White Recruited Applicants to the NCAA Clearinghouse in 1997 by Self-Reported Family Income

	No. of African American Applicants	% of African American Applicants	No. of African American Ineligible	% of African American Ineligible	No. of White Applicants	% of White Applicants	No. of White Ineligible	% of White Ineligible
Greater than $80,000	568	9.3	52	9.2	9,562	31.8	200	2.1
$50,000 to $79,999	1,080	17.7	153	14.2	8,814	29.3	311	3.5
$30,000 to $49,000	1,431	23.5	287	20.1	5,665	18.8	373	6.6
Less than $30,000	2,269	37.3	630	27.8	2,526	8.5	225	8.9
Missing	741	12.2	181	24.4	3,498	11.6	151	4.3
Total	6,089	100.0	1,303	21.4	3,006	100.0	1,260	4.2

Note: African Americans constitute 14.1% and Whites constitute 69.5% of the applicant pool.

student-athletes. According to table 11.1, recruited African American high school seniors who have a family income of more than $80,000 are more than four times as likely to be declared ineligible as White potential student-athletes at the same level of family income. Similarly, lower income seems to have a greater impact on eligibility rates for African American than for White athletes. The impact of race differences in socioeconomic status on rates of eligibility may be even more pronounced when we take into consideration that income underestimates the level of racial stratification that exist in this country. Oliver, Shapiro, and Farley (1996) point out that racial differences in socioeconomic status that focus exclusively upon current earnings and income overlook a key dimension of racial stratification: Whites have much more command over financial assets than African Americans. Whites compared to African Americans are much more likely to have savings to offset economic setbacks, to inherit assets, to benefit from housing appreciation, and to own businesses (Blau & Graham, 1990; Horton, 1992; Menchik & Jianakoplos, 1997). On any indicator of socioeconomic status, African Americans, on average, are poorer than Whites, and the data suggest that this factor has an adverse consequence for potential African American student-athletes.

Impact of Initial Eligibility Requirements on African American Male Athletes

Finally, it is important to note that much of the discussion around the impact of initial eligibility requirements on African American student-athletes has been implicitly gendered. Intercollegiate athletics is a much more important path to higher education for African American male athletes than it is for African American female athletes. While 1 out of 9 African American males on NCAA Division I campuses is an athlete, that ratio is only 1 out of every 50 for African American women athletes (NCAA, 1995a). Historically, African American women athletes (as well as other women athletes) have had fewer opportunities to compete in intercollegiate athletics. As a result, there have been fewer visible examples of African American women who were able to use athletics as a vehicle of upward social mobility for young African American girls to emulate. One reason for these relatively few opportunities for African American female athletes is that women's sports rarely have generated revenues for their institutions. An examination of the demography of intercollegiate athletics suggests that African Americans, regardless of gender, tend to be afforded greater opportunities to participate in intercollegiate athletics only when their participation helps to generate revenue. According to the NCAA (1995a), African American male student-athletes in Division I constitute most of the athletes in the revenue-generating sports of football (51%) and basketball (65%), but only 9% of the male athletes in non-revenue-generating sports. Similarly, Division I African American female athletes constitute 37% of the women basketball players, but only 11% of the athletes in the non-revenue-producing sports. (The proportion of African American women athletes in nonrevenue sports are even smaller (6%) if one excludes track and field.) An interesting question is whether African American female athletes will experience similar issues and trends as their male counterparts as women's basketball continues to gain in exposure and profitability.

How does the NCAA's initial eligibility legislation adversely impact African American student-athletes' educational opportunities when these rules do not preclude potential student-athletes from attending college, but simply determine who is eligible for an athletic scholarship? Some argue that the same opportunities that are available to other people who are interested in going to college are available to the student-athlete who is declared ineligible. In reality, the options for these individuals to attend a four-year institution are greatly reduced. The fact that a disproportionate number of these individuals are coming from poorer backgrounds means that they cannot afford to go to school without significant financial assistance. In most cases, their academic record suggests that they will not be competitive for an academic scholarship. At present, we do not have any definitive data on what happens to student-athletes who are declared ineligible, although the NCAA research committee is in the process of investigating the fate of those athletes who are declared ineligible. Those who are unable to find alternative avenues to a higher education do pay a significant lifetime financial penalty. According to recent information from the United States Bureau of Census, the median income of African American individuals eighteen and older with a bachelor's degree was $13,233 higher than the income of African Americans with a high school diploma or its equivalent (Day & Curry, 1998).

Summary

The structural barrier argument leads to several recommendations for various constituencies: Member institutions of the NCAA would be better served if they focused more of their efforts on improving student-athletes' educational opportunities once they are on-campus, instead of focusing on their selection of student-athletes. The fact that African American athletes historically have and continue to graduate at rates higher than African American nonathletes (NCAA, 1995b) despite coming to college with lower test scores and high school GPAs (Center for the Study of Athletics, 1988), suggests the possibility of effective intervention aimed at the student-athletes' experiences once they are on campus.

In the interest of providing greater equity in access to higher education, NCAA member institutions would be well served to send their admissions officers with their football coaches when it is time to recruit new students. While many of the high schools that produce a number of the African American student-athletes are not necessarily the strongest schools academically, these schools do produce valedictorians and other honor students who deserve an opportunity for an education. By employing such a strategy, universities will go a long way toward having student bodies that are more representative of the general population.

The African American community must reevaluate intercollegiate athletics as an avenue for upward mobility. While there is little evidence that an overemphasis on athletics is a major factor in African American student-athletes' lower academic performance compared to Whites, there is little reason to predict that NCAA initial eligibility requirements will be relaxed in any significant way. The African American community must find ways to place greater pressure on society to provide other avenues of access to higher education besides athletics. Individual African American athletes who demonstrate an athletic aptitude and who harbor hopes of getting a college education need to utilize their athletic skills to gain entree to and take the greatest advantage of educational opportunities that many private high schools and preparatory schools offer. Finally, and most importantly, we as a society must decide whether we want every American child to have equal access to a higher education. If so, we as society must first recognize, and then remedy the reality that every American child does not have access to the same quality of education at the primary and secondary level.

In many ways, the issues surrounding the initial eligibility of African American student-athletes mirror those that face our educational system in general. In both instances, there is a tension between issues of personal responsibility and structural inequities as primary causal forces in students' academic performance. With respect to intercollegiate athletics, it is clear that both advocates of the motivational argument and the structural barrier argument would agree that significant reform is needed. As such, intercollegiate athletics is uniquely situated to provide innovative solutions to what may be the major dilemma of higher education in the next century: the problem of striving for academic excellence while at the same time providing equal access to all citizens. One thing is certain regarding the NCAA's reform efforts. The elementary and secondary educational playing field is not level. Hence, any reform effort that targets student-athletes' motivation without also addressing structural inequities in our education system is destined to exacerbate those inequities.

Notes

The authors would like to thank Drs. James S. Jackson, and Steve Boker, and members of the NCAA Workgroup at the University of Michigan for suggestions and critical input.

1. A ruling in March 1999 by a federal judge in Philadelphia invalidated Proposition 16. The court ruled that the use of absolute minimal test scores discriminated against African Americans since they, on average, score lower than Whites. At the time of the printing of this chapter, it was unclear as to the ramification of the ruling regarding the legality of using the SAT or the ACT as criteria for initial eligibility. Lawyers for the NCAA immediately sought an injuction to delay the implementation of the ruling until their appeal could be heard. It seems likely that regardless of the ultimate outcome of the appeal that some form of initial eligibility requirements will be implemented across institutions

References

Ashe, A. (1989). Is Proposition 42 racist? *Ebony, 44,* 138–140.

Blau, F. D., & Graham, J. W. (1990). Black-white differences in wealth and asset composition. *Quarterly Journal of Economics, 105,* 321–339.

Center for the Study of Athletics (1988). *Report No. 1: Summary results from the 1987–88 national study of intercollegiate athletes.* Palo Alto, CA: American Institutes for Research.

Center for the Study of Athletics (1989). *Report No. 3: The experiences of African American intercollegiate athletes at NCAA Division I institutions.* Palo Alto, CA: American Institutes for Research.

Day, J., & Curry, A. (1998). *Educational Attainment in the United States: March 1997* (United States Bureau of the Census, Current Population Reports, Series P20–505), Washington, DC: United States Government Printing Office.

Edwards, H. (1979). Sport within the veil: The triumphs, tragedies, and challenges of Afro-American involvement. *Annals, AAPSS, 445,* 116–127.

Ervin, L., Saunders, S. A., Gillis, H. L., & Hogrebe, M. C. (1985). Academic performance of student-athletes in revenue-producing sports. *Journal of College Student Personnel, 26* (2), 119–124.

Hashway, R. M., Clark, J., Roberts, G. H., & Schnuth, M. L. (1990). An econometric model of the Scholastic Aptitude Test performance of state educational systems. *Educational Research Quarterly, 14* (4), 27–31.

Honea, M. (1987, September). No pass, no play . . . a counterproductive and dysfunctional policy. *Texas Coach,* 32–34.

Horton, H. D. (1992). Race and wealth: A demographic analysis of black homeownership. *Sociological Inquiry, 62,* 480–489.

Kiger, G., & Lorentzen, D. (1986). The relative effect of gender, race, and sport on university academic performance. *Sociology of Sport Journal, 3,* 160–167.

Lederman, D. (1991, March 27). College athletes graduate at higher rate than other students, but men's basketball players lag far behind, a survey finds. *Chronicle of Higher Education, 37,* 28, A1, A35–38.

McArdle, J. J., & Hamagami, F. (1994). Logit and multilevel logit modeling of college graduation rates for 1984–85 freshman student-athletes, *Journal of the American Statistical Association, 89,* 1107–1123.

Menchik, P. L., & Jianakoplos, N. A. (1997). Black-white wealth inequality: Is inheritance the reason? *Economic Inquiry, 35,* 428–442.

Morton, S., Richardson, B., & Vizoso, A. (1994). Academic standards for interscholastic athletic participation. *North Carolina Educational Policy Research Center.* (ERIC Document Reproduction Service No. Ed 375 116).

National Collegiate Athletic Association (NCAA) (1984). *Study of freshman eligibility standards: Executive summary.* Reston, VA: Social Sciences Division, Advanced Technology.

National Collegiate Athletic Association (1991). *NCAA research report 91–04: A graphic display of initial eligibility rules applied to 1984 and 1985 freshman student-athletes.* Overland Park, KS: NCAA Publications.

National Collegiate Athletic Association (1992). *1991–1992 NCAA division I graduation-rates report.* Overland Park, KS: NCAA Publications.

National Collegiate Athletic Association (1993). *NCAA research report 92–02: A statistical comparison of college graduation of freshman student-athletes before and after proposition 48.* (ERIC Document Reproduction Service No. Ed 381 044).

National Collegiate Athletic Association (1995a). *1995 NCAA division I graduation-rates report.* Overland Park, KS: NCAA Publications.

National Collegiate Athletic Association (1995b). *NCAA research report 93–01: Cohort trends in college academic performances of 1984–88 freshman student-athletes.* (ERIC Document Reproduction Service No. Ed 381 045).

National Collegiate Athletic Association (1998). *NCAA research report 98–04: Characteristics of NCAA division I recruits, including ethnic and income-level groups in the 1996–97 NCAA initial eligibility clearinghouse.* Overland Park, KS: NCAA Publications.

Oliver, M. L., Shapiro, T. M., & Farley, R. (1996) Black wealth/white wealth. *Contemporary Sociology, 25,* 472.

Peterman, L. E. (1986, December). Increased eligibility requirements fail to produce higher grades, study shows. *National Federation News,* 16–19.

Purdy, D., Eitzen, D. S., & Hufnagel, R. (1982). Are athletes also students? The educational attainment of college athletes. *Social Problems, 29,* (4), 439–448.

Sellers, R. M. (1992). Racial Differences in the predictors for academic achievement of student-athletes in division I revenue producing sports. *Sociology of Sport Journal, 9* (1), 48–60.

Sellers, R. M. (1993). Black student-athletes: Reaping the benefits or recovering from exploitation? In D. Brooks & R. Althouse (Eds.), *Racism in College Athletics.* Morgantown, WV: Fitness Information Technology.

Sellers, R. M., Kuperminc, G.P., & Waddell, A.S. (1991, Fall). Life experiences of African American student-athletes in revenue producing sports: A descriptive empirical analysis. *Academic Athletic Journal,* 21–38.

Shapiro, B. J. (1984). Intercollegiate athletic participation and academic achievement: A case study of Michigan State University student-athletes, 1950–1980. *Sociology of Sport Journal* (1), 46–51.

Walter, T., Smith, D. E. P., Hoey, G., & Wilhelm, R. (1987). Predicting the academic success of college athletes. *Research Quarterly for Exercise and Sport, 58,* 2, 273–279.

Race and Sport and Youth in America

A Conversation with Terrence Barnum

*T*erry Barnum *played fullback for the University of Southern California's (USC) intercollegiate football team. He was selected for the All-
Academic Pac-10 Conference Team in 1994 and 1995. He currently works
as a Department Business Manager at the College of Letters, Arts, and Sciences at USC and is studying for a doctorate in education.*

Ed.: Kenneth L. Shropshire offers that, compared to White athletes,
African American athletes are disproportionately expected to be role mod
els. Have you felt yourself to be the object of expectations because of being
a successful African American athlete?

TB: I can see how it has affected my life. In American society, a large
number of times, when you see African American men who are doing something successful and noteworthy, it is in the athletic arena, or in the music
industry. So when African American youth look for role models, these are
the images that they are constantly bombarded with. You rarely see an
African American businessman being spotlighted. I think this does put a disproportionate amount of pressure on athletes who have been successful. I
have felt—although no one told me—that it was my obligation to serve as
a good role model and to provide youth coming up today with something
that they could point to. I also tried to temper that. Every time I had some
exposure with young people, I tried to talk to them about nonathletic things
as well. Over 99 percent of people don't get a chance to play sports at the
professional level, and 90 percent of people don't get a chance to play sports
at the collegiate level. I was lucky enough to experience playing intercollegiate football, but even for me it didn't work out to the extent that I would
have hoped. If life were my dream, I would be playing in the Super Bowl on

187

Sunday. For the 90 percent of the population who have to do something else, the earlier they are told that it is OK to do something else, and that it is possible to be as successful doing something else, the better.

Ed.: Do you see a difference for African American compared to White athletes with respect to the pressure to be a role model?

TB: I think the off-the-field behavior of African American athletes is much more followed and watched. In 1994, while we were beginning to prepare for a bowl game, the *Los Angeles Times* (Sandoval, 1994) ran a story about student-athletes who had a police record. It named students at different colleges with criminal offenses. The story included what essentially equated to mug shots of guys who were my teammates, and the article described things that many of them had done before they ever came to college. I don't remember there being a White student in that article. I think that is where Black athletes feel pressure. It is assumed that, were it not for athletics, odds are you would be a criminal. And that criminal element or predisposition still lives within you, so you are going to be watched to see if that criminal element comes to light at some moment of weakness. I don't think that same assumption is made of White athletes.

Ed.: What are ways to get messages to young people that there are other ways to be successful besides sports and music?

TB: I don't fault sending an athlete who has been successful into the community to get kids interested in doing well in school. But, in time, maybe you can send the Harvard graduate who is a stockbroker on Wall Street. He can show these youngsters that he tangibly does have the elements of success, that he drives a Lexus and lives in a big mansion. And, he didn't do it through athletics but through using his mind and other talents.

You do need to understand more than putting the ball in the hole. Basketball players Patrick Ewing and Michael Jordan and Grant Hill went to some of the best universities in the country and they played for coaches who demanded that they go to class and do well, that they get the most out of an education. You are not going to hear about these guys being broke, nor are you going to hear about off-the-court antics. But the average kid is not going to recognize this distinction because it is not what he is fed.

Ed.: What does it mean to kids when the African American athlete behaves outrageously, misbehaves, or gets in trouble with the law?

TB: Because we are so connected to the media, it all depends on how it is framed. If there is a chance that the athlete is not totally at fault, that perhaps he was tricked or trapped in behavior, or that the allegations are false, then I think that young people hang on to the belief that he really didn't do it. It's just the system, or White society, trying to bring him down.

If an athlete doesn't deny that he made an error in judgment, I think the reaction of the youth is a little different. For some, the person might become a hero, particularly if he is able to go on and play well. If the athlete makes an error in judgment off the field and doesn't recover athletically, he is really just forgotten and becomes just another person in the community.

Contrast Lawrence Phillips and Randy Moss. They were at the same crossroads. Lawrence Phillips, who is as gifted a running back as anybody, made a comeback at Nebraska after being suspended. He was a high draft pick. He was on his way to becoming a hero. Then he ran into problems with the police again, things he couldn't really deny. It got to the point that his pro career just fizzled. He did get a second chance with the 49ers. He made it work for a while, but continued to get in trouble off the field and eventually washed out. The hero that was Lawrence Phillips in the making just kind of died.

Randy Moss of the Vikings was at the same crossroads. Through a little bit of good luck, he got drafted by a team with a coach who could help him and with other stars on the team, which helped him to keep his whole reality in perspective, that while he was a very big talent, he was not everything. Having learned that he could be successful, he realized that he did not need to do that other stuff. Lawrence Phillips and Randy Moss: both of them were in the same position, one made some good choices, and now he is a hero.

Ed.: Academic scandals have inspired NCAA reform of intercollegiate athletics. Sellers states that the implicit assumption underlying these reforms is the motivational hypothesis. That is, the problem is a lack of motivation; thus, if standards are raised, then student-athletes will be motivated to study harder to meet those standards. Sellers then goes on to suggest ways that this analysis may be flawed.

TB: I think that an unrecognized aspect of the problem is that high schools have defined success as getting their players accepted into college. They feel that if their student-athletes can get accepted into college, then they have done their job. But these students arrive at college not equipped to compete with National Merit scholars, and therefore they are not destined to have a successful academic experience. Some of these student-athletes were never exposed to the SAT before being expected to take it.

Ed.: Sellers and Jackson also sounded a concern about African American student-athletes experiencing isolation on campus.

TB: I think that isolation occurs because of how we introduce student-athletes to us, to our community. It is very easy for a student-athlete to never see any other part of the institution or meet anyone else outside of the Athletic Department until their first day of class. They are first contacted by the

Athletic Department. They are pursued by the Athletic Department. The Athletic Department shows them the institution through an athletic lens. And with athletic departments now being asked through the NCAA to give more and to provide more to student-athletes, there is no need to get involved in anything outside the Athletic Department. The Athletic Department has tutors for you; they feed you; they provide clothes in the form of athletic gear; they help you register for classes; they do all of these things that the normal student has to go to different entities around the university to get. They perpetuate the student-athlete's experience of being told everything that they have to do. They don't teach the skills of getting connected as a student on campus. Of course there's going to be isolation.

Ed.: Do you think it's different for the African American student-athlete?

TB: Yes, because not only do you experience the isolation that every student-athlete does. But now on top of that, you are a racial minority. So when you go to class, not only is no one in class experiencing what you are experiencing, but also no one even looks like you. Odds are that no one had the life experiences before getting there that you had. Also, when an African American athlete walks into class and he's the only African American and he's big and the professor knows that he is an athlete, and all his classmates know that he is an athlete, at least some figure that he is only there because of his athletic ability. That too is isolating and gets attached to racial stereotypes.

Ed.: Both Greenfield and Jackson posit that athletic participation is special because people of different races are on the same team and are directing their efforts toward a common goal. Did you find intergroup relationships on the team to be in accord with this theory, that being on a team in pursuit of a common goal fosters intergroup cooperation and diminishes discrimination?

TB: I think feeling that you are all on the same team is directly connected to winning and losing. I can give an example. Early in the 1998 football season, UCLA was undefeated, on their way to playing for a national championship. They lost to Miami, a team they should have beaten. The defense, who had predominantly Black players on it, played horridly. They had not been playing well the entire year, but they played particularly poorly this game. The offense, who were predominantly White, played well. They had played well all year, but they played particularly well this game. What came out in the newspaper the week after the loss was that there was some strife because some of the members of the team wished to wear black wristbands as a protest against the prohibition of affirmative action in the University of California system (Adande, 1998; Howard-

Cooper, 1998). Coach Toledo, who is White, said that he thought this had no place on the field. They argued about it all week. They had two team votes including a vote in the locker room before going out for the game. The team voted not to wear wristbands, but it wasn't an overwhelming vote. So a good portion of the team felt slighted. After the vote, they go out and lose the game.

What role did this divisiveness on the team play? I don't know personally. Obviously UCLA didn't block; they didn't tackle; they didn't do a lot of things that go along with winning a football game. They went on and a month later played for the Rose Bowl and lost that one too. Was there a carryover? I don't know. But having played intercollegiate athletics at that same level, had an issue like that come up before a big game, it absolutely would have had an effect. It's hard to play next to a guy who you personally feel doesn't care about issues that are important to you.

Ed.: What else can coaches do to help overcome divisions?

TB: Having a diverse coaching staff helps. If you have a staff that is all White, you're going to run the risk of alienating non-White players. Coaching, just by the nature of the job, is a position of authority. And if you have only White men in a position of authority telling young Black men what to do, that conjures up a whole bunch of images and feelings and emotions that are going to be detrimental to the team's success.

Ed.: Jackson talks about how people have multiple identities—an athletic identity, a racial identity, a gender identity. He proposed that on the athletic field, the athletic identity becomes more salient than the racial identity. In fact, the wristband incident is a good example of racial identity intruding on the athletic field.

TB: My personal view is [that] sports is one of the good things that this country has, in that it comes the closest to being a color-blind atmosphere as you're going to get in America. When you really have a team that's successful and that's working together, you find guys—Black, White, Hispanic, Asian—they're all there for one common goal, and I don't know you can say about other aspects of our country right now. I think that it's very tragic when race does take away from that unifying effort. Being a Black man in America, I know that race is inevitable, and I'm going to be reminded that I am Black every single day. Just because I might be playing professionally or in intercollegiate athletics at the highest level, with the world watching me, doesn't mean that I'm any less Black or that people are not going to remind me to any extent. I just think they do it in different ways. What helps is when you have your teammates and your coaches of different races coming together and saying we all want to win. If the Black guy can help us win, fine. If the White guy can help us win, fine. But that's what we all want to do. Now, after the game is over, we may all go our separate ways. We have the right to do that. But while we're here, we're going to leave all of that outside, regardless of our color, and we're going to concentrate on this. You come inside the room to work on being a team. That's what you are working on. All the other stuff does not matter; that's what you are working on. Sports—unlike any other aspect of society—has the potential to break down those walls.

References

Adande, J. A. (1998, October 10). File away conspiracy theories. *Los Angeles Times,* D1, D8.

Howard-Cooper, S. (1998, October 8). Protest vote may have been distraction before Miami loss. *Los Angeles Times,* D6.

Sandoval, G. (1994, October 29). What, and when, should a coach know if a player is in trouble. *Los Angeles Times,* C1, C11.

PART IV

Violence On and Off the Playing Field

Is the Problem Sport Culture or Society?

This concluding section is organized around a central issue for theorists and practitioners who seek to understand and ameliorate the problem of sports violence on and off the playing field—is there something unique to the culture of sport that sets it apart from the larger societal forces underlying violence of all kinds? This is an important debate because it has direct practical implications for the design of intervention programs. For example, if we assume that there is something unique about sport culture, then we narrow our intervention focus to its distinctive values and norms. If, however, we see sport violence as only a reflection of larger social forces, then we design intervention programs for athletes and their coaches, promoters, fans, and families that parallel those designed for nonathletes.

Fragmented inquiry and inadequate communication between researcher and practitioner—of the kind that we are trying to overcome in this volume—undermines our ability to understand the relative roles of sports-specific culture or sports as a reflection of larger societal influences. Researchers from fields as varied as sociology, criminology, psychology, epidemiology, and cultural studies share a concern for understanding the causes of violence; yet, their inquiries into the problem are rarely informed by each other's perspectives and research findings. Moreover, violence researchers often do not even consider sport or how their models extend to athletes. Further fragmentation arises as a result of sport violence analysts' tendency to specialize in either violence on or off the field, in male-male or male-female violence, or in player or crowd violence.

Our aim in this concluding section is to begin a process of crossing disciplinary boundaries and specialized concerns and engaging both researchers and practitioners. Taken together, the chapters pose the issue of whether sports violence is a unique case, to what extent sports violence reflects a more general societal problem, and to what extent general theories of violence help us to understand sports violence. This juxtaposition of chapters is intended to illustrate the advantages of a cross-disciplinary conversation that might better guide the development and implementation of sports violence intervention programs.

The criminologist Malcolm W. Klein and the psychologist Susan B. Sorenson, lead off by suggesting important connections that can be made between what is known about the causes of all illegitimate violence and violence in sport. They summarize criminological and social psychological research literatures, and suggest concepts from the study of violence that may be particularly applicable to understanding sports violence. Practitioners could beneficially adapt these concepts to informing intervention programs.

Kevin Young, a sociologist working from a cultural studies perspective, deals directly with the implications of taking a criminological approach to the study of violence on the field. He joins "player" and "crowd" violence in an in-depth exploration of why they remain outside the social control mechanisms of the criminal courts. Why, for example, is violence on the sports field tolerated, even implicitly legitimated, when the same acts outside the cultural contours of sport would be actively prosecuted by the judicial system?

Chapters 14 and 15 by Michael A. Messner and Mark A. Stevens and by Donald G. McPherson should be read as a pair, as they offer directly opposed answers to the question of whether sports violence is/is not distinctive. Messner and Stevens argue that there is something unique. They suggest that the institutional context of sport is a site of exaggerated "masculinity" wherein misogyny, homophobia, and interpersonal violence are normative. Messner, a sociologist and cultural studies analyst, and Stevens, a clinical psychologist, nicely bridge the researcher-practitioner divide as they explore the implications of their position for the design of effective intervention programs for male college athletes.

McPherson, a former professional football player working in the Mentors in Violence Prevention Program, argues that there is nothing unique in the culture of sport that accounts for violence on the part of male athletes. For example, the intervention program described by McPherson, and earlier by Jackson Katz, is premised on the notion that off-the-field violence against women by male athletes is caused by the sexism and denigration of women in the larger society. As such, one would not assume that there is anything special about sport culture that needs correction; rather, the intervention task is to sensitize male athletes to how they have absorbed larger societal views on women that men generally employ to justify their violence against women.

We conclude this section with an interview with Billy P. Weiss, an epidemiologist who directs the Violence Prevention Coalition of Greater Los Angeles. Weiss stresses the importance of building a multidisciplinary network of researchers and practitioners to address the violence problem in or out of sport. In this interview, we return to several themes raised in the Klein and Sorenson chapter; namely, setting the issue of sport violence in context of the prevalence of violence as a social problem—especially as a cause of death among young people—and social psychological issues surrounding the appropriateness of male athletes as role models.

We also return in the course of this interview to the central theme of this book—the paradox of sport as both "cause" and "cure" of undesirable behavior on the part of youth, including violent behavior. Weiss poses a germane quandary. On the one hand, sport is a tool with more than half of her participating community groups using sport as the site for their intervention programs. On the other hand, Weiss indicates resistance to using male sport celebrities for role modeling or fund-raising efforts, a resistance based upon the difficulty of finding exemplars appropriate to the violence intervention mission—celebrities who do not carry the baggage of notoriety through violence.

TWELVE

Contrasting Perspectives
on Youthful Sports Violence

MALCOLM W. KLEIN AND SUSAN B. SORENSON

In this chapter we examine two differing perspectives on the question of whether sports violence is endemic to sport culture or reflective of the larger culture. Each perspective derives from different disciplinary approaches and literatures. The criminological perspective generally implies that youth violence in sports is more or less predictable on the basis of what is known about youth violence more generally, while the social psychological perspective suggests that sports—especially team sports—contain elements that might exacerbate normal levels of violence.[1] We conclude with a discussion of how the research agenda might be expanded to move us to a better understanding of the relationships between sport, violence, and the larger society.

The Criminologist's Perspective

From the viewpoint of criminology, youthful violence (as contrasted to aggression, assertiveness, or inadvertent harm, as might be expected in "contact" sports) is delinquent or criminal behavior defined as such by law.[2] It is usually interpersonal and intentional, although intentionality in an emotional setting is often difficult to establish. Youthful violence is usually described by such terms as *assault, robbery, manslaughter,* and *murder*. Normally one does not use these terms when describing sports violence, but for the criminologist sports is only one of many settings to which the terms apply. The illegal behavior is not altered by its location on the ball court or field, anymore than by its location in a classroom, shopping mall, or alley. Furthermore, violence of various kinds is part of the panoply of illegal acts that youth may commit, and so may be classed along with theft, burglary, substance abuse, graffiti writing, habitual truancy, and running away from home. What applies to crime and delinquency generally, applies as well to violent behavior. Sports violence, by this token, is better understood in the context of illegal behavior more generally, about which we know a great deal. Moving from the more to the less obvious, we can cite the following illustrative patterns:

1. Youthful illegal behavior—therefore violence and sports violence—is primarily a male phenomenon, by ratios variously estimated from 2 to 1 up to 5 to 1, male to female.

2. Illegal behavior is more common among Whites because Whites are more common, but it is disproportionately more common among minority populations, such as African Americans and Latinos in the United States, aborigines in Australia and in Canada, and Eastern European and North African immigrants in Western Europe. It is not the specific race or ethnicity that is important, but the state of being disenfranchised or marginalized. In the United States, for example, African Americans are 12 percent of the population but contribute up to 42 percent of juvenile homicide arrests and 50 percent of juvenile violence arrests. For Black youth aged 15 to 19, the firearm death rate is 49.2 per 100,000 as contrasted with the White rate of 5.1 per 100,000. There remains controversy as to what part of those disproportions is attributable to the offenders and what part to the agents of control.

3. Beyond age, gender, and race, there are other stable risk factors for crime, and violence specifically, at every level of analysis. There are individual risk factors such as measured intelligence, school performance, prior abuse, selected personality variables, and social attitudes and values. There are family factors such as family conflict, family criminal history, poverty, supervision of children, and number of children (but not family structure). There are peer factors such as number of delinquent friends, free time with friends, and being a "loner" (low risk). And there are neighborhood risk factors such as exposure to violence, informal social organization, presence of public gathering spots, and physical structure of open spaces.

4. Furthermore, these risk factors can be elevated by the violence they foster: The relationship is often reciprocal. Family conflict, for example, can lead a youngster to spend more time with peers who will lead him or her into a level of illegal or violent behavior that will, in turn, increase the level of family conflict. Violence not only begets violence in return; it reinforces itself.

5. Violent acts are less common than property crimes, substance use, and other delinquencies. The more persistent offender is the more versatile offender and therefore, by simple probability, the more likely to commit violent acts as well. Rather than seeking clues to, or predictors of, violence specif-

ically, we do better to seek clues for predictors of *chronic* or *versatile* offending. This yields earlier clues than waiting around for the violence to occur.

6. The peak years of youthful violence are *not* necessarily the later adolescent or early adult years. Self-reported (admitted) assaults peak in *early* adolescence, although arrests for these acts peak in late adolescence. Society responds differently to younger and older offenders. This contrasts with such acts as murder and substance abuse that accelerate into early adulthood. However, while it is also the case that White/Black differences in youthful violence involvement are not strong, Black rates of chronicity and persistence into adulthood accelerate more than do White rates.

7. Early onset of delinquency and early onset of violence both predict more chronic youth involvement in crime and violence. Bullying behavior in school, often scoffed at as a serious issue, thus takes on importance as a predictor of more serious future involvement.

8. The past several years have seen a marked drop nationally in levels of juvenile crime of almost all sorts. The exception, unfortunately, is seen in a marked increase in the most serious juvenile violence. This increase is highly correlated with an increase in homicide—especially homicide involving firearms. Also, the increase in firearm violence is disproportionately associated with males and with Blacks (and some say drug sales, but this is in some dispute).

9. There is a strong linear relationship between age on the one hand and offending with peers on the other. The oft-cited finding that delinquency (including violence) is primarily a group phenomenon is supported by the dramatic figures reported by Farrington for English youth, as seen in table 12.1. Consider the implications for *team* sports.

10. Finally, and discouragingly, of all industrialized nations, the United States reports the highest rates of violence. Most dramatic is the contrast between the United States and its close geographic and cultural neighbor, Canada, as shown in figure 12.1.

Self-reported or admitted violence rates comparing various cities in the United States and abroad show the American city, Omaha, to be second only to Athens in the prevalence of various categories of juvenile violence, and above the rates in Germany, Ireland, Belgium, Italy, and Finland (Junger-Tas, Terlouw, & Klein, 1994). We know of no comparative data on sports-related violence in these or in other countries, but a reasonable extrapolation from general violence rates would certainly yield higher sports violence rates for the United States.

In the United States, sports involvement is higher among males, disproportionately higher in organized team sports among Blacks, and higher in the adolescent years. The data reported here on youthful crime and violence therefore suggest that sports-related violence, especially in team

Table 12.1
Youth Violence as Peer Violence

Age	Alone	With Others
10–13	25%	75%
14–16	39%	61%
17–20	45%	55%
21–24	57%	43%
25–28	70%	30%
29–32	84%	16%

Note: Co-offending is most common for assault and alcohol use. Overall, co-offending decreases with age.

sports, will also project a more male, young, and minority or Black image. It may well be, then, that our public image of violence in sports is merely a reflection of the larger pattern, and not specific to sports in any important way. If we know how sport demographics relate to crime demographics, we may conclude that the issue for sports analysts is not a special issue: Sports violence is what we should expect it to be.

The Social Psychologist's Perspective

The last sentence, however, is at odds with certain dimensions of the sports experience. The predictive power of early onset and chronicity of violence, for example, suggests that proper socialization in prepubescent periods should have reduced the depredations of basketball players Bill Lambeer, Latrell Sprewell, football player Lawrence Phillips, boxer Mike Tyson, and skater Tonya Harding. Coaches' attention to the societal norms relevant to team sports in early adolescence, when assaultive behavior is peaking, should have precluded the need for sanctioning cheap shots and hard slides at the college level. Instead, we have "excused" overly aggressive behavior because it occurs in a contact sport; sports governing authorities have applied their own rules in defiance of legal statutes, in effect announcing that "normal violence," punishable in the alley, is acceptable in the arena; sports announcers have applauded "great hits" and focused their cameras on the ice hockey brawl (see the rest of the chapters in this section for specific illustrations). The early bully will find a home in sports, simply by watching what is allowable in sports. We learn criminal and violent values and behavior in much the same way as we learn much prosocial behavior—by example.

This preceding paragraph is, in essence, a foray into some central concepts of social psychology. What these social psychological notions tell

Figure 12.1
Average Young Homicide Offender Rates:
Canada, 1961–1990, United States, 1965–1990

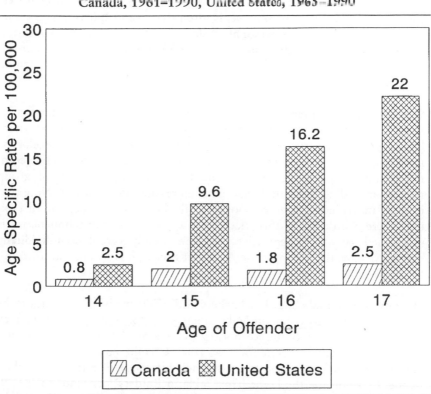

Data from J. C. Howell, B. Krisberg, J. D. Hawkins, & J. J. Wilson (Eds.) (1995). *Sourcebook on serious, violent, and chronic juvenile offenders* (Thousand Oaks, CA: Sage)

us is that whatever may be the "normal" levels of aggression and violence in a youthful population, and however these may be disproportionately displayed by different genders, ages, and ethnicities, the sports context has a special character that exacerbates them. There are other such concepts, equally applicable to the world of sports, which suggest to us that the context of sports will, if anything, increase the likelihood of violent behavior. Consider the following five examples:

Peer norms. The tendency for youth to offend or be arrested in the company of others, as seen in table 12.1, reflects the conflict between family and peer attachments. As young people slowly alter the balance toward peers, the social norms and behavioral expectations of those peers become paramount. If drawn toward peers who endorse competitive, assertive, or aggressive norms—as is often the case in sports—then something approaching interpersonal violence can be expected to result. Trash-talking, hard body contact, and aggression that would be considered violence off the court become socially legitimated and reinforced on the court.

Communication patterns. Research suggests that communication that is shared, interactive, and fully networked among group members yields higher group consensus around social norms, along with higher productivity. The emphasis on *team* play in sports includes quick and effective communication between the players, and thus the augmentation of group norms—including those that legitimate aggression and violence. Note that in more individually oriented sports—with the obvious exception of boxing—there is little use of this effect. Thus when a golfer or tennis player is sanctioned for overly aggressive behavior, usually verbal or individually expressive as in the tossing of one's club or racket, it is so singular as to call forth special attention.

Stereotyping and labeling. Linebackers and defensive backs are said to be a bit wild. Cameras focus on Mike Singletary's focused eyes and on Jack Tatum's vicious hits. Some ice hockey players are labeled *enforcers,* and traded from team to team for that role. Certain baseball pitchers are known for their willingness to brush back hitters or to retaliate for close pitches by returning the favor. The Oakland Raiders' penchant for penalties has earned them generations of labels as a dirty team. Regardless of the extent to which these depictions are fair and accurate, they persist and fail to yield significant sanctions. They are found acceptable within the broad range of the normative expectation of the sport. They are, to the participant and to the rabid fan, widely endorsed roles.

Role modeling. Social learning theorists remind us that one potentially powerful source for learning one's behavior is to copy that of admired leaders. Prelaw and premed students mimic their successful elders. Fictional characters from the Lone Ranger to Mighty Mouse set standards for their young apprentices in the audience. We have in mind the critical role that coaches may play in establishing standards of appropriate conduct and setting limits on questionable conduct. Coaches George Allen and Bobby Knight, and promoter Don King can present models that stretch or go beyond the limits, but they are admired and emulated by their recruits. We think of the college football coach whose halftime exhortation to his losing team was to "go out there and shove the f——— ball up their f——— asses; now let us kneel and pray."[3]

Group cohesiveness. One of the defining group level constructs of social psychology is cohesiveness, that elusive proxy for the glue of interrelationships that enhances both the "we" feeling in groups and their productivity. Criminologists have applied the notion effectively to the strength and persistence of street gangs, whose opposition to authority structures and intense rivalries with other gangs are signal parts of their existence. The parallel to sports teams is obvious. Even in those sports where team scores are little more than the accumulation of individual points, as in swimming and diving, or college level tennis or track and field, the competition in dual and multiple-school meets is made manifest by coaches, and all the more so when engaging traditional rivals. Employing team spirit to enhance individual performances is commonplace, although it still pales in the face of purely group sports where team cohesiveness can effectively rationalize all kinds of illicit behavior in the pursuit of victory. As some zealots are fond of saying, "winning is everything."

Thus, even as we encourage team spirit, mutual support, and healthy competition, even as we supply and laud the images of successful athletes and hire enthusiastic coaches, we may inadvertently contribute to unwanted sports violence. Violence becomes the "victim" of well-intentioned practices, being exaggerated beyond the bounds of competitive assertiveness. As a test, we would urge keeping an eye on the future of women's ice hockey, so successfully introduced in the 1998 Olympics as a minimum contact sport.

Expanding the Horizons of Future Research on Sport, Violence, and Society

Key to understanding sport violence is *clear definition of the problem.* Are we interested in sports violence or in the violence-prevention potential of sports? Sports have been heralded as a way out for young people—out of a neighborhood, out of adverse life experiences and circumstances, out of poverty. Proponents of golden gloves, midnight basketball, and other recreational programs claim that sports are one way to prevent youth from becoming involved in criminal and other antisocial activities. Yet others characterize competitive sports in terms sometimes used to describe military combat training. Athletes are depicted as victims of a socialization process that dehumanizes them and their rivals, and violence is presented to them as an expected outcome. In any case, those interested in sport as a violence-prevention tool need to consider the violence-activation potential of at least some sports. Each perspective can offer examples of individual cases in which "his life was turned around" by sports, or "he was a fine young man until" he played a certain sport. Although intuitively appealing, dueling case studies will contribute relatively little to our understanding of sports and violence beyond the specific instance. Various research strategies can help assess these competing perspectives.

Ecological studies might note the association between the rise in participation in organized sports and the increase in homicide rates in the nation. But causal inference would, of course, not be possible. Likewise, one study observed that emergency department visits by women for injuries increase when the local football team wins (White, Katz, & Scarborough, 1992). Both findings are open to numerous interpretations because of the widely acknowledged ecological fallacy, namely, simply because there is an observed association at the population level does not mean that there is an association at the individual level.

Longitudinal (cohort) studies could examine young people, some of whom engage in competitive sport and others who do not. By observing the athletes and nonathletes over time, one could assess the temporal sequencing of sports and violence, an important step toward determining causation. An obvious limitation to the use of longitudinal designs is that self-selection would operate by the very nature of the phenomenon. Specifically, only certain youth would have the requisite body build, skill, interest, leisure time, and so on, to participate in sports. Thus, they will differ from the outset from those who do not possess these characteristics.

Cross-sectional and case control studies, likewise, are open to the same self-selection bias. Using comparison groups such as contact versus noncontact versus no sport involvement groups would help illuminate certain issues although self-selection biases remain.

Closer examination of *athletes' behavior off the field and community reactions* when that behavior entails violence could help us to answer important questions. Are athletes at higher risk of becoming involved in community (i.e., not sports-related) violence? Are there differential sanctions for athletes who do commit violence in the community? Are the violent activities of high-profile athletes evaluated comparably to similar behaviors by nonsport celebrities? All of the remaining chapters in this section raise issues and observations that bear upon these questions with respect to boys and men. However, as higher proportions of girls and women have participated in organized sports since the enactment of Title IX which supported their equality of opportunity, we could also examine whether there has been a concomitant rise in women's participation in violent activities. These are but a few of the questions that could be investigated.

Criminological and social psychological perspectives on sport violence overlap to some extent around *the issue of norms*. Norms, the unwritten as well the written rules of society, define expectations for behavior in a range of circumstances. Likewise, the rules and expected etiquette in competitive sports shape behavior on the court and on the field. The rules of each sport, although relatively clear-cut, are sufficiently flexible to allow for a range of behavior. For example, although it is against the rules to intentionally injure another player, "taking out" a key member of the opposite team sometimes is a tacit goal. The task is to do so within the rules of the game. Certain teams and certain players are reputed to consistently push the limits of the rules which, in turn, shapes the social norms of a sport such that aggressive and sometimes violent on-field behavior may become more expected and more tolerated. We need to know more about the actual normative boundaries of sport violence that are in practice on the playing field, though they may not be in the rule books.

Another normative phenomenon that may be worthy of future research concerns the norms for talking to and about your opponent. *Trash talking* about an opponent prior to a game has been added to the repertoire of athletes' intimidation tactics. As this form of intimidation of competitors becomes more widely practiced and more accepted, at least two questions may be asked: Does trash talking increase the likelihood of event violence? Does trash talking about opponents carry over to verbal intimidation in other sectors such as male athletes' interactions with women?

We close with this simple thought: Multiple perspectives can be useful—indeed necessary—in the attempt to describe and understand sports-associated violence. Each contributes, but the synergy of several disciplines is clearly required if we are to be able to tease out the complex relationships between sport, violence, and society.

Notes

1. In this chapter, we limit ourselves principally to participant violence and do not cover spectator violence or media coverage of either.

2. Data reported in this section, unless otherwise noted, are taken from various publications of the United States Department of Justice, from longitudinal studies of youth violence in Denver and Rochester, and from two recent volumes: Howell, Krisberg, Hawkins, & Wilson (1995), and Loeber & Farrington (1998).

3. The incident was observed and reported by one of this book's editors, during a conversation about coaching as a character-building exercise.

References

Howell, J. C., Krisberg, B., Hawkins, J. D., & Wilson, J. J. (Eds.) (1995). *Sourcebook on serious, violent, and chronic juvenile offenders.* Thousand Oaks, CA: Sage.

Junger-Tas, J., Terlouw, G.J., & Klein, M. W. (Eds.) (1994). *Delinquent behavior among young people in the Western world.* Amsterdam: Kugler Publications.

Loeber, R., & Farrington, D. P. (Eds.) (1998). *Serious and violent juvenile offenders.* Thousand Oaks, CA: Sage.

White, G. F., Katz, J., & Scarborough, K. E. (1992). The impact of professional football games upon violent assaults on women. *Violence and Victims, 7,* 157–171.

THIRTEEN

From "Sports Violence" to "Sports Crime"

Aspects of Violence, Law, and Gender in the Sports Process

KEVIN YOUNG

Introduction and Definitional Concerns

The primary purpose of this chapter is to explore the question of why sports-related violence enjoys relative immunity from criminal sanction in North American society. When it comes to classifying and responding to participant violence in sport, it is clear that social control processes are affected by the fact that sport carries enormous cultural legitimacy and appeal. This chapter examines the question of legitimacy in light of what appear to be shifting scales of social and legal tolerance toward matters of interpersonal violence connected to sport. Questions of how these scales may be "gendered" are also raised.

Before moving to the particular focus of this chapter—the controversial issue of how we think about assaultive acts committed by athletes—some brief observations on definitional matters are in order. Far too often people fail to explain clearly what specific aspect of "sports violence" they are exploring (Coakley, 1988/1989). If there is one thing I can say with absolute confidence after studying in this area for several years (Smith & Young, 1987; White & Young, 1997; Young, 1986, 1988, 1990, 1991, 1993, 1994, 1997, 2000; Young & Smith, 1988/1989; Young & Wamsley, 1996; Young & White, 1995; Young, White, & McTeer, 1994), it is that the concept of "sports violence" is extremely slippery. Like other aspects of the social process such as "culture," or "family," or "crime," everyone thinks they know what sports violence is until challenged to define it or, even more troublingly, faced with having to do something *practical* about it. This is true not only for ordinary members of the public but also for sports organizations themselves and for those responsible for upholding the law of the land, including the police and the courts.

At the simplest level, most people usually conceive of sports violence as falling into two categories—"crowd violence" (which can involve both crimes against persons and property) and "player violence" (usually injurious player-player contact incurred during the context of a game). If we broaden the traditional parameters of sports violence to include violent acts *related to sport* (and I think there are good *sociological* reasons to do so),[1] it becomes clear that our subject may be far more heterogeneous than simply acts of violence perpetrated by athletes or members of sports crowds. High-profile cases of violence related to sport in the last few years include not only the injurious and occasionally fatal practices of rioting soccer fans (witness, e.g., crowd "troubles" at the recent World Cup in France, 1998),[2] and the usual spate of on-field assaults and catastrophic injuries done by and to athletes (cf., White & Young, 1997), but also

- a pipe bomb explosion at the 1996 Centennial Olympic Games in Atlanta that killed two people and injured over a hundred others (*Sports Illustrated,* August 5, 1996, 22–31);
- the stabbing of a professional female tennis player—the Monica Seles case (*Sports Illustrated,* July 17, 1995, 18–26);
- the involvement of a world class female figure skater in the off-ice assault of an opponent—the Tonya Harding/Nancy Kerrigan case (*Time,* January 24, 1994, 34–38);
- the rape conviction and jail term of a world boxing champion (Mike Tyson) who is known to have made the claim "I like to hurt women" (*Sports Illustrated,* July 31, 1995, 62–74);
- the murder trial of an American football hero—the O.J. Simpson case (*Newsweek,* July 11, 1994, 20–27);
- the depressingly common involvement of male athletes in sexual assault against women (see Benedict & Klein, 1997; Crosset, Benedict, & McDonald, 1995; Melnick, 1992);
- male athletes' involvement in what *Sports Illustrated* has called "sport's dirty little secret" (July 31, 1995, 62), that is, partner abuse by such athletes as footballers Warren Moon and Vance Johnson, golfer John Daly, English soccer players Paul Gascoigne and Stan Collymore, boxer Sugar Ray Leonard, basketball player Robert Parish, and baseball player Jose Canseco;

- cases of harassment, stalking, and threats throughout the world of sport, such as the case of champion figure skater Katarina Witt, which have spurned a thriving muscle-for-hire security industry (*USA Today,* July 14, 1995, 3C);[3]
- scandals throughout numerous levels of Canadian hockey regarding the sexual abuse of young boys, some of whom, now as adults, are just beginning to go public with their stories (see the discussion of the widely documented Sheldon Kennedy case and the "Maple Leaf Gardens scandal" in Donnelly, 1999).[4]

These incidents probably represent only the tip of the proverbial iceberg of acts of violence related to sport. They are not normally thought of as "sports violence." They are all, however, clearly intentionally injurious or otherwise threatening acts that cannot be divorced from the sports process, and such acts only begin to make sense when the *socially, culturally,* and *historically* embedded character of sport is closely scrutinized. The domestic violence examples also underscore the fact that the problem of violence in sport interfaces with problems of violence elsewhere in society (see Klein & Sorenson in this volume). With this caveat in mind, it is violence *on the field* and the way that it is responded to formally and legally that I am concerned with in this chapter. There are many parallels, particularly with respect to issues of gender and law, in the cases listed here and in the ones I will describe.[5]

Defining Player Violence

One of the most widely adopted typologies of player violence was developed by the Canadian sociologist Michael Smith who, like the British sociologist Eric Dunning,[6] was a pioneer in the field of sports violence study. In his 1983 book, *Violence and Sport,* Smith classified player violence into four basic categories, the first two being relatively legitimate and the last two relatively illegitimate in the eyes of both sports administrators and the law:

Brutal Body Contact

Brutal body contact includes what Smith called the "meat and potatoes" of our most popular sports, such as tackles, blocks, body checks, collisions, hits, and jabs. Depending on the sport being examined, these are all acts that can be found within the official rules of a given sport.

Borderline Violence

Borderline violence involves acts prohibited by the official rules of a given sport but that occur routinely and are more or less accepted by many people connected with the game. Examples might include the fistfight in hockey; the late hit and personal foul in football; the wandering elbow in basketball, soccer, and road racing; the high tackle, the rake (the violent use of cleats against skin), and the scrum punch (a punch hidden from officials in the formed scrum) in rugby; and the "beanball" (a pitch aimed deliberately at a batsman's head) or "knock-down" pitch in baseball. Importantly, all of these actions carry potential for prompting further violence—the bench-clearing brawl in hockey, or retaliatory fighting in any one of these other sports. Historically speaking, sanctions imposed by sports leagues and administrators for borderline violence have been notoriously light.

Quasi-Criminal Violence

Quasi-criminal violence violates the formal rules of the given sport, the law of the land and, to a significant degree, the informal norms of players. This type of violence usually results in serious injury that precipitates considerable official and public attention. Quasi-criminal violence in ice hockey includes "cheap shots" or "sucker punches" that often elicit in-house suspensions and fines.

Criminal Violence

Criminal violence includes cases so seriously and obviously outside the boundaries of both the sport and social acceptability that they are handled as criminal from the outset. The broadly cited Canadian case used by Smith is that of Toronto teenage hockey player Paul Smithers who, in 1973, assaulted and killed an opponent in the arena parking lot following a local game.

Smith's typology addresses what Ball-Rokeach (1971, 1980) would call the question of the "legitimacy of violence"; that is, the legitimation/delegitimation process with regard to what is perceived as acceptable violence and what is not. Since the late 1960s and the early 1970s era, for example, there appears to have been a shift in what is categorized as legitimate and illegitimate sports violence, no doubt prompted by shifting scales of public and legal tolerance when it comes to forms of interpersonal violence in general.[7] For example, using Smith's categories, incidents considered a decade ago as quasi-criminal violence, borderline violence, or even brutal body contact are being more closely scrutinized in some quarters today and, where litigated, may be dealt with under criminal rather than civil law.

Recent Sports "Crimes"

Apparently shifting scales of public and official tolerance have been brought into sharp relief by several highly publicized cases from a number of international contexts. Recent cases suggest a trend, at least in some Western industrial societies, toward legal intervention into, and the criminalization of, sports violence:

The Jimmy Boni Case (February 1994)

Boni, a Canadian-raised player in the Italian Hockey League, retaliated, when punched, by slashing his opponent, Miran Schrott, in the chest with his stick. Schrott never regained consciousness and died of cardiac arrest. Initially charged with intentional homicide and facing up to eighteen years in prison, Boni eventually pleaded guilty to the reduced charge of manslaughter and was fined $1,800 Canadian (*Macleans,* February 28, 1994, 11).

The Howard Collins Case (December 1994)

Rugby player Howard Collins was sentenced to up to six months in jail for stomping an opponent's head during a top-level game played in Wales between Welsh rugby teams Pencoed and Cardiff Institute. The head wound suffered by his opponent, Christian Evans, required ten stitches and plastic surgery (*Calgary Herald,* December 22, 1994, D2).

The Eric Cantona Case (February 1995)

Manchester United star Eric Cantona was charged with common assault for his "kung-fu" style assault on a taunting Crystal Palace fan during a regular Premier League soccer game in England. Following a guilty plea, the French player was sentenced to two weeks in jail (*Calgary Herald,* March 24, 1995, D3).

The Duncan Ferguson Case (May 1995)

A Scottish soccer player with three previous convictions for assault was sentenced to three months in jail for head-butting an opponent during a Scottish Premier Division game in April 1994. Ultimately, Ferguson served forty-four days in a Glasgow prison. This is thought to be the first case of an international player in British soccer being jailed for an on-field incident (*Toronto Star,* May 26, 1995, C10; *Calgary Herald,* October 12, 1995, C1).

The Simon Devereux Case (February 1996)

British rugby player Simon Devereux was found guilty on charges of grievous bodily harm and was jailed for nine months by an English court for punching his opposing captain, Jamie Cowie. His jaw broken in three places, Cowie spent five nights in a hospital and was forced out of the game for eight months (*Sun*, February 23, 1996, 16).

The Charlottetown Hockey Case (February 1996)

With only thirty seconds left in overtime in a Canadian varsity play-off game between the University of Moncton and the University of Prince Edward Island, a controversial goal prompted twelve Moncton players to swarm the referee, punch him, and spear him with their sticks. It took over a dozen police officers to restore order. The Atlantic Universities Athletic Association banned two players each for five years, and another player for two years. Criminal charges, including assault, were imposed.

These cases, drawn from professional or top-level amateur sport, are examples of player violence entering the jurisdiction of either civil or criminal law in a way that did not occur in earlier decades of the twentieth century. Over the same brief period, dozens of similar incidents at the amateur and recreational level, including college and high school, have resulted in criminal charges (often of assault), litigation, and prosecution across North America. Sociologically, then, it seems important to ask how player violence cases have been treated by the courts across time, and to what extent social and legal responses have shifted.

Historical Shifts in Responses of Authorities to Player Violence

Traditionally, the courts in most countries have considered player violence outside of their respective jurisdictions. In the United States and Canada, for example, literally hundreds of assault charges have been thrown out of court and "not guilty" decisions rendered because athletes are assumed to *consent* to a certain amount of force used both by and against them, as well as to the risk of injury (see the contributions by McPherson and by Messner & Stevens in this volume). Nonetheless, legal involvement in sports violence cases in Britain and America can be traced back at least to the turn of the century (Barnes, 1988; Young & Wamsley, 1996). In most cases, however,

> not guilty verdicts were rendered on the occasionally explicit grounds that sports leagues should police themselves and that the State should not intervene in seemingly self-regulating sports communities where the rules, it was argued, were clearly delineated, where a certain amount of risk was assumed voluntarily, and where competition was monitored by qualified officials. (Young & Wamsley, 1996, p. 53)

At the root of contemporary legal struggles over the parameters of acceptable sports conduct is the issue of consent or what in legal jargon is known as *volenti non fit injuria*—in other words, "voluntary assumption of risk."

Such is true in National Hockey League (NHL) case law (Reasons, 1992). An outdated but well-known and still widely cited example, the 1969 *R. v. Green* case showed evidence that Ted Green of the Boston Bruins came off the boards and swiped his opponent Wayne Maki with the back of his glove. Maki retaliated by chopping Green on the head with his stick. In Horrow's (1980) account, "Green sustained a serious concussion and massive hemorrhaging. After two brain operations, he regained only partial sensation and has never recovered 100 percent" (p. 19). While charges were brought against both players, Green, having used a "self-defense" argument, was acquitted with the following judicial assessment:

> No hockey player enters onto the ice of the National Hockey
> League without consenting to and without knowledge of the
> possibility that he is going to be hit in one of many ways once
> he is on the ice . . . we can come to the conclusion that this is
> an ordinary happening in a hockey game and (that) the play-
> ers really think nothing of it. If you go behind the net of a
> defenceman, particularly one who is trying to defend his zone,
> and you are struck in the face by that player's glove, a penalty
> might be called against him, but you do not really think any-
> thing of it; it is one of the types of risks one assumes. (Hor-
> row, 1980, p. 186)

In brief, players have traditionally been understood to either express or imply consent to certain levels of force used against them *except* in cases of extraordinarily savage and injurious attacks. This is key. As tolerated as sports violence cases have been historically, their presence in tort and criminal law, coupled with what appears to be a decreasing social tolerance toward certain aspects of violence in society, has led litigators to more stringently reevaluate sports offenses as "excessive" and "unjustifiable" (White, 1986). In this sense, contrary to its legal conventions, then, *volenti non fit injuria* does not imply *absolute* consent, but consent *only as a matter of degree.*

To date, case law indicates that charges and convictions for assault causing bodily harm are most widespread, although criminal charges of common assault, and even manslaughter and homicide are being heard (Reasons, 1992; Young, 1993; Young & Wamsley, 1996). Along with boxing, hockey appears most frequently in criminal reports, especially in Canada. Indeed, as Reasons notes, "it may be said that Canada leads the common law world in criminally prosecuting its athletes for criminal violence" (p. 8). While the amateur game seems particularly cluttered with "hockey crimes," similar cases may be found at the professional level. In one of the most documented cases, Dino Ciccarelli of the Minnesota North Stars was convicted in an Ontario court. Among other evidence proving *mens rea*, Ciccarelli told the court that in using his stick violently, he was "probably trying to intimidate" the plaintiff. Although the latter was not seriously hurt, Ciccarelli was convicted on charges of common assault.

Explaining Legal Reluctance to Prosecute Sports Violence

Sociolegal Explanations

Sociolegal explanations for the traditional reluctance of the courts to prosecute sports violence cases have again been neatly summarized by Smith (1987) who identified seven key explanations for the relative immunity of player violence to legal sanction:

1. That the courts have more important things to do like prosecuting "real" criminals
2. That the leagues themselves are in the best position to effectively control player misbehavior
3. That civil law proceedings are better suited than criminal proceedings for dealing with an injured player's grievances
4. That it is unfair to prosecute an individual player while ignoring those who may have aided, abetted, or counseled that player
5. That it is unfair to prosecute a player when the law is unclear as to what sports violence is
6. That it is almost impossible to reach a guilty verdict anyway
7. That prosecuting athletes does little to solve the wider social causes of violence

It is likely that these views will continue to reflect popular thinking in the world of sport, in the public at large, and perhaps also in the courtroom. The role of the media in "framing" sports violence issues for the public is key here (Ball-Rokeach & Loges, 1996; Young, 1986, 1990; Young & Smith, 1988/1989). Despite the prevalence of these views, more punitive attitudes on the part of both sports authorities and the law on the player violence issues seem to be emerging. A process of delegitimation of some aspects of extreme sports violence does seem to be underway. The following observations serve to update Smith's sociolegal explanations for the traditional reluctance of the courts to prosecute player violence to capture what may be a trend toward delegitimation:

1. Criminologists have known for a long time that, in countries like Canada and the United States, justice systems are predisposed to policing so called street crime. For example, there remains in both countries a widespread concern with youth crime and youth violence. While it may be some time before large sections of the public are willing to view athletes behaving violently in the same light as "real" criminals, it seems likely that the sheer numbers of athletes being charged with assault may have affected public perceptions. Often sensational media attention to sports assault cases, such as the ones listed earlier, may have encouraged public perceptions of such acts as "real" violence.

2. The argument that "in-house" policing is the most effective means to monitor player violence is a controversial one. It seems reasonable to argue that the leagues and clubs are in the most informed and nuanced positions to judge the magnitude of an offense relative to the rules and traditions of the game. On the other hand, we know from the criminological literature that self-regulating professional organizations entrusted with policing themselves (e.g., lawyers, doctors, and the police) sometimes abuse that privilege by meting out only tokenist punishments to appease public concern. Likewise, sociological research has uncovered processes of "nonenforcement," "covert facilitation," and "cover-ups" with respect to sports violence cases (Young, 1993). Moreover, we also know that there are numerous ways in which violent practices are rewarded in sport—financially, occupationally, and within the specific culture of the game. To my knowledge, no one has conducted a systematic study of whether in-house punishments (warnings, suspensions, fines, etc.) are increasing in sport, but impressionistic evidence suggests that this may be the case.

3. The courts have traditionally viewed civil law proceedings as more appropriate than criminal proceedings in dealing with the grievances of injured players in assault cases. Again, this approach stems from the view that a certain amount of physical damage should be expected in sport and from the English common law notion of *volenti non fit injuria*. While it probably remains the case that most injury cases are dealt with in civil law, criminal law is also being viewed as an appropriate venue, as an already large number of cases on both sides of the Atlantic suggests.

4. The view that it is unfair to prosecute individual players for their actions while ignoring those who may have assisted in the teaching or promotion of those acts (e.g., coaches or owners) prevails. Courts also continue to invoke the philosophy of legal individualism that tends to shift the onus of criminal responsibility from an organization (e.g., a sports team or a league) to a particular player. However, there are recent cases where courts have decided against sports teams rather than against an individual

player, and these may be precedent setting cases. For a discussion of the
legal implications of matters such as "vicarious liability" and "foreseeabil-
ity," see Young (1993).

5. Legal systems on both sides of the Atlantic continue to approach
sports violence cases inconsistently and with great variability. Despite
recent pressures on sports organizations and the courts to examine more
closely and thus define more clearly some related aspects of sports behavior such as sexual harassment, it is probably fair to argue that among the
public, sports organizations, the courts, as well as scholars, definitions of
what constitutes "sports violence" remain less than clear.

6. The argument that one should avoid sports violence litigation
because it is impossible to get a guilty verdict may strike the reader as missing the point. However disagreeable one finds this logic, it is nevertheless
true that the decision to litigate is often premised on the perceived chances
of receiving a favorable decision in court. In this sense, it is very likely that
at the level of the aggrieved player or the prosecution, courts may be
avoided due to the perception that the justice system would not be sympathetic to the case. However, it is also true that many cases *have* reached the
court and *have* resulted in guilty verdicts. In other words, where sports
"crimes/assaults" are concerned, there are already many precedents in law.
To date, we have no record of the extent to which these cases are growing,
but anecdotal evidence seems to point in this direction—at least for
Canada, England, and the United States.

7. The argument that prosecuting violent athletes is a "Band-Aid"
solution to the problem because it does little to solve wider causes of violence is crucial. As a sociologist, and following Smith, I accept the proposition that player violence is socially and culturally embedded, such that
criminalizing individual cases is likely to achieve very little unless similar
antiviolence intervention/transformation/reeducation occurs elsewhere in
the wider community (see McPherson, chapter 15 and Messner & Stevens,
chapter 14).

In sum, a sociolegal approach highlights something of a paradox on
this matter. While there seems to be an increasing degree of social and legal
intolerance to forms of player violence, there remains an ongoing reluctance on the part of the the courts to actually prosecute athletes for assault
and for other sports "crimes."

Gender Explanations

Any attempt to explain player-player assault and sports violence requires
us to focus our attention on gender dynamics; first, to account for why so
many male athletes have been willing to risk health and safety in accept-

ing violent sports roles and, second, to explain the possible complicity of legal structures in defining sports violence as legally tolerable, and even as socially valuable. Only a cursory examination of early Canadian sports violence case law is needed to validate these claims. For example, in the 1911 Ontario case of *R. v. Wildfong and Lang* in which two men were charged with engaging in a prizefight, Judge Snider was unequivocal in his views on the value of sports as a physical and social training ground for boys and men:

> I wish to make it clear that I am as much opposed to prize-fighting and brutality and intentional injury in boxing, football, hockey or lacrosse, as any person can be. At the same time I feel confident that it will be a long time before Parliament will think it wise to so hedge in young men and boys by legislation that all sports that are rough and strenuous or even dangerous must be given up. Virility in young men would soon be lessened and self-reliant manliness be a thing of the past.[8]

In his closing remarks, Snider went on to consolidate the philosophy of Muscular Christianity by citing Lord Bramwell from the 1878 British *R. v. Bradshaw* case: "I have no doubt that the game was in any circumstances a rough one but I am unwilling to decry the manly sports of this country, all of which are no doubt attended with more or less danger and roughness."[9]

At the turn of the century, legal decisions such as these gave sports officials, organizers, and sport promoters (who were exclusively male at the time) the power to police their own affairs, legitimizing the creation of distinct rules regarding violent conduct within sport, and codes of appropriate masculinity outside of sport. In this sense, it may be argued that the early Canadian state was implicated in the management of gender relations, and specifically in galvanizing what Donaldson (1993) has called the "public face" of hegemonic masculinity.

Prompted by the more gender sensitive climate of the current era, the *explicitly* gendered assumptions of early sports assault litigation appear to have been seriously toned down. The traditionally patriarchal trappings of law may now be articulated in more subtle ways. It may be speculated that courts would be less tolerant of woman-to-woman sports assault on the grounds that aggression and femininity are still viewed as mutually exclusive. Because sport and society in general have been so efficient at excluding women from sport, especially the more physically risky sports, there is insufficient case law to assess this possibility.

Feminist work on sport and gender (e.g., Bryson, 1987; Messner & Sabo, 1990, 1994) urges us to understand male tolerance of violence, risk, and injury linked to sport as a *constitutive* social process through which

serious injury and disablement become reframed as *masculinizing*. In this
way, the cultural meaning of sports violence and living with injury is linked
with larger ideological issues of gender legitimacy and power (see Messner
& Stevens in this volume). For example, Theberge (1990) and Lenskyj
(1990) argue that aggressive expressions of male power serve to consolidate the apparently compulsory heterosexualism of sport, as well as to
reproduce the subjugation of "less forceful" femininities. The risks and violence of male sports culture carry enormous symbolic weight, rather than
being understood as mere rituals associated with sport, they now reflect
wider forms of gender ordering.

Violent sports conduct, together with what Messner and Sabo (1990)
have called the "pain principle" of sport, appear to be defined by many
male athletes as rich in rewards and masculinizing potential. Players allow
their work lives to be manipulated because salaries and public adoration
make it all seem worthwhile. Masculinization born of violence and aggression is ephemeral and often accompanied by considerable disablement as
may be seen in the burgeoning literature on sports injury (cf. Curry &
Strauss, 1994; Nixon, 1993; Young & White, 1995; Young, White, &
McTeer, 1994).

Summary

As we enter the twenty-first century, there is increasing evidence of changing (i.e., more punitive) attitudes on the part of both sports authorities and
the law to the issue of player-to-player violence. Litigation of sports
assault, or what has provocatively been tagged as "sports crime" not only
by sociologists but interestingly enough by the Government of Canada,[10]
appears to be on the rise in Canada and elsewhere. What Michael Smith
defined as brutal body contact and borderline violence over a decade ago
is increasingly prompting injured athletes to step forward as private liti-
gants to initiate not only civil, but also criminal, charges. At the same time,
nonlegal forms of intervention (fines, suspensions, and generally closer
policing practices) based on principles of deterrence are increasingly being
adopted by sports clubs, leagues, and organizations. But, for all of this, it
would be a mistake to assume that legal intervention into sports violence
has been uncontested or unilinear; this is clearly not the case. In general,
sports violence is still defined ambiguously, at best, and there remains little
agreement among sports leagues and authorities as to the limits of aggressive, injurious, or otherwise risky sports conduct.

Player violence in sport continues to be treated differently by the law
from other forms of violence, and most sports organizations continue to
regulate themselves. Fines imposed on violent players, though increasingly

punitive, remain relatively mild, and suspensions inconsistently applied and often tokenist. Also, while civil and criminal *charges* against violent athletes may also be on the increase, *prosecutions* remain rare and sentences light. In the aforementioned common assault case, Dino Ciccarelli's conviction was followed by only one day in a Toronto jail, of which he spent less than two hours in a cell signing autographs (*Sports Illustrated,* September 5, 1988, 34). Even in cases where the conduct of athletes *away* from the arena has drawn widespread legal and public disapproval and has resulted in conviction and imprisonment (e.g., the Mike Tyson rape case), the sports-aggression-masculinitiy nexus appears so culturally meaningful that top-level athletes are able to rebound and actually profit from publicity around the case.

The courts remain particularly unwilling to prosecute the more serious charges laid against athletes. Sports violence case law across the twentieth century demonstrated a routine reduction of murder charges to manslaughter and other commutations. Massive variability within and across societies in the implementation of the law in sports assault continues to undermine the integrity of legal intervention per se. For example, in two of the British cases mentioned earlier involving intentional assaults, one player (Simon Devereux) was sentenced to nine months in jail, and the other (Eric Cantona) had his two-week jail term commuted to community service. Complicating this sociolegal quagmire further still, there is little evidence that criminalizing sports violence actually *works* in any practical sense to reduce the phenomenon.

Despite high-profile international sports law cases, there is considerable evidence that the notion of *volenti non fit injuria* endures at the center of public and legal tolerance of sports violence. In other words, one of the main causes of the still widespread tendency to excuse sports violence lies in the concept of implied consent. From this position, it comes as no great surprise that when player violence becomes redefined as sports *assault* and is litigated, a series of commonsense rationalizations (and legal defenses [Young, 1993]) kick in to defend the violent dimensions of sport. As former England rugby "hard man" Mike Burton proclaimed in his overly literal interpretation of the Simon Devereux incident, "Every tackle in a game of rugby is a common assault"[11] (*Sun,* February 23, 1996, 42).

In answering the question, "Why does violence in sport enjoy relative immunity from criminal sanction?" there are social, cultural, and historical factors at work that enter into the quite technical matter of determining consent. Legal intervention into sports assault cases remains problematic due to the intersection of sport, manliness, and profit in our culture. The reverence that we have for sport (including its violent and injurious aspects); the

220 *Young*

seductive revenues that sports businesses promise owners, communities, and governments; the aggressive requirements of appropriate masculine role performance, and the trust that we place in professional organizations together determine that player violence remains institutionalized and continues to elicit rewards.

The gender process has also limited antiviolence forays by the law into sports organizations. Students of gender will quickly observe, for instance, that both sport and law have historically operated as male-defined and male-controlled institutions. Even the most perfunctory examination of participation rates, employment possibilities, and general decision making is strongly suggestive of heavy patriarchal baggage in both athletic and legal domains. Compounding the already complicated task of distinguishing between acceptable and unacceptable sports behavior, this fact perhaps helps us explain the relative leniency of the law to participant violence in sport.

Notes

1. Far from representing a "world apart" (a common aspect of popular thinking about sport), sports issues, including violence issues, are very much connected to values, practices, and norms in the wider society.

2. The 1998 World Cup, held in France, witnessed numerous outbreaks of violence, including clashes between English and Tunisian fans and between German fans and the French police. The latter resulted in one police officer having his skull smashed with a signpost. At the time of writing, the overall "hooligan count," which at the very least involves the detention of hundreds of fans from a number of countries, is unclear (*Globe and Mail,* June 24, 1998, A1–11).

3. Among a long list of male and female athletes from a range of sports who report being stalked, harassed, or threatened is the figure skater Katarina Witt. In 1992, an obsessed fan was charged on seven counts of sending obscene and threatening mail, and was sentenced to three years in a U.S. psychiatric hospital. It was revealed that Harry Veltman II had, among other things, followed Witt around the world attempting to distract her as she skated in competition (*USA Today,* July 14, 1995, 3C).

4. In early 1997, the world of Canadian ice hockey was stunned by claims made by a National Hockey League player—Sheldon Kennedy—that his junior coach had sexually abused him on over three hundred occasions. After a short trial, the hockey coach Graham James was sentenced to three years in jail. At the time of writing, police have received literally dozens of calls from male hockey players across the country who allege being abused by older men connected with the sport.

5. What I am suggesting here is that gendering processes occurring in sport or law are reflections of gendering processes taking place in the wider society.

6. See Elias and Dunning (1986) and Dunning (1999) for substantive and theoretical samples of this important work.

7. In both Canada and the United States, for example, there has recently been a swing to the political Right with respect to punitive responses to street crime. In Canada, public outrage in the wake of numerous incidents of youth violence has been such that punitive sanctions have grown increasingly severe, and an exhaustive revamping of the Canadian Young Offenders Act is underway to toughen the legislation.

8. Canada Court Records, Wildfong and Lang, from *R. v. Bradshaw, 14,* Cox CC, 83.

9. Ibid.

10. In response to injuries in ice hockey (including paralyses), the Government of Canada released an advertisement in the late 1980s that contained a photograph of an empty hockey arena with the caption "The Scene of the Crime." The Ministry of Fitness and Amateur Sport has since allowed this particular advertising campaign to lapse, but it remains a fascinating attempt to relabel and transform public thinking on the Canadian national game.

11. A "hard man" is a player who accepts the risky and physical aspects of rugby at any cost.

References

Ball-Rokeach, S. (1971). The legitimation of violence. In J. F. Short & M. E. Wolfgang (Eds.), *Collective violence* (pp. 100–111). Chicago: Aldine.

Ball-Rokeach, S. (1980). Normative and deviant violence from a conflict perspective. *Social Problems, 28,* 45–62.

Ball-Rokeach, S., & Loges, W. E. (1996). Making choices: Media roles in the construction of value choices. In C. Seligman, J. Olson, & M. Zanna (Eds),. *The psychology of values: The Ontario symposium* Vol. 8 (pp. 277–298). Mahwah, NJ: Erlbaum.

Barnes, J. (1988). *Sports and the law in Canada.* Toronto: Butterworths.

Benedict, J., & Klein, A. (1997). Arrest and conviction rates for athletes accused of sexual assault. *Sociology of Sport Journal, 14,* 86–95.

Body of Evidence. (1994, July 11). *Newsweek, 124,* 20–25.

Bryson, L. (1987). Sport and the maintenance of masculine hegemony. *Women's Studies International Forum, 10,* 349–360.

Coakley, J. (1988/1989). Media coverage of sports and violent behavior: An elusive connection. *Current Psychology: Research and Reviews, 7,* 322–330.

Crosset, T., Benedict, J., & McDonald, M. (1995). Male student-athletes reported for sexual assault: Survey of campus police departments and judicial affairs. *Journal of Sport and Social Issues, 19,* 126–140.

Curry, T., & Strauss, R.H. (1994). A little pain never hurt anyone: A photo-essay on the normalization of sports injuries. *Sociology of Sport Journal, 11,* 195–208.

Donaldson, M. (1993). What is hegemonic masculinity? *Theory and Society, 22,* 643–657.

Donnelly, P. (1999). Who's fair game?: Sport, sexual harassment, and abuse. In P. White & K. Young (Eds.), *Sport and gender in Canada* (pp. 107–129). Don Mills, Ontario: Oxford University Press.

Dunning, E. (1999). *Sport matters: Sociological studies of sport, violence and civilization.* London: Routledge.

Elias, N., & Dunning, E. (1986). *Quest for excitement: Sport and leisure and the civilizing process.* New York: Basil Blackwell.

Head butt earns soccer player three months in jail. (1995, May 26). *Toronto Star,* p. C10.

Horrow, R. (1980). *Sports violence: The interaction between private law-making and the criminal law.* Arlington, VA: Carrollton Press.

Lenskyj, H. (1990). Power and play: Gender and sexuality issues in sport and physical activity. *International Review for the Sociology of Sport, 25,* 235–246.

Lister, V. (1995, July 14). Danger stalks athletes. *USA Today,* p. C3.

Melnick, M. (1992, May/June). Male athletes and sexual assault. *Journal of Physical Education, Recreation and Dance,* 32–35.

Messner, M., & Sabo, D. (1990). *Sport, men and the gender order: Critical feminist perspectives.* Champaign, IL: Human Kinetics.

Messner, M., & Sabo, D. (1994). *Sex, violence, and power in sports: Rethinking masculinity.* Freedom, CA: Crossing Press.

Nack, W., & Munson, L. (1995, July 31). Sport's dirty secret. *Sports Illustrated, 83,* 62–74.

Nixon, H. (1993). Accepting the risks of pain and injury in sport: Mediated cultural influences on playing hurt. *Sociology of Sport Journal, 11,* 79–87.

Opening Notes/Passages, Fined. (1994, February 28). *Macleans, 11.*

Price, S. L. (1995, July 17). The return. *Sports Illustrated, 83,* 22–26.

Price, S. L. (1996, August 5). Stained games. *Sports Illustrated, 85,* 22–31.

Reasons, C. (1992). The criminal law and sports violence: Hockey crimes. Unpublished manuscript, University of British Columbia, Vancouver.

Rugby player sentenced (1994, December 22). *Calgary Herald,* p. D2.

Smith, M. (1983). *Violence and sport.* Toronto: Butterworths.

Smith, M. (1987). *Violence in Canadian amateur sport: A review of literature*. Report for Commission for Fair Play. Ottawa, Ontario.

Smith, M. D., & Young, K. (1987). *Violence in Canadian amateur sport: An annotated bibliography*. Report to the Commission for Fair Play, Minister of State Fitness and Amateur Sport. Ottawa, Ontario.

Smolowe, J. (1994, January 24). Tarnished victory. *Time, 143*, 50–54.

Soccer player jailed (1995, October 12). *Calgary Herald*, p. C1.

Soccer star gets two weeks in jail (1995, March 24). *Calgary Herald*, p. D3.

Theberge, N. (1990). Gender, work, and power: The case of women in coaching. *Canadian Journal of Sociology, 15*, 59–75.

Thug rugby star jailed 9 months (1996, February 23). *The Sun*, p. 16.

White, D. (1986). Sports violence as criminal assault: Development of the doctrine by Canadian criminal courts. *Duke Law Journal, 36*, 1030–1034.

White, P., & Young, K. (1997). Masculinity, sport and the injury process: A review of Canadian and international evidence. *Avante, 3*, 1–30.

Young, K. (1986). The killing field: Themes in mass media responses to the Heysel Stadium riot. *International Review for the Sociology of Sport, 21*, 253–267.

Young, K. (1988). Sports crowd disorder, mass media, and ideology. Unpublished doctoral dissertation, McMaster University, Ontario.

Young, K. (1990). *Treatment of sports violence by the Canadian mass media*. Report to Sport Canada's Applied Sport Research Programme. Ottawa, Ontario.

Young, K. (1991). Sport and collective violence. *Exercise and Sports Sciences Reviews, 19*, 539–587.

Young, K. (1993). Violence, risk, and liability in male sports culture. *Sociology of Sport Journal, 10*, 373–396.

Young, K. (1994, March). *Sports violence: Its nature and extent in North America*. Keynote address presented at the VIII Annual Futures Conference on Sports Violence: Issues for Law Enforcement. Office of International Criminal Justice, University of Illinois at Chicago.

Young, K. (1997). Women, sport, and physicality: Preliminary findings from a Canadian study. *International Review for the Sociology of Sport, 32*, 297–305.

Young, K. (2000). Sport and violence. In J. Coakley & E. Dunning (Eds.), *Handbook of sport and society* (pp. 382–408). Thousand Oaks, CA: Sage.

Young, K., & Smith, M. D. (1988/1989). Mass media treatment of violence in sports and its effects. *Current Psychology: Research and Reviews, 7*, 298–312.

Young, K., & Wamsley, K. (1996). State complicity in sports assault and the gender order in twentieth century Canada: Preliminary observations. *Avante, 2,* 51–69.

Young, K., & White, P. (1995). Sport, physical danger, and injury: The experiences of elite women athletes. *Journal of Sport and Social Issues, 19,* 45–61.

Young, K., White, P., & McTeer, W. (1994). Body talk: Male athletes reflect on sport, injury, and pain. *Sociology of Sport Journal, 11,* 175–195.

FOURTEEN

Scoring without Consent

Confronting Male Athletes' Violence Against Women

MICHAEL A. MESSNER AND MARK A. STEVENS

In recent years, increased public attention has focused on incidents of violence against women perpetrated by high-profile college and professional male athletes. Although not long ago, accusations of sexual assault, sexual harassment, or wife abuse by a high-profile athlete may have been ignored, downplayed, or considered to be outside the frame of legitimate media coverage (Messner & Solomon, 1993), the issue of athletes' violence against women has now moved squarely into the realm of public and media discourse (McDonald, 1999). As reporters move to cover accusations (and sometimes convictions) of male athletes assaulting women, they have turned to scholars of sport with a key question, Are male athletes more likely than nonathletes to engage in acts of sexual violence against women, or do we just notice it more when some athletes assault women, because of their high-profile status?[1]

The question of male athletes' relationship to violence against women is difficult but important to answer. Some activists who work with athletes on violence prevention (e.g., Donald McPherson in this volume), argue that men's violence against women is a broad social problem that is proportionately reflected, like all other social problems, in sport. Perhaps fearing that pointing the finger at high-profile athletes will reinforce destructive and oppressive stereotypes of African American males as sexual predators, these activists prefer instead to pull male athletes into positions of responsibility to educate peers to prevent violence against women.[2]

Although programs based on these assumptions, like the Mentors in Violence program discussed by McPherson in chapter 15, are laudable, it is important to examine whether or not they are based on sound assumptions. Faulty assumptions can limit or undercut effectiveness. An examination of recent research on the relationship between athletic participation and violence against women is illustrative. A number of studies of college athletes in recent years have pointed to statistically significant relationships between athletic participation and sexual aggression (Boeringer, 1996; Fritner & Rubinson, 1993; Koss & Gaines, 1993). In what is widely considered the most reliable study to date, Crosset, Benedict, and McDonald (1995) surveyed twenty universities with Division I athletic programs, and found that male athletes, who comprised 3.7 percent of the student population, were 19 percent of those reported to campus Judicial Affairs Offices for sexual assault.[3] Crosset (2000) argues that researchers probably use too broad a brush in their examination of "men's sports" and violence against women. Vast cross-sports differences are found. Koss and Gaines (1993) found a much stronger relationship for men's "revenue-producing sports," and Crosset, Ptacek, McDonald, and Benedict (1996) found that the majority of reported assaults concerned athletes in "contact sports" (e.g., basketball, football, and hockey). These data suggest the danger of "clumping all sport environments together under the rubric of athletic affiliation" (Crosset, 2000). When the focus is on specific kinds of athletic contexts, we may be able to better understand the causes of some athletes' violence against women, and thus intervene more effectively.

Crosset (2000) argues that although empirical research does show a correlation between participation in certain kinds of sports with violent and misogynous attitudes and behaviors, more research is needed to establish clear causal connections. He concludes that the current debate over whether athletes commit more violence than nonathletes do against women is "unproductive." It "detracts from the fact that some athletes are violent against women," a fact that calls for active prevention efforts. Crosset's pragmatic point is well taken, and we take it a step further. It is important to confront male athletes' violence against women not only because "some athletes are violent against women," but also because the world of sport is a key institutional site for construction of hegemonic masculinity, and thus a key site for its contestation (Bryson, 1987; Kidd, 1990; Messner, 1988). The institution of sport tends not only to "reflect," but also to *amplify* everything about masculinity that is generally true in the larger gender order. Values of male heroism based on competition and winning, playing hurt, handing out pain to opponents, group-based bonding through homophobia and misogyny, and the legitimation of interpersonal violence as a means to success are all values undergirding hegemonic masculinity in the larger gender order that are amplified in men's sport. Thus, confronting these issues within sport may not only help make the world safer for some women, but a fundamental confrontation with the root causes of athletic men's violence against women may have a positive ripple effect throughout the larger gender order.

It is necessary to distinguish between direct and complicit involvement. The vast majority of male athletes *do not engage* in violence against women, but an unknown, and certainly larger, percentage are complicit by their silence. We argue that intervention strategies must confront the root causes of men's violence against women, and that a key way to accomplish this is to provide a context in which the "silent majority" of men move affirmatively away from being complicit in a culture of misogyny, homophobia, and violence.

The question of what enables, encourages, or even rewards certain men's violence against women is a complex one. Broad, contextual factors such as the degree to which boys experience life as a pedagogy of legitimate violence (Canada, 1995), combined with the degree of gender inequality in the culture or community (Sanday, 1981) can enable or constrain men's violence against women. Researchers have only begun to explore possible linkages between men's violence against women with the experience of some men—especially in homosocial (same sex) institutions like sports, the military, or fraternities—of being routinely rewarded for successfully using their bodies as weapons against other men (Messner, 1992; Nixon, 1997). Furthermore, researchers have begun to explore links between male athletes' violence against women with their experience of being rewarded for ignoring their own pain and injuries and "giving one's body up for the team" (Messner, 1992; Sabo, 1994a; Young & White, 2000). With these issues in mind, we will focus this chapter on one key element underlying male athletes' violence against women: the peer group dynamics of the team. Following our analytic discussion of these dynamics, we will raise some critical questions about educational intervention strategies with male athletes.

Locker-Room Talk, and Actions

In a riveting and insightful news account of the infamous 1989 Glen Ridge gang rape case, a journalist, Bernard Lefkowitz (1997) describes how twelve popular White high school athletes lured a seventeen-year-old "slightly retarded" girl into a basement. The dynamics of the sexual assault that ensued are instructive for our purposes here: First, the boys set up chairs—theater style—in front of a couch. As some boys sit in the chairs to watch, others lead the girl to the couch and induce her to begin to give oral sex to one of the most popular and respected boys. As this happens, one sophomore boy notices "puzzlement and confusion" in the girl's eyes, turns to his friend and says, "Let's get out of here" (Lefkowitz, 1997, p. 23). Another senior baseball player "feels queasy" and thinks, "I don't belong here," and climbs the stairs to leave with another baseball player. On the way out, he tells another guy, "It's wrong. C'mon with me," but the other guy stays (p. 24). In all, six of the young men leave, while six—five seniors and one junior—remain in the basement. As the girl is forced to continue giving oral sex to the boy, other boys laugh, shout encouragement to their friends, and derisively shout, "You whore!" at the girl (p. 24). One boy decides it would be amusing to sexually abuse her with a baseball bat. As he does this (and follows it with a broomstick), the girl hears one boy's voice say, "Stop. You're hurting her," but another voice says, "Do it more" (p. 25). Later, the girl remembers that the boys were all laughing, while she was crying. When they were done, they warned her not to tell anyone, and concluded with an athletic ritual of togetherness by standing in a circle and clasping "One hand on top of the other, all their hands together, like a bas-ketball team on the sidelines at the end of a timeout" (p. 25).

In his description and analysis of the Glen Ridge community in which the boys and their victim grew up, Lefkowitz points to a number of factors that enabled the gang rape to happen. These include many of the factors that the recent social scientific literature on men, sexual violence, and sport has pointed to

1. the role of competitive, homophobic, and misogynistic talk and joking as a form of "dominance bonding" in the ath-letic male peer group;
2. "voyeuring" whereby boys set up situations where they seduce girls in places and situations in which their friends watch the sex act, and sometimes take an active part in it;
3. the suppression of empathy—especially toward girls who are the objects of the competitive male dominance bonding that boys learn from each other;
4. a "culture of silence" among peers, families, and the larger community that enables some men's sexual violence against women.

In examining these four enabling factors, we keep in the forefront Lefkowitz's observation that the actual physical assault in the case he reported was conducted by four football players and wrestlers. Two others, apparently, sat and watched—perhaps laughed and cheered—but did not actually physically join in the assault. The other six boys who left the scene as the assault was beginning felt uncomfortable enough to leave, but they did not do anything significant at the time to stop their friends. They did not leave the basement and report the assault to parents, teachers, or the police, and they all refused throughout the subsequent years of litigation to "turn on" their male friends to provide incriminating evidence. It is the *complicity* of these boys that is the centerpiece of our analysis. As R. W. Connell (1995) has argued, the dominant or "hegemonic" form of masculinity is usually expressed and embodied by a relatively small proportion of men; what helps hegemonic masculinity sustain itself in a system of power relations is the consent of many women, but especially the complicity of other men—some (or many) of whom may be uncomfortable with some or all of the beliefs and practices that sustain hegemonic masculinity. Although legal interventions in sexual assaults obviously need to target the behaviors of boys and men who are perpetrators, intervention strategies that aim to prevent future sexual assaults should also target those boys and men who may be marginal to the group, but whose complicit silence enables their teammates' assaultive behaviors.

Sexual Talk and Dominance Bonding

Gary Alan Fine (1987) found that one important way in which eleven- and twelve-year-old boys in Little League Baseball learn to bond with each other is with sexually aggressive banter. Wood (1984) argues that this sort of competitive sexual talk among boys is a sort of group pedagogy through which boys are "groping toward sexism" in their attitudes and practices toward girls and women. These same tendencies are evident among postadolescent and young adult men. In a study of talk in a college men's athletic locker room, Curry (1991) observed a dominant mode of conversation inclined toward the dual themes of competition and boasting of sexual conquests of women. Such conversation is characterized by high volume—it is clearly intended as a performance for the group—and by its geographic and discourse centrality. This kind of locker-room talk has consequences. First, as Curry's (2000) subsequent research of college athletes' violence in a sports bar shows, aggressive talk can often be connected to violent off-the-field actions. And, according to Farr (1988), sexually aggressive talk provides a means of "dominance bonding" for young males that can later spill over into non-sports-related occupations. Internal hierarchies are constructed and contested as the boys and young men simultaneously mark the boundaries of the "insider" and the "outsider" (e.g., women, gay men, and nonathletic men). And dominance bonding—based as it is on humorous, aggressive, sometimes violent talk about sex—has an erotic base to it, as Lyman's (1987) research on joking among fraternity members indicates.

Curry's (1991) locker-room study suggests another important discourse dynamic. On the margins of the locker room, other men were engaged in other kinds of conversations. They spoke in hushed tones about personal issues, even insecurities about dating or relationships with girlfriends. These quiet and private conversations stand in contrast to the loud and public conversation that dominates the locker room. We speculate that these more personal conversations remain private partly because boys and young men have had the experience of being (or seeing other boys) humiliated in male groups for expressing vulnerability, or for expressing care for a particular girl (Sabo, 1994b).

The main policing mechanisms used to enforce consent are misogyny and homophobia: Boys and men who may have made themselves vulnerable by revealing personal information are often targeted as the symbolic "women," "pussies," and "faggots" on athletic teams (and, indeed, in many other male groups). A key part of the group process of dominance bonding is that one or more members of the male group are made into the symbolic debased and degraded feminized "other" through which the others can bond and feel that their status as "men" is safely ensured. Early on, most boys learn to avoid offering themselves up as targets for this kind of abuse. The power of this group dynamic was illustrated in Messner's (1992) interview with a former athlete who, during his successful athletic career, had been a closeted gay man. One of the best ways in which this man found to keep his secret was to participate in what he called "locker-room garbage" talk about sexual conquests of women.

"Voyeuring": Women as Objects of Conquest

Lefkowitz (1997, pp. 183–184) shows that by the time they were teens, the "jocks" of Glen Ridge used more than talk for their erotic dominance bonding. They would sometimes gather together in a home when parents were away to watch pornographic films and masturbate together. The next step was the development of a group form of entertainment that they called "voyeuring" whereby a plan would be made for one guy at a party to "convince a girl to go upstairs to a bedroom for a sexual encounter." But first, "his buddies would go up and hide in a closet, under the bed, or behind a door" where they could watch. Sex with a girl, for these guys, was less an intimate encounter with a valued human being than it was the use of a woman's body as a platform for sexual performance for one's male buddies. It was, in Lefkowitz's words, "a way for these guys to create their own porn movie" (p. 184). Though it is difficult to say how widespread similar voyeuring among male athletes might be, this erotic bonding dynamic is found elsewhere. For instance, the California White high school football players known as the "Spur Posse" had multiple sexual encounters with girls and young women to see who could "score" the most times (Messner, 1994). Similarly, Sanday's (1990) research suggests that misogynistic denigration of women and erotic male bonding underlie fraternity gang rapes.

A key to understanding the group process by which males use women's bodies to erotically bond with each other is that most heterosexual boys and young men go through a period of intense insecurity and intense discomfort when learning to establish heterosexual relations with girls and women. Former male athletes reported that when they were in high school or even in college, talking with girls and women raised intense anxieties and feelings of inadequacy (Messner, 1992). They dealt with feelings of "lameness" with young women primarily by listening to and watching their male peers deliver a "rap" to women. As these men immersed themselves in the peer pedagogy of heterosexual relations, they learned to put on a performance for girls which, surprisingly for some of them, seemed to "work." Their successful utilization of this learned dramaturgy of the heterosexual "come-on" allowed them to mask or overcome a sense and appearance of insecurity and "lameness." It also intensified—at a deep psychological level—adherence to the group process of erotic dominance bonding with other members of the male peer group by collectively constructing women as objects of conquest.

Suppression of Empathy

An important lesson that an athlete—especially one in the more aggressive "combat sports"—must learn in order to survive and thrive is to suppress empathy for one's opponent (Messner, 1992). Nixon's (1997) research suggests that male athletes who learn to accept that their participation in sports will routinely result in injuries to others are more likely to engage in physical aggression outside of the sport context. Cross-cultural research on rape has pointed to the importance *of the degree and type of contact that boys and men have with girls and women* as variables that correlate with rates of rape. Rape rates tend to be higher in societies with rigid divisions of labor between the sexes, especially where these divisions are marked by male dominance and female subordination (Sanday, 1981). Homosocial (same sex) bonding among men, especially when it is the sort of sexualized dominance bonding just discussed, is a very poor environment for the development of empathy for women. Lefkowitz (1997) observes that the boys most central to the Glen Ridge rape grew up without sisters in families dominated by strong male figures. Their peer group, family, and community experiences taught them that boys' and men's activities were more highly prized than those of girls and women. "The immediate environment," Lefkowitz argues, "did not cultivate great empathy for women" (p. 28). In contrast, some of the boys who left the scene due to their discomfort with the gang rape were unable to suppress their empathy for the victim. Most of these boys grew up in homes with sisters.

The Culture of Silence

A question that plagued Lefkowitz in his examination of the Glen Ridge rape was why the six boys who left the scene remained complicit in their silence, both the day of the rape, and during the subsequent years of litigation. At least some of these young men were very uncomfortable with what happened—even thought it was "wrong"—but nobody in the group raised a hand or voice to stop it. The case "broke" when another male athlete who had not been at the scene of the assault reported to teachers that he had overheard other guys laughing and bragging about the rape. This African American whistle-blower felt excluded from the tightly knit, high-status clique of White athletes. A second nonparticipant young man became an activist in a quest to see that the jocks did not get away with their crime. He was a long-haired *Gigger,* a term used to identify the small minority of radical, artsy, antijock crowd at the school. Both of these boys—one an athlete, one not—were *outsiders* to the dominant athletic male peer group. Those inside—even those who were marginal within the group—maintained a complicit silence that enabled the assault to occur.

This culture of silence is built into the dynamics of the group's spoken and unspoken codes and rituals. Boys have years of experience within the group that has taught them that there are rewards for remaining complicit with the code of silence, and indeed, there are punishments for betraying the group. A whistle-blower might be banished from the group, be beaten up, or he might remain in the group, but now with the status of the degraded, feminized "faggot" who betrayed the "men" in the group.

Empowering Marginal Discourses

How might coaches, teachers, counselors, and parents intervene with young male athletes to encourage changes in the attitudes and relations that lead to assaults on girls and women? Confronting a male athletic team, especially as an adult "outsider," is a daunting task. The difficulty of this task is compounded by the fact that all too often, professionals are brought in to consult with athletic departments and to run workshops with athletes because assaultive behaviors have already occurred. There is often in these situations an atmosphere of resentment and defensive silence among the athletes. The intervention strategies discussed in the next section aim to use what little time there is to provide a safe place for talk, but also an enabling place for the emergence of new forms of talk. We explicitly try to "decenter" the dominant misogynistic conversation, while empowering the non-sexist conversations that might otherwise remain marginal.

Contextual and Facilitation Issues

Male student-athletes approach our workshops in much the same way that most people anticipate spending an evening at traffic school. They resent having to attend, anticipate a critical finger being pointed in their direction, and often enter the room with an air of unfriendliness and bravado. On the other hand, we have found a detectable amount of curiosity hidden beneath this veneer of aloofness. Understanding male student-athletes' resistance while expanding their curiosity helps the engagement process. The facilitator needs to be prepared for a unique type of intimidation that may take the form of loud side conversations, off-the-wall questions, insider jokes, and loud silences accompanied by nonexpressive staring. We have attempted to meet these challenges by using a variety of facilitation tools designed to create a safe learning environment, which reduces resistance and increases positive engagement.

- *Get Their Attention:* We provide statistics, show some video clips, and ask rhetorical questions, such as, "How many of you would like to know with 99 percent certainty that you will never be accused or convicted of being a date or acquaintance rapist?" Almost all participants raise their hands in response to this question. With most eyes on the facilitators, we then tell them that there are some simple principles and practices to use in order to know when one has full consent, and that we will be discussing these later on in the workshop.
- *Self-Disclosure:* We strategically and selectively share our own personal sexual and athletic experiences to create a safe context for risk-taking and to lessen the us-versus-them mentality.
- *Reward Honesty:* Participants are more verbal when they feel that they are respected and will be heard. When they are rewarded for taking the risk of sharing their thoughts and feelings, even if they happen to be "politically incorrect," they engage the workshop instead of shutting down.
- *Be Firm, But Flexible:* Groups of male student-athletes can be quite loud, and this group dynamic can create a chaotic

learning environment. We try to demonstrate that we expect them to treat us with the same respect that they treat their coaches. On the other hand, we find that it is important to allow room for laughter and for some level of chaos, and even to join in at appropriate times.

- *Respectfully Challenge:* Participants often present opinions that need to be challenged. It is an essential part of the educational process to find ways to challenge the participants in a manner that will lead to continued dialogue. One way to accomplish this is to become curious, rather than critical, concerning how a participant developed a certain opinion or belief.

The Workshop Agenda

Increasing empathy. Empathy is the ability to take into consideration and respond accordingly to the feelings of another person. Empathy allows one to measure the impact and consequences that a certain behavior will have on another human being. Men who sexually violate others have been shown to have limited empathy skills (Stevens, 1993). We have argued that athletes are often immersed in peer contexts in which they are rewarded for suppressing their empathy toward others. Increasing empathy skills is thus key to the success of any rape prevention program, but especially important when dealing with male student-athletes. Most men give little thought to how the fear of rape can be so incredibly consuming for women. Additionally, most men are unaware of the fact that most women feel neither flattered nor safe when whistled at or made the target of lewd propositions and ogling. In fact, many men have been socialized to view such behavior as essential to the mating ritual, as well as an important component of the bonding process in the male group. Furthermore, men have been systematically taught—partly, but not exclusively within athletics—to hide, avoid, or deny their own feelings of pain, embarrassment, or hurt. When boys are told not to cry, they are also being denied the opportunity to learn how to empathize and feel for the other. We employ a variety of tools and exercises to help motivate men to improve their empathy skills:

1. *Imagining a world without rape:* We ask the group to imagine what their life would be like if there were no such thing as rape. We then ask them to imagine how women would feel and act if they knew there was no such thing as rape.

2. *Being bullied:* We ask the participants to recall an experience when they were threatened or picked on by someone
   who was bigger or more powerful. We ask them to describe
   how they felt after the attack.

3. *What if this happened to your sister or girlfriend?* After we
   ask the participants to discuss the variety of ways that they
   try to "hit on" or "pick up" women, we ask them to imagine other guys using the same behaviors toward their sisters
   or girlfriends. In response to their discussion of their feelings and reactions, we attempt to pierce the implicit
   Madonna-whore view of women that often pervades male
   peer groups. We challenge them to be aware of the fact that
   every woman has a brother, a boyfriend, and/or other family who cares about her.

Gaining full consent. Sexual assault cannot occur if there is full and mutual
consent. How to know that full consent exists is a complicated process. We
approach this problem by suggesting the concept of a "consent table" upon
which certain variables need to be clearly placed before one can be certain
that consent exists. These variables include permission, sobriety, a truthful
statement of one's intentions, and any other information that would influence one's decision to become sexually involved. Making these variable
explicit *before* becoming fully sexually involved tends to run against the
grain of men's taken-for-granted notions of a "proper sexual script." Most
men have been taught to believe that they just automatically "know" when
a woman is aroused and willing to become sexually involved. The idea of
asking for permission or clarification of some ambiguity seems unroman-
tic, and seems to raise the risk of rejection. Several exercises are designed
to clarify the importance of having unambiguous consent. For example, we
relate various scenarios, and ask them to discuss whether consent was clear
in each scenario. Two of our most successful are as follows:

The traffic light metaphor. We begin by asking the men how they respond
as drivers to a red, yellow, or green light. They usually say that they know
what to do with a red or green light, but when approaching a yellow light,
there is often a moment of confusion, usually followed by their speeding up
rather than slowing down. Sexual encounters, the men tell us, are far too
often experienced as a yellow light. We extend the metaphor by noting that
a yellow light is supposed to signal a driver to slow down and show caution; speeding up is a major cause of crashes in intersections. We explain
that a sexual encounter is very much like an intersection—ripe with both
excitement and danger—a "yellow light" should be a sign that danger

looms, and that one should slow down; show caution. We ask participants to brainstorm ways they can respond to yellow light situations in ways that are respectful and that assure consensual sex.

Speaking out. We have found that many men are disgusted when they see other men verbally and/or physically degrade women. Yet when confronted with this reality, they often say nothing or signal their approval. One root of this complicit silence is that men are afraid of other men. As with most all-male groups, male student-athletes are reluctant to break the silence for fear of being humiliated, ostracized, or beaten up. One way that we confront this issue in workshops is to utilize the concept of team loyalty. For instance, we ask them what is likely to happen *to the team* if, at a party, two or three of their teammates take a very drunk woman into a room and have sex with her when she is clearly not in a condition to give her full consent. Isn't it part of the loyalty to the team, to each other, and to themselves to bravely step in and stop something like this from happening? Responses to these sorts of questions suggested that some of the previously more marginal men on the teams are empowered to speak out. And, interestingly, when one teammate does speak out—at least in the context of the workshop—others on the team seem to listen, and other marginal teammates then feel empowered to add their voices to the mix.

Summary

Current intervention programs with male athletes (e.g., the University of Massachusetts Mentors in Violence Program, Athletes for Sexual Responsibility at the University of Maine, as well as our work in various colleges) need to be empirically evaluated to assess their effect, if any, on sexist attitudes and dynamics of male athletic peer groups that enable the assaultive behaviors of some male athletes. We suspect that interventions that are not organically linked to long-term institutional attempts to address men's violence at its psychological, peer group, and organizational roots will have little, if any, effect. At their best, such programs may provide a context in which some individual boys and men are empowered to remove themselves from the role of passively complicit (but not fully comfortable) participants in the daily practices that feed an athletic rape culture. Boys and young men who have suppressed empathy for girls and women might be reawakened and validated, especially if they come to understand the links between their own marginalization within the male peer group and that group's denigration and victimization of women. These young men might be moved to risk "breaking the silence" to speak out against the dominant discourse and practices of the group. The result of this might be that a few girls and women—and indeed, some boys and men—will be safer than they might otherwise have been.

But intervention programs that do not directly confront these contextual factors are unlikely to radically alter the annual reproduction of sport as a pedagogical site for boys' and men's learning of violence against women. In fact, "rape awareness sessions" for athletes may serve as a school or university's public relations window dressing, while allowing the athletic department and its teams to continue with business as usual. A commitment to address the root causes of men's violence against women will ultimately run up against the need to fundamentally rethink both the dominant conceptions of gender in the society, as well as the specific ways that gender difference and hierarchy continue to be constructed in sport.

Notes

1. Benedict and Klein (1997) compared arrest and conviction rates of male collegiate and professional athletes accused of felony sexual assault with national crime data, and concluded that when athletes are accused of sexual assault, they are more likely than nonathletes to be arrested or indicted, but significantly less likely to be convicted.

2. It is important not to dodge questions related to race, violence, and men (see Klein & Sorenson in this volume). When data reveal that college athletes in revenue-producing sports have higher rates of sexual assaults against women, the term *athletes in revenue-producing sports* can become a thinly veiled code word for *Black* male athletes, and thus a way to perpetuate racist stereotypes of Black males as sexual predators. It is our position that the apparent overrepresentation of Black male college athletes charged with sexual assault is due to their dramatic overrepresentation in football and basketball. In high school, where White males are more highly represented in the student-athlete population, some of the most egregious examples of sexual assault by athletes have involved White males, for instance, the gang rape described in this chapter.

3. Crosset and his colleagues also surveyed reports to campus police departments and found that male athletes were more likely to be reported for sexual assault than male nonathletes, but the difference was not statistically significant. They argue that college women are more likely to report assaults to Judicial Affairs than to campus police, and so the (statistically significant) data from the former are a better reflection of reality than the data from the latter.

References

Benedict, J., & Klein, A. (1997). Arrest and conviction rates for athletes accused of sexual assault. *Sociology of Sport Journal, 14*, 73–85.

Boeringer, S. D. (1996). Influences of fraternity membership, athletics and male living arrangements on sexual aggression. *Violence Against Women, 2*, 134–147.

Bryson, L. (1987). Sport and the maintenance of masculine hegemony. *Women's Studies International Forum, 10*, 349–360.

Canada, J. (1995). *Fist stick knife gun: A personal history of violence in America.* Boston: Beacon.

Connell, R. W. (1995). *Masculinities.* Berkeley: University of California Press.

Crosset, T. (2000). Athletic affiliation and violence against women: Toward a structural prevention project. In J. McKay, D. F. Sabo, & M. A. Messner (Eds.), *Masculinities, gender relations, and sport* (pp. 147–161). Thousand Oaks, CA: Sage.

Crosset, T. W., Benedict, J. R., & McDonald, M. (1995). Male student-athletes reported for sexual assault: A survey of campus police departments and judicial affairs offices. *Journal of Sport and Social Issues, 19*, 126–140.

Crosset, T., Ptacek, J., McDonald, M., & Benedict, J. (1996). Male student-athletes and violence against women: A survey of campus judicial affairs offices. *Violence Against Women, 2*, 163–179.

Curry, T. (1991). Fraternal bonding in the locker room: Pro-feminist analysis of talk about competition and women. *Sociology of Sport Journal, 8*, 119–135.

Curry, T. (2000). Booze, boys and bars: The social psychology of public violence among college athletes. In J. McKay, D. F. Sabo, & M. A. Messner (Eds.), *Masculinities, gender relations, and sport* (pp. 162–175). Thousand Oaks, CA: Sage.

Farr, K. A. (1988). Dominance bonding through the good old boys' sociability group. *Sex Roles, 18*, 259–277.

Fine, G. A. (1987). *With the boys: Little league baseball and preadolescent culture.* Chicago: University of Chicago Press.

Fritner, M. P., & Rubinson, L. (1993). Acquaintance rape: The influence of alcohol, fraternity membership and sports team membership. *Journal of Sex Education and Therapy, 19*, 272–284.

Kidd, B. (1990). The men's cultural center: Sports and the dynamic of women's oppression/men's repression. In M. A. Messner & D. F. Sabo (Eds.), *Sport, men and the gender order: Critical feminist perspectives* (pp. 31–42). Champaign, IL: Human Kinetics.

Koss, M., & Gaines, J. (1993). The prediction of sexual aggression by alcohol use, athletic participation and fraternity affiliation. *Journal of Interpersonal Violence, 8*, 94–108.

Lefkowitz, B. (1997). *Our guys*. New York: Vintage Books.

Lyman, P. (1987). The fraternal bond as a joking relationship: A case study of sexist jokes in male group bonding. In M. S. Kimmel (Ed.), *Changing men: New directions in research on men and masculinity* (pp. 148–163). Newbury Park, CA: Sage.

McDonald, M. (1999). Unnecessary roughness: Gender and racial politics in domestic violence events. *Sociology of Sport Journal, 16,* 111–133.

Messner, M. A. (1988). Sports and male domination: The female athlete as contested ideological terrain. *Sociology of Sport Journal, 5,* 197–211.

Messner, M. A. (1992). *Power at play: Sports and the problem of masculinity*. Boston: Beacon.

Messner, M. A. (1994). Riding with the spur posse. In M. A. Messner & D. F. Sabo, *Sex, violence and power in sports: Rethinking masculinity* (pp. 66–70). Freedom, CA: Crossing Press.

Messner, M. A., & Solomon, W. S. (1993). Outside the frame: Newspaper coverage of the Sugar Ray Leonard wife abuse story. *Sociology of Sport Journal, 10,* 119–134.

Nixon, H. L. II (1997). Gender, sport, and aggressive behavior outside sport. *Journal of Sport and Social Issues, 21,* 379–391.

Sabo, D. (1994a). Pigskin, patriarchy and pain. In M. A. Messner & D. F. Sabo (Eds.), *Sex, violence and power in sport: Rethinking masculinity* (pp. 82–88). Freedom, CA: Crossing Press.

Sabo, D. (1994b). The myth of the sexual athlete. In M. A. Messner & D. F. Sabo, *Sex, violence and power in sport: Rethinking masculinity* (pp. 36–41). Freedom, CA: Crossing Press.

Sanday, P. (1981). *Female power and male dominance: On the origins of sexual inequality*. New York: Cambridge University Press.

Sanday, P. (1990). *Fraternity gang rape: Sex, brotherhood and privilege on campus*. New York: New York University Press.

Stevens, M. (1993). College men and sexual violation: Counseling process and programming considerations. In L. Whitaker & J. Pollard (Eds.), *Campus violence: Kinds, causes, and cures* (pp. 239–258). Binghamton, NY: Haworth.

Wood, J. (1984). Groping toward sexism: boys' sex talk. In A. McRobbie & M. Nava (Eds.), *Gender and generation* (pp. 54–84). London: Macmillan.

Young, K., & White, P. (2000). Researching sports injury: Reconstructing dangerous masculinities. In J. McKay, D. F. Sabo, & M. A. Messner (Eds.), *Masculinities, gender relations, and sport* (pp. 108–126). Thousand Oaks, CA: Sage.

FIFTEEN

Sport, Youth, Violence, and the Media

An Activist Athlete's Point of View

DONALD G. McPHERSON

The purposes of this chapter are to challenge the view that the "male locker room" is a distinctive breeding ground of misogyny, to draw attention to the effects of television upon sports culture, and to describe the effects of my experience in a program designed for athletes that seeks to combat misogyny and sexism. I make the argument that there is nothing distinctive about male sports culture that predisposes male athletes to violence against girls and women.

The Male Locker Room

It has long been assumed that the male sports locker room is a breeding ground for misogyny. The presumption is that the locker room is distinctively wrought with lewd comments, exaggerated stories of sexual exploits, and aggressive male behavior that promotes men's violence against women. In reality, locker-room behavior and attitudes are brought into that environment by boys and men who have been raised in a culture that has taught and nurtured those attitudes and behavior. Many young boys are raised in a culture that teaches and supports misogyny. This is a culture that teaches women to protect themselves against rape and sexual assault, but does very little to tell boys why sexist behavior is wrong. The lack of female presence and influence in the locker room allows such attitudes to be expressed free of admonishment. Still, the assumption prevails that there is something special about the male sports locker room that promotes sexist behavior.

241

Without question, the male locker room is a stage for the verbose braggart and the foul-mouthed joker. However, the locker room is no different from many other all-male environments that exclude women as a general practice. Whether it's in corporate boardrooms, construction sites, or health club locker rooms, the behavior is similar. What makes them similar is the lack of female presence and/or the clear understanding that this is a male-dominated environment. The few females who entered these environments have had to endure the prevailing attitudes. As more and more females come into corporate boardrooms, law firms, and constructions sites, these environments may become less vulgar and misogynous. Basic privacy rights have enabled the locker room to remain relatively free of female intrusion and, therefore, relatively unchanged.

Cultural Roots of Misogyny and Violence Against Women

Our entire culture must be examined in order to identify the developmental roots of misogyny and male violence against girls and women. In particular, we need to examine the views and beliefs of those who own the advertising, marketing, and television industries. The success of American sports as a form of entertainment and business is due in large part to the power of the mass media and, in particular, television. Television advertising and marketing agents have changed the function of sport in American culture. Once considered recreation and education, sport now serves a completely different function in our culture. Today, financial considerations play at least as large a role as educational and developmental considerations in athletes', families', and coaches' decision making. Businesses see only the entertainment and financial value of sports venues. Sport is packaged as an entertainment consumer item for sale.

What is sold, however, is more than entertainment and the products endorsed by networks, leagues, and athletes. As consumers of "sport," we buy the nostalgia, not the cultural reality, of what we loved most about classical sport. We substitute team merchandise for the values of teamwork and sportsmanship. But most of all, we buy the attitudes of those who sell us these products. The images and attitudes of commercial advertising have become fundamental elements of our sport culture. Their messages teach a win-at-all-costs attitude that undermines the traditional values of sport. The attitudes of "savage" capitalism communicated through the media now dominate discourse on sport.

This presents a perplexing dilemma for organizations, like Northeastern University's Center for the Study of Sport in Society, which develop programs designed to use sport to address social issues. How can one effectively intervene to reduce sports violence, and gender violence in particular, when violence not only sells, but also has become part of the definition of good entertainment?

The Mentors in Violence Prevention Program

Developed in 1993 at Northeastern University, the mission of the Mentors in Violence Prevention (MVP) program is to reposition gender violence as a men's issue. The MVP program was created by Jackson Katz and Art Taylor of Sport in Society, and Ron Slaby of the Education Development Center in Newton, MA. Historically, men's violence against women has been considered a women's issue. Women bore the sole responsibility of dealing with sexual harassment, sexual assault, battery, rape, and the like. By calling these problems "women's issues," questions about male socialization practices that contribute to gender violence were excluded from the discussion.

The MVP program is designed to bring men into the discussion of gender violence prevention. Its goals are to identify and educate male athletes to lead other men in discussion regarding issues of male responsibility, bystander behavior, and leadership. Major training aims include raising awareness about how men have been socialized to view women as "less than" men, and to hold misogynous attitudes and behavior. Awareness training is followed by action-oriented training in the important role of bystander behavior—the actions and reactions of those who witness misogynous attitudes and actual instances of men's violence against women. The goal is to activate bystander behavior that expresses disapproval of such attitudes and behavior. The focus on bystander behavior is designed to avoid resistance that would be elicited from a focus on the athlete himself. An assailant or perpetrator focus would suggest that trainers regard all male athletes as actual or potential aggressors against women.

A Personal Case in Point

When I was first introduced to the Mentors in Violence Program, I didn't consider myself to be an oppressive or abusive man, but I was uninformed. I had just retired from a seven-year professional football career and was more interested in issues of racial equality in sport because of my personal experiences. However, as I examined my own socialization, and the process of my own understanding of gender, I realized how my sense of masculinity had been developed through my experiences as an athlete. I also became keenly aware of how our entire culture supports and perpetuates sexist mores.

While examining my experiences as a boy and as a young athlete, I thought of the behavioral expectations placed on me and on many other young boys during sport participation. I thought especially about the ways in which behavior is enforced by other males. I considered the language that is used to shame boys. One expression had haunted me—"you throw like a girl." This is an expression that virtually every male athlete has heard. It takes different forms in nonsport related endeavors (e.g., "you are a sissy"); however the meaning and understanding is consistent. Girls are less than boys, and to be considered "girl-like" is an insult. Boys learn these attitudes at critical stages of psychological and emotional development of gender identification and understanding of gender roles. I learned that if we, as boys and men, consider girls and women to be less than us, then we are more likely to disrespect, disregard girls and women and, ultimately, to emotionally abuse them. I saw a connection between misogyny and other forms of oppression. Nazi Germany, American slavery, civil war in countries such as Bosnia, and the age-old conflict in the Middle East are all examples of oppression based on the notion of superiority of one group over another.

Another lesson of sport concerns pain and emotional expression. Coaches and teammates often discourage the expression of physical or emotional pain. Such expression is treated as a sign of weakness that could undermine team success. In parallel fashion, demonstrations of the ability to ignore feelings, especially physical and emotional pain, are often rewarded and extolled in sport participation.

I can recall a particular game, while playing quarterback in college football, when I suffered a third-degree separation of my left shoulder. As the medical staff cut my jersey and shoulder pads from my torso, I protested while the doctor taped a pad on my shoulder and taped my clavicle back in place. My protest was because he wrapped it too tight, thereby limiting my ability to fully use my left arm, and my effectiveness on plays to the left. With total disregard for the pain and for my physical well-being, I thought I would continue to play. It didn't matter that the only thing holding my arm to my body was flesh, as all the ligaments in my shoulder had been torn away from the bone. In my mind I could not lie down; I could not miss a play. I was taught that pain must be ignored in competition. Today I'm more aware and understand that if I can ignore my own pain, then I am less capable of acknowledging the pain I inflict on other people. Moreover, denial of pain can generalize to a general inability to acknowledge the feelings of others.

When the denial of pain is coupled with the lessons of female inferiority, a dangerous combination of attitudes and beliefs is formed that can lead to emotionally abusive and physically violent behavior against women. In defense of sport, I must say that my sexist attitudes came from many other influences in my life. Older boys of my youth bragged of sexual encounters, and a more conservative patriarchal society taught the inferiority of women. Television exaggerated these lessons.

Extending the Locker Room

Through the media we consume millions of images that instill ideas, influence behavior, and affect what we consider to be "normal" and "deviant" behavior. In many cases, we become desensitized due to the sheer number of times that we witness recurring themes, sex and violence, in particular. Even our daily news programs are consumed with violence and stories of sexual exploitation. We observe objectification of women and gratuitous sex and violence as staples in advertising, music television, daytime television, and even children's video games. Scholars and researchers continually debate the "chicken and egg" question. Does television violence cause societal violence, or is television merely a window on our culture? As we remain embroiled in this debate, sexist and objectified images and messages continue to flood the minds of our youth, probably lessening their ability to see others' and, in particular, women's pain. Our adherence to the First Amendment rights of the media keeps us at arm's length from addressing how the media nurtures and reinforces negative and potentially dangerous attitudes.

When I retired from football in 1994, I left the locker-room environment behind. However, I did not escape many situations where the verbose braggart held center stage, and I encountered many examples of misogynous behavior. In fact, as I assumed the life of a nonathlete, I noticed that the "real world" was less structured and disciplined than the regimen of professional athletics from which I came. And as I looked more closely at what many considered to be "sports culture," I realized that what they referred to as sports culture was a media version of that culture. The notion that sports is all about men, and all for men, is central to the way that sports television sells its products. The fantasies commonly held about the lives of professional athletes have become part of the created sports culture. Ironically, this media-created culture works to reinforce the worst sexism and misogyny of the locker room.

In the created sports culture of the media, the male audience is made to feel comfortable in an atmosphere void of female presence and feminist thought. The result is an environment that I call the "extended locker room." Unlike the real locker room, the focus of the extended locker room is not driven by the complexities of the game. It is driven by the economics of business where what sells is of paramount importance. In the extended locker room, submissive women and gratuitous sexual stimulation sell. The viewer becomes a voyeurist participant in misogyny. Women are to be seen (looking good, of course) as they serve as ornamental enhancement to the sports experience, holding the attention of men while selling products and reinforcing sexist attitudes. Certain themes and female roles are consistent. One dominant theme of the extended locker room is the presentation of women as the "ultimate prize." They fill the breaks in action and maintain a level of simulation for the male viewer. Women are often scantily clad supermodels who are submissive and silent in their portrayed acceptance of the sexist rules of the created sports culture. Feminine qualities are mocked and trivialized. Women's show of emotions or care for daily domestic maintenance are mocked, while men hide from their domestic responsibilities, their emotions, and ultimately their female counterparts.

An additional dangerous element in the created sports culture, is alcohol. The promotion and sale of beer is commonplace. A beer commercial graphically illustrates what the environment of the extended locker room suggests. It begins with a caveman sleeping on a flat rock. He has an empty beer bottle in his hand as he dreams of the "supermodel" prancing in his direction. Her hair is done to perfection, and she bounces out of her bikini in sync with her slow motion stride and the romantic music of her anticipated arrival. At this untimely moment, the caveman is awakened by a cavewoman who looks a great deal like her primitive mate. Face-to-face with his mirror-image mate, he knocks himself on the head with the empty beer bottle. Rendering himself unconscious enables him to continue his dream about a woman who does not exist in his world. How many men sit in imaginary escape of their female partners as they engross themselves in televised sporting events accompanied by objectified versions of women whose place is to entertain the male without making the kinds of emotional demands that a wife makes?

It would be far too convenient and simplistic to blame the scourge of men's violence against women solely on the actual or the media-created "locker-room mentality." However, as we live in a society that is witnessing an apparent rise in youth violence, and gender violence in particular, we must examine the social influences that are teaching such behavior. The enormous growth of American sport as an entertainment venue cannot be ignored. It saturates the lives of our youth through video games, marketing, advertising, and the mass media.

Summary

The violent behavior we are witnessing in our youth (young boys, especially) must be traced to their teachers. Far too often we look at the actions of children and blame them, as if they have invented violence and misogyny. As adults (not just parents), we must accept the responsibility of what we teach and what we choose not to teach our children. We must also understand the many ways in which they learn very important social lessons via our own behavior, not only what we do, but also what we don't do. By failing to confront real and created sports culture, we endorse and reinforce violent, hateful, and prejudiced attitudes and behavior, including misogyny and men's violence against women and girls.

Sport and Youth-Violence Prevention

A Conversation with Billie P. Weiss

B*illie P. Weiss is Director of The Violence Prevention Coalition of Greater Los Angeles, a program that she developed in her work at the Los Angeles Country Department of Health Services. She holds a Master's Degree in Public Health from the University of California at Los Angeles and brings the perspective of an epidemiologist to the youth and violence issue.*

In 1997, 1,291 homicides were reported (452 were gang related).

Nearly 21,000 cases of domestic violence were prosecuted in the City of Los Angeles.

Paramedics annually respond to 25,000 calls due to acts of violence, almost twice as many as for heart attacks. (Violence Prevention Coalition of Greater Los Angeles brochure, *Violence Is Preventable*)

Ed.: When and why was the coalition established?

BW: I started working in the Los Angeles County Department of Health Services as an epidemiologist in 1981. From the ongoing public health surveillance we did, I noticed that violence was the number one cause of death and disability among young people, especially young men of color. From an epidemiological point of view, violence was an epidemic, but it was not recognized as such. Community agencies were not dealing with this problem in any focused way. My boss, Dr. Shirley Fannin, supported my desire to get some funding to do something about it. We got a grant from the State Department of Health Services. I, along with a number of public health, medical, law enforcement, and other colleagues, met to develop a

249

strategy to deal with the problem. We discovered that there were a number of uncoordinated groups trying to intervene with respect to gang violence, domestic abuse, child abuse, and other violence-related problems.

Ed.: Was violence even defined as a public health problem at that time?

BW: It was just beginning. In the public health community, only a handful of people had taken a long enough look to know that you could measure and monitor the violence epidemic; there were certain characteristics of victims and perpetrators that you could identify, so there might be places to intervene.

Ed.: As the program has developed, what are its primary goals?

BW: The primary goal is to work with a multidisciplinary network to reduce the level of violence in communities—to develop a community-based violence prevention infrastructure. To do this, we had to create an awareness of violence as a public health issue; that is, that violence is preventable, that there are places where you can intervene, and that people working together can change the community's perceptions about violence. We now have over nine hundred participating grassroots organizations, and serve as a technical and educational resource to the law enforcement, business, health care providers, media, and legislative professionals concerned with violence prevention.

Ed.: About how many of your participating organizations use sports in their violence prevention activities?

BW: Of those that are directed to youth, I would say at least half. Last year, for example, we sponsored a basketball tournament that brought together community organizations that serve youth living in housing projects or in group homes with a lot of learning-disabled kids—many of these are gang prevention programs. It's interesting that many gang members are smaller than average and, thus, don't get selected as participants in organized team sports. Every participating team got a trophy or a ribbon and participants really seemed to feel empowered. Off the court, there was little interaction between kids from different neighborhoods, but there was little or no problem with shoving or punching on the court. We had about a hundred eighty kids participate and expect even more this coming year.

Ed.: These were all males?

BW: There were a few girls, but not many. We had hoped for more.

Ed.: How else does sport play a part?

BW: Many organizations that provide computer training, tutoring, and mentoring encourage their adult members to take their mentees to sporting events as a way of bonding.

Ed.: A number of professional athletes have suggested that their job is to excel in their sport, not to serve as models for youth. Do you seek out professional sport role models to sponsor or advertise your programs?

BW: Because fund-raising is one of our activities, we are always on the lookout for celebrity sponsors. However, our efforts to find appropriate professional athletes have not been successful. Too many of them have been found to be violent in their personal lives—especially violence against women—and that is no role model for the message we are trying to get out.

Ed.: Can we separate the larger world from the sports world when it comes to violence? By this I mean how do the conflicts present in the larger world come into play in sport?

BW: Gender separation and marginalization of females is probably the most obvious way. We need to do a better job of integrating boys and girls in the same sports activities. In general, girls tend to participate more in individual sports activities like swimming and gymnastics, and these tend to be less violent than the boys team sports like football. It's true that boys and men commit most of the violence, and too much of that is violence against women. Maybe boys should be encouraged to participate in more individualized sports where they are more likely to develop anger management and other cognitive-behavioral skills.

Ed.: Do you think that the way conflicts are settled in professional sport may be sending the wrong message to youth?

BW: Yes. Every once in awhile you'll see something that puts forth the model that sports is supposed to be—about sportsmanship—about controlling your anger in the sports arena. It's so uncommon that it becomes a major media event. It becomes the exceptional case that defines the norm; namely, not controlling your anger, not resolving conflicts nonviolently— like hitting your opponent over the head with your hockey stick.

Ed.: In chapter 12, Malcolm W. Klein and Susan Sorenson discuss criminological, social psychological, and public health approaches to violence. From a violence intervention point of view, which of these seem most useful?

BW: The criminological approach where you punish people has not been very effective. If it were effective, we should have much less crime, and we should not have a violence epidemic—we've locked up more people than any other country in the world—but it continues. My sense is that people who don't have the skills to deal with their situation resort to violence. Children can and do learn these skills in anger management programs in the schools. I guess this suggests a public health approach to identify the risk factors associated with violence and, then, a social psychological strategy of intervention.

Ed.: Implicit in your remarks is a challenge to the idea that we should push kids into sport as a way to let them sow their wild oats and, for the guys, to give them a way to innocently keep their testosterone in check. Am I reading you correctly?

BW: Contact sports present a particular dilemma for violence prevention programs. On the one hand, it seems logical to encourage especially boys to be involved in physical activities. On the other, these boys watch professional athletes solving their conflicts on and off the field through violent means. They do not seem to learn anger control techniques; rather they see angry athletes in football and other contact sports expressing their anger in violent ways. I worry that this is teaching them violence as a normative way to express their frustrations or to resolve interpersonal conflicts. As someone trying to teach young boys and girls how to control their anger, this raises a question in my mind about whether we should be encouraging the groups we work with to allocate their scarce resources to getting high-risk youth involved in contact sports. Individual sports activities like track and field seem more desirable as in general they do not see professional athletes in these kinds of sports being so violent.

Ed.: Michael Messner and Mark Stevens in chapter 14 suggest that there is almost a sick association between masculinity and sports injury; that is, boys are taught to put their bodies in danger and to play when injured to demonstrate their masculinity. As a public health specialist concerned with injury prevention, what do you think of this argument?

BW: I just don't understand teaching someone that their body and their health mean so little that they should give it up for a contest. I have a child who was a pitcher in little league and when he developed elbow problems, a doctor suggested that he shouldn't pitch anymore. The coach called me and said, "I need him to pitch." When I said he's not supposed to be pitching, the coach said, "Well, I need him." The coaches are pushing these kids to do things that are not in their best interests. Superficially, the kids may get the message that they are important, but underneath that is the deeper message that they are not valued as people, only as instruments to satisfy other people's goals.

Ed.: Kevin Young [in chapter 13] discusses the legal principle of *volenti [non fit injuria];* that is, the idea that athletes assume the risk of serious bodily injury when they agree to participate. Do you see this kind of attitude in young people, and also in their parents' reactions?

BW: I see it myself when we are out watching. I do think it's a pervasive idea. However, I don't think it's acceptable. Isn't it counter to what we are trying to teach children with regard to how to avoid violence-related injury?

Ed.: The last question I have concerns rape prevention programs designed especially for male athletes. Don McPherson [in chapter 15] discusses his experiences as a participant and trainer in programs that use consciousness-raising and empathy training to counter the objectification of women. Are you familiar with these programs?

BW: A good number of our programs deal with rape prevention. I think the approach sounds promising. What I've noted about the gang rape that reportedly goes on in sports, is that it's not very different from street gang rapes. So I see a connection between the world of sport and the gang world when it comes to the problem of rape.

Conclusion

This volume is, to no small extent, an outcome of the editors' felt need to bridge usually fragmented domains of inquiry into sport both within academia and between academic and practitioner worlds. Our hope is that this volume will serve as evidence that bridging is possible and productive.

Voices Heard

The breadth of voices heard is in the service of telling a nuanced story about the up- and downsides of sport as an institution, an institution that has important consequences for participants, fans, and for the larger society. Represented in this volume are practitioners and academics from many different orientations and worlds. Among the practitioners, there are specialists in violence prevention, rape prevention, sports journalism, and youth-mentoring programs. Many practitioners, of course, are professionals in their own right, and they stay in touch with their respective fields through the literature and professional meetings. The working conditions of the practitioner are at least as varied as the academics. The practitioner may work in city, county, state, or federal government agencies; the non-profit sector; or in corporate settings. Among the academic contributors, we have clinical, cultural, social, and sport psychologists, communication and media scholars, criminologists, specialists in education and educational psychology, gender and race studies analysts, kinesiologists, physical education specialists, and sociologists working from cultural studies or social science perspectives. Their workplaces vary widely in terms of being located within education, humanities, social science, and medical colleges.

Academic Conversations: Barriers and Potentials

Part of the reason for the wide dispersion of academics interested in sport studies is the absence of an institutional unit, such as a sports institute,

255

where scholars with shared interests can come together. Only a few of our contributors are located in such institutes. Another barrier to conversation across academic disciplines and work settings is the fact that we come to the study of sport with very different concerns. Social and clinical psychologists, for example, are primarily concerned with the potentials of sport as a venue for learning, whether that be the learning of socially desirable behaviors (e.g., life skills) or attitudes (e.g., racial tolerance) or socially undesirable behaviors (e.g., violence) or attitudes (e.g., misogyny). All too often, researchers focused upon learning socially desirable behaviors do not engage those concerned with the learning of socially undesirable behaviors.

In contrast to scholars operating from a psychological orientation, sociologists and cultural studies analysts are much less interested in what particular individuals are learning from sport. Their focus is upon understanding how the institution of sport shapes cultural beliefs and practices and, in so doing, advantages or disadvantages major racial, gender, and class groups. Most problematic to these analysts are the downsides of sport participation, whether they be the promotion of violence, racism, sexism, or economic inequality. Despite their shared emphasis on the downsides of sport, differences in methodological orientation (e.g., cultural studies vs. social science) often prevent these scholars from engaging each other.

There are good reasons for academics of all stripes to engage each other's concerns and arguments. Doing so in conferences, journals, and in publications, such as this book, may not only prod us to less fragmented inquiry, but may also discourage polarization into either the critic's or the advocate's corner. Our own personal biographies suggest a more ambivalent positioning. While we differ in our concerns and perspectives, one thing we seem to share is a personal history of participation in sport. In addition to the participation of the editors noted in the introduction to this volume, contributing authors note the role of sport in their biographies. For example, Jay Coakley has long-term involvement in sport as a player and as a coach; Marty Martinson was a college athlete who went on to coach intercollegiate volleyball; Steven J. Danish has coached high school and college basketball; Donald G. McPherson and Robert M. Sellers were all-American collegiate football players, and Terry Barnum was a member of the all-Academic Pac-10 Conference football team; Mary Jo Kane won a junior women's golf title in her high school days in Bloomington, Illinois; and Kevin Young has had long-term involvement in soccer as both a player and coach. Our experiences of the pains, as well as the pleasures, of sport certainly came in different proportions depending upon our social characteristics. For most of us, however, it was not an entirely positive nor negative set of experiences.

Academic-Practitioner Conversations: Barriers and Potentials

Equally, if not more, important than the joining of academic voices is the insight and discipline offered by more direct communication between academics and practitioners. The fact that practical problems in communities require solutions on a more immediate schedule than that typically embraced by academic scholars makes such communication difficult. One natural way for practitioner-researcher contact is through evaluation research of programs that employ sport as either an intervention activity or as an intervention context. However, this avenue of contact is usually not pursued because agencies that fund sport or sport-related programs are rarely interested in supporting efforts to seriously evaluate the outcomes of sport participation. Another obstacle to communication is that academics have few incentives to draw out the specific implications of their research for sport policies and practices. Publication venues, for example, are often devoted to either analysis or application, and most of them are targeted to specialized audiences.

This volume contains some rare examples of bridging between research and practice. One key source of influence is coaches and physical education teachers. Jim McKay suggests proposals for teaching future physical education instructors, by including in their education a confrontation with how media frame sportsmen and sportswomen and what that means for the teacher of sport. Lawrence A. Wenner recommends a Sports Violence Profile, encompassing dangerous practices allowed by current rules, bad sportsmanship, and exploitation of sports violence. Steven J. Danish shows how to use collegiate athletes as instructors of sports skills and life skills to adolescents, and Marty Martinson describes how to develop a mentor program. The programs targeted to male athlete violence against women and girls featured in this volume (e.g., the Mentors in Violence Program discussed by Donald G. McPherson) afford another starting point for the joining of academic theory and sports violence prevention. More generally, these examples of bridging afford a beginning for two-way exchange of academic and practical knowledge about the problems and possibilities that sport offers youth.

Another bridge between academics and practitioners was established once the editors committed themselves to include a practitioner's voice in each section of this book. The anticipation of conducting an interview with a person who was either trying to employ sport as a means to a desirable social end or was in the business of telling sport stories, proved beneficial in the editing process. Each of us had to view the chapters written by academics from the eyes of the practitioner we were to interview.

Joining Voices

When we consider this volume as a whole in terms of what the practitioner could learn from the work of academics and what academics could learn from practitioners, we can identify several major themes.

The most general is the need to take a critical stance that maintains an appreciation of both the upsides and downsides of sport in our society. Part and parcel of a critical stance is the ability to entertain the idea that the way a sport has been constructed as an activity may have positive effects for some participants or fans, but undesirable effects on others. For example, boys may build self-esteem and develop teamwork skills through participation at the same time that they learn to devalue girls and women. Sport as a means to other ends, such as affording a context for interracial understanding also has to be examined critically, as this outcome requires more than being on the same playing field.

Another thematic implication of the research is that coaches are pivotal in the process. Coaches should be carefully selected and trained to play their important socialization roles. Indeed, we need to think of coaches, whether they are in a school or an extramural context, as teachers of young people. There are serious staffing and financial difficulties in obtaining coaches who have both the sport and the mentoring skills required. Foundations and governmental or nonprofit agencies might help to overcome these difficulties by investing in efforts to develop serious training programs for paid and volunteer coaches.

Inequalities of access to sport participation come in many forms and are a pressing issue. While we debate the upsides and downsides of sport for what young people are learning and for our society at large, most youth welcome the opportunity to participate. Profound inequalities of access exist along lines of class, race, gender, and urban/rural residence, and these go beyond sheer participation rates to the quality of participation. Poor urban youth, for example, may not have access to organized and safe after-school sport, to quality coaches, or to quality equipment. Practitioners working in central urban areas have to consider who is left out by virtue of these inequalities of access. Some foundations (e.g., the Amateur Athletic Foundation) seek to address access issues, but this remains a profound problem that needs more clear articulation by people working especially in government agencies.

A common theme throughout this volume is that media stories matter. Young people may or may not have access to direct participation in sport, but they have wide access to indirect participation through the media. The question of what young people are learning from their media consumption of sport events and from the numerous uses of sport celebrities in advertising is of great concern to academics. For practitioners who employ sport as an activity or context for intervention with youth, it is important to consider how media sport stories might be operating against their intervention aims. It may be necessary to deal directly with media messages when they undermine or contradict intervention goals. It is probably unrealistic to expect the commercialization of sport that is evident in the media to decline, but it may be possible for practitioners to work more directly with sport journalists who are sensitive to the issue of the effects of their stories upon young people.

Adult athletes may not like to be put in the position of role models, but once they gain celebrity status, it is hard to avoid. Black athletes, in particular, object to a double standard whereby they are criticized for not accepting a heavier burden than the White athlete to serve as a role model. Their point is well-taken. Nonetheless, the evidence suggests that celebrity athletes of all colors are important role models for youth. Practitioners need to take this into account when designing programs for training and counseling such athletes.

It is hard to contain rule-breaking behavior to the sport field, and it is important to examine the values and norms that underlie a rule-breaking sport culture. What participants and fans learn on and around the field of play carries over to their behavior off the field. While instances of off-the-field violence and sexual assault receive much media attention, the more basic problem concerns the values and norms that underlie these behaviors. When those values and norms endorse racism, misogyny, or the use of illegitimate violence to attain personal ends, it should not be surprising that athletes will evidence these beliefs in their relationships off the field. Coaches, parents, and other teachers need to be made especially aware of these issues. Judges also need to take them into account in their rulings concerning athletes' rule violations.

Missing Voices

One important voice that is generally not included in the study of sport and is, therefore, missing from this volume, is the voice of the youth who we study or seek to serve. For example, it would be desirable in future research to systematically study how young people interpret media representations of sport with respect to gender, race, violence, and other socially important messages. It would also be desirable to conduct studies that capture young people's perspectives on the role of sport in their everyday lives.

Another voice that deserves more attention in academic inquires is the non-White and non-Black sport participant, particularly in urban areas with substantial Latino, Asian, Middle Eastern, and other ethnicities. For example, among recent immigrants we would expect to find culturally specific preferences for sports that do not receive the same amount of attention from academics and practitioners as paid to dominant culture sports, such as football and basketball. In any case, the challenges of our increasingly diverse society press us to be more inclusive in our examinations of sport as a site of cultural negotiation.

Finally, the voices of people who consider sport as an end in itself, not just as a means to an end, need to be included. In the process of arguing the importance of sport as an institution, we should not lose sight of the play value that sport can offer. The seriousness with which we treat sport is in no way inconsistent with its play and entertainment value. Play, after all, is an essential element in our development and in our ability to lead a fruitful and rewarding life.

About the Contributors

Sandra J. Ball-Rokeach, Ph.D., is Professor in the Annenberg School for Communication at the University of Southern California. Her books include *Violence and the Media* (GPO, 1969); *Media, Audience, and Social Structure* (Sage, 1986); *The Great American Values Test: Influencing Belief and Behavior Through Television* (Free Press, 1984); and *Theories of Mass Communication* (Longman, 1989). Dr. Ball-Rokeach has been a Fulbright and Rockefeller Fellow, coeditor of *Communication Research*, and is presently a board member of the McCune Foundation and The Southern California Injury Prevention Research Center.

Sarah Banet-Weiser, Ph.D., is Assistant Professor at the Annenberg School for Communication at the University of Southern California. She has written a book on beauty pageants and national identity, *The Most Beautiful Girl in the World: Beauty Pageants and National Identity* (University of California Press, 1999), and is now working on a manuscript that looks at the cultural politics of women and sports, with a focus on the WNBA.

Ioakim P. Boutakidis is a doctoral student in developmental psychology in the Department of Psychology at the University of California, Riverside. His current research interests involve the effects of language use within immigrant families.

Crystal F. Branta, Ph.D., is Associate Professor in the Department of Kinesiology at Michigan State University. Her research has focused on a longitudinal study of children's growth and motor skill development and the needs of children in low economic urban communities.

Kendrick T. Brown, Ph.D., is Assistant Professor of Psychology at Macalester College in St. Paul, Minnesota. His research interests include the influence of skin tone bias on African Americans' psychological well-being, the role of prejudice in policy endorsement, and the effects of inter-

261

racial athletic contact on the racial attitudes of collegiate student-athletes.

Tony N. Brown, Ph.D., is Assistant Professor of Sociology at Vanderbilt University. He is also a member of the Program for Research on Black Americans at University of Michigan. His research interests concern the impact of race and racism on adult mental health. In particular, he is interested in the psychological cost of racism for African Americans as well as the mental health benefits that some Whites receive as a consequence of racism.

Tabbye M. Chavous, Ph.D., is Assistant Professor in the Department of Psychology and in the Combined Program in Education and Psychology at the University of Michigan. Previously, she has published works examining the congruence between student motivation research and NCAA admissions policies. Her overall research interests lie in issues of person-environment fit and minority student development, particularly the impact of institutional policies, structures, and climate on the educational and life experiences of African Americans in both secondary and higher education settings.

Jay Coakley, Ph.D., is Professor of Sociology at the University of Colorado, Colorado Springs and author of *Sport in Society: Issues and Controversies* (7th ed., McGraw-Hill, 2001). He has played at many levels of organized sports, including city leagues in Chicago and varsity high school and college sports. He has coached youth sports and is widely sought as a consultant to youth sports programs. His research on youth sports, conducted over the course of nearly three decades, has been published in academic journals and in magazines read by coaches and youth sport leaders.

Steven J. Danish, Ph.D., is Director of the Life Skills Center and Professor of Psychology, Preventive Medicine, and Community Health at Virginia Commonwealth University. He is a licensed psychologist and a Diplomate in Counseling Psychology of the American Board of Professional Psychology as well as a registered sport psychologist of the Sports Medicine Division of the United States Olympic Committee. He has coached both high school and college basketball and is author of over 120 articles and 8 books.

Helen M. Davis has an M.Ed. and a Certificate of Advanced Standing from Harvard University and an M.S. in Ed. from Bank Street College of Education. She has worked with children from kindergarten through high school, both as a teacher and as a researcher. She was a Fulbright fellow to Costa Rica, and currently is a doctoral candidate at the Harvard Graduate School of Education in Human Development and a Staff Research Associate at the University of California, Los Angeles.

Martha E. Ewing, Ph.D., is Associate Professor in the Department of Kinesiology at Michigan State University and member of the Institute for the Study of Youth Sports. A sport psychologist, her research interests include achievement motivation, parental pressure, and improving sport opportunities in urban areas.

Lori A. Gano-Overway, Ph.D., is Adjunct Assistant Professor in the Department of Health and Human Performance at Austin Peay State University. Her research interests are in the areas of goal perspective theory, participation motivation, and sportspersonship.

Margaret Gatz, Ph.D., is Professor of Psychology at the University of Southern California and Coordinator of the Steering Committee for the Study of Sport in Society. She served as USC's Faculty Athletic Representative to the NCAA and to the Pacific-10 Conference from 1986 through 1993, and from 1991 through 1998, she was on the National Collegiate Athletic Association's Research Committee. Author of over 120 publications, she is known for her interest in public policy and program evaluation with respect to mental health and preventive interventions.

Patricia M. Greenfield, Ph.D., is Professor of Psychology at the University of California, Los Angeles. She is internationally known for her research on culture and human development, including the influence of electronic media—television, radio and video/computer games—on cognitive development. Her most recent books, all co-edited or co-authored, include *Cross-Cultural Roots of Minority Child Development* (Lawrence Erlbaum, 1994), *Interacting with Video* (Ablex, 1996), and *Bridging Cultures between Home and School* (Lawrence Erlbaum, 2001). She is the 1992 winner of the American Psychological Foundation Distinguished Teaching Award and the American Association for the Advancement of Science Award for Behavioral Science Research.

James S. Jackson, Ph.D., is the Daniel Katz Distinguished University Professor of Psychology, Director of the Research Center for Group Dynamics' Program for Research on Black Americans, Research Scientist at the Institute for Social Research, Director of the Center for Afroamerican and African Studies and former Chair of the Social Psychology Program at the University of Michigan. Since 1989, he has served on the Data Analysis Research Committee of the National Collegiate Athletic Association, serving as chair from 1994 to the present. He publishes regularly on African American mental health, adult development and aging, and race and ethnic relations.

Mary Jo Kane, Ph.D., is Professor in the College of Education and Human Development and Director of the Tucker Center for Research on Girls & Women in Sport at the University of Minnesota. She holds the first Distinguished Professorship related to women in sport and physical activity—The Dorothy McNeill Tucker Chair for Women in Sport and Exercise Science. She is a sport sociologist who is an internationally recognized scholar on the media's treatment of female athletes. She is particularly interested in the media's focus on sportswomen's femininity and physical/sexual attractiveness versus their accomplishments as highly skilled athletes. As a high school student, she won the city-wide junior women's golf title.

Shelley Keiper is a doctoral student in social psychology at the University of Michigan. Her research interests include the effects of academic support and social support for intercollegiate student-athletes.

Malcolm W. Klein, Ph.D., is Professor Emeritus of Sociology and founder and past Director of the Social Science Research Institute at the University of Southern California. Dubbed "dean of gang research," he has won the principal awards from both the American Society of Criminology and the Western Society of Criminology. He is author or editor of 12 books and over 80 articles, as well as recipient of 55 grants and contracts from federal, state, local, and international agencies. His book, *The American Street Gang* (Oxford University Press, 1995), has received wide recognition by scholars, legal practitioners, and the media.

Jim McKay, Ph.D., is Associate Professor in the School of Social Science, The University of Queensland, St. Lucia, Queensland, Australia, where he teaches courses on gender and popular culture. He is former editor of the *International Review for the Sociology of Sport.* His most recent books are *Men, Masculinities, and Sport* (Sage, 2000) with Michael Messner and Donald Sabo, and *Globalization and Sport: Playing the World* (Sage 2001) with Toby Miller, Geoffrey Lawrence, and David Rowe.

Donald G. McPherson is Associate Director of Athletes Helping Athletes at Adelphi University. He worked previously as National Director of Mentors in Violence Prevention, conducting workshops throughout North America with high school and college athletes concerning violence prevention, sportsmanship, leadership, and community service. In 1987, as quarterback at Syracuse University, he led the nation in passing. He was a consensus all-America selection and winner of over 18 national player of the year honors. He played professionally in the National Football League and in the Canadian Football League.

Warde Manuel, M.S.W., is Associate Athletic Director with the University of Michigan Athletic Department. He oversees the Academic Success Program for student-athletes, and assists in the administration of football and men's basketball and hockey. He was a letter winner in football and track at the University of Michigan.

Michael A. Messner, Ph.D., is Associate Professor of Sociology and Gender Studies at the University of Southern California. He is a former high school and college athlete, a former youth league coach and referee, and a frequent speaker and consultant on issues related to sports media, male athletes and violence, and gender equity in sports. His books include *Power at Play: Sports and the Problem of Masculinity* (Beacon Press, 1992); *Sex, Violence, and Power in Sports: Rethinking Masculinity* (Crossing Press, 1994); *Politics of Masculinities: Men in Movements* (Sage, 1997); and *Taking the Field: Women, Men, and Sports* (forthcoming). He has conducted three studies on "Gender Stereotypes in Televised Sports" for the Amateur Athletic Foundation of Los Angeles, and is past President of the North American Society for the Sociology of Sport.

Kimberly D. Pearce is a Ph.D. Candidate in the School of Kinesiology and Leisure Studies at the University of Minnesota. She is also an affiliated scholar with the Tucker Center for Research on Girls & Women in Sport. Her research interests include gender and race in leisure and sport, the development of full human potential through leisure and sport, and critical research methodologies.

Vern D. Seefeldt, Ph.D., is Professor Emeritus in the Department of Kinesiology and retired Director of the Institute for the Study of Youth Sports at Michigan State University. He initiated the longitudinal Motor Performance Study and founded the Youth Sports Institute, and is a member of the American Academy of Kinesiology and Physical Education.

Robert M. Sellers, Ph.D., is Associate Professor in the Department of Psychology at the University of Michigan. He was an all-American football player while an undergraduate at Howard University. As Principal Investigator of the Student-Athlete Life Stress Project, he has published research examining the life experiences of student-athletes with a particular focus on the psychosocial development of the African American student-athlete. In addition, he has published in areas of stress and coping and African American racial identity.

Kenneth L. Shropshire, J.D., is Professor and Chair of Legal Studies at the Wharton School of the University of Pennsylvania and formerly Acting Director of the University's Afro-American Studies Program. He is the author of several publications related to race, law, and the business of sports, including the award-winning book, *In Black and White: Race and Sports in America* (New York University Press, 1996).

Susan B. Sorenson, Ph.D., is Professor in the School of Public Health at the University of California, Los Angeles. Her research focuses on the epidemiology of violence, and she has published articles on homicide, suicide, sexual assault, spouse abuse, child abuse, and youth violence. A consistent theme in her work is the intersection of gender and ethnicity as related to risk of, and exposure to, violence. For the past five years, She has directed a graduate-level training program in public health approaches to violence.

Mark A. Stevens, Ph.D., is Psychologist and Coordinator of Training at the University of Southern California Student Counseling Services and Adjunct Professor in the Counseling Psychology program at USC. Previously, he was Staff Psychologist at the Ohio State University, where he was the first cochair of the Men's Rape Prevention project. At USC, he founded the CARE (Creating Attitudes for Rape-Free Environments) Program.

Lalita K. Suzuki, Ph.D., is an Assistant Research Psychologist at the University of California, Los Angeles. Her current research interests include cross-cultural and ethnic psychology, parent-child relations, and children's educational software development.

Lawrence A. Wenner, Ph.D., is the Von der Ahe Professor of Communication and Ethics in the College of Communication and Fine Arts at Loyola Marymount University in Los Angeles. His research has focused on critical assessments of media content, ethical dimensions of race and gender portrayals in advertising, audience experiences with television in the family context, and the values and consumption of mediated sports. Author of 5 books and over 60 journal articles and book chapters, his recent books include *MediaSport* (Routledge, 1998); and, with Leah VandeBerg and Bruce Gronbeck, *Critical Approaches to Television* (Houghton-Mifflin, 1998). He is a former editor of the *Journal of Sport and Social Issues*.

Kevin Young, Ph.D., is Senior Research Fellow in the Department of Physical Education, Sports Science and Recreation Management at Loughborough University, Great Britain. He is coeditor of *Sport and Gender in Canada* (Oxford University Press, 1999) and teaches classes in the sociology of sports, criminology, and youth crime. He is currently Vice President of the International Sociology of Sport Association. He played high school and university soccer and rugby on both sides of the Atlantic and has coached children's soccer for many years.

Author Index

267

Subject Index

273

SUNY series, Sport, Culture, and Social Relations
CL Cole and Michael A. Messner, editors

List of Titles